SECOND EDITION

ADVERTISING
CONCEPT AND COPY

GEORGE FELTON

W. W. NORTON & COMPANY
NEW YORK • LONDON

For Karen

Book design and composition by Gilda Hannah
Manufacturing by Everbest
Production manager: Leeann Graham

Library of Congress Cataloging-in-Publication Data

Felton, George, 1947–
    Advertising: concept and copy / George Felton.—2nd ed.
      p. cm.
    Includes bibliographical references and index.
    ISBN 13-978-0-393-73159-0
    1. Advertising. I. Title.

HF5823.F43 2005
659.1—dc22

                                                    2005051298

W. W. Norton & Company, Inc., 500 Fifth Avenue, New York, NY 10110
www.wwnorton.com

W. W. Norton & Company, Ltd., Castle House, 75/76 Wells Street,
London W1T 3QT

0 9 8 7 6 5 4 3

CONTENTS

It's God's
favorite beer.
Oops. Sorry.
That's "Bob's."

ree-dimensional
rared imaging
o hunt in total darkness.

Fortunately, we close at 6 p.m.

FROM HERE,
IT LOOKS LIKE
YOU COULD USE SOME
NEW UNDERWEAR

BAMBOO LINGERIE

Italy gave us the Mafia. They also gave us these. Let's call it even.

Vespa

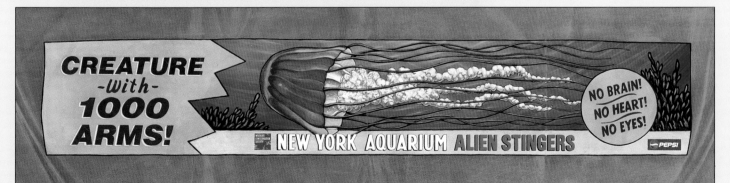

CREATURE
-with-
1000
ARMS!

NEW YORK AQUARIUM ALIEN STINGERS

NO BRAIN!
NO HEART!
NO EYES!

PEPSI

PREFACE

How this book is organized, and why

If you're new to the book, you'll see that I've divided it into three parts. The first two sections correspond to a natural sequence in the solving of an advertising problem: first you create a strategy, then you execute it. The last section offers suggestions for making those executions memorable.

Part 1, Strategy, operates on the premise that the selling idea beneath an ad's surface determines its success. You get that good idea by researching your client's product, understanding who buys it and why, and studying the marketplace in which it competes. In doing those things you'll discover the problem that your advertising must solve, you'll find the strategic approach that best solves it, and you'll be able to write the creative brief that focuses this strategic thinking into specific advertising objectives.

Now, how to put that strong selling idea into action? How to express it? Part 2, Execution, examines the tools at your command, from the elements of print advertising—headlines, visuals, body copy—to the wide variety of media and advertising genres available to you. These are the means by which you turn strategic thinking into real-world effectiveness. Thus the movement of the first two sections: what are you going to say, and how are you going to say it?

Part 3, The Toolbox, is what it sounds like: a place to find problem-solving tools. Here I discuss basic principles of creativity and follow that with techniques that advertising professionals have used, over and over, to produce attention-getting, persuasive work. I hope you'll try these techniques when the blank page looms too large. They're more specific and therefore more helpful than the earnest advice copywriters give themselves and get from others to "think."

As a copywriter, you're expected not only to write well but to think well—generating unusual, provocative ideas, visual as well as verbal ones. How this is done is a great mystery, of course, and no book can tell you enough. But especially in Part 3, The Toolbox, I've tried to give you the best advice I can find on developing your creativity. After all, that's what you're selling.

What I've kept and what I've changed

I've rewritten this book to make it better and more useful. I've kept what's good and improved it, cut what's weak or strengthened it, and updated everything. Most obviously, I've updated the ads themselves. Although principles of persuasion don't change, the look and language of ads certainly do, and there's nothing more exciting than fresh work. (That said, great ads are timeless, which is why I'm reprinting some classics, too.)

Updates also include new sections on guerrilla advertising, interactive media, international and multicultural advertising, and postmodern advertising. Since not all problems can be solved with a quick, visual joke, I've strengthened the discussion of some of the longer copywriting forms (brochures, direct mail, and catalog writing). I've also added the following chapters to the Toolbox: How to Write a Headline; Human Truth; and Grace Notes. In the chapter titled How to Write a Headline, I discuss at length headlines, slogans, theme lines, and naming, not just because these are so often the crux of the matter for writers but also because they demonstrate the principles of persuasion briefly enough that you can get a good look at them. Advice in this chapter can, I hope, extend to much of the writing you'll do in advertising, however short or long.

The many people who have helped me

Writing a book may seem the most solitary of tasks, and in some ways it is, but it is also the labor of many hands and minds.

I want to thank all the companies, advertising agencies, and design studios whose work I have borrowed. Many people let me interrupt their already busy lives, then hunted through the back of their minds, the bottom of drawers, or the deep reaches of hard drives to find ads I requested, and often to suggest ones I hadn't. Many of them also helped me acquire the permissions necessary to show these ads to you. I am in debt also to the clients, creative directors, art directors, copywriters, designers, photographers, and illustrators—among them Columbus College of Art & Design (CCAD) alumni Christopher Cole, Steve Stone, Mark Suplicki, and Crit Warren—who thought up this brilliant work in the first place. It's the best thing in here. I'm equally indebted to the many people whose insights and ideas I quote in this book. They have thought it and said it better than I ever could, and the book is richer for their presence.

I thank my students at CCAD, whose energy and ideas got me started on this book in the first place. I also thank my colleagues in advertising, design, and liberal arts at CCAD for their insight and inspiration. To the librarians at the Packard Library, who knew where things were when I so frequently didn't, I extend my thanks. Bruce Hager and Maria Spiess of Tom Faist's terrific IT staff came to my aid happily, readily, and I'm sure way too often, solving digital mysteries with their own kind of magic; I couldn't have created this book without them. I thank the College for granting me a sabbatical, which has given me the time to finish this edition, time for which I am grateful. Without the excellent copyediting of Alice Vigliani and the graceful design of Gilda Hannah, this book would not be nearly as good. Without the encouragement and skill of my editors at W. W. Norton, Nancy Green and Andrea Costella, this second edition simply would not be.

GEORGE FELTON
Columbus, Ohio

PART ONE

STRATEGY

> We place a lot of importance on strategy. It's not worth anything to be creative if you're not going to make that turnstile turn. Creative and strategy are so integral, one depends on the other.
>
> —Jean Robaire,
> art director, Stein Robaire Helm

A great ad is a wonderful thing; it's why you love advertising. But what you're looking at is only half of what's there, and the part you can't see has more to do with that ad's success than the part you can. Before those surface features (the terrific headline or visual or storyline or characters or voiceover or whatever) can work their wonders, the ad has to have something to say, something that matters. Either it addresses real consumer motives and real consumer problems, or it speaks to no one. To make great ads, then, you have to start where they start: with the invisible part.

1 ▪ Creating an Advertising Strategy

Advertising based on a sound strategy but executed poorly is as dull as another snowy day in January. Advertising executed brilliantly but based on a weak strategy may be entertaining—but it won't work. So you have to do the whole job, not just half. Strong strategy. And strong execution.

—Ron Anderson,
executive vice president, Bozell & Jacobs

First things first

Probably the greatest danger you'll face as a copywriter is trying to get to the ad too fast. You'll rush for a headline or selling idea before making sure it works. And since most great ads do employ some kind of a twist (you can't just put clichéd ideas in clichéd places), it's tempting to start playing with language and image right away, trying to create some "pop," usually with puns, double entendres, and other jokes. But cleverness is useless if you're saying something beside the point. Until you discover the real reasons—whatever they may be—that people buy this or that good or service, you create ads for no one.

So great ads really begin with the grunt work, the legwork, digging around in the issues, getting up to speed on the selling situation, working to know enough even to begin playing with the language.

If, for example, you're creating advertising against teen-age drinking and driving, writing headlines like "Don't drive yourself to drink" or "Don't take the car for a spin if your head's spinning" or "How can you stay in a single lane if you're seeing double?" is a waste of time. The real problems of drinking and driving are elsewhere, and you need to understand them. Why, in the face of repeated warnings and omnipresent advertising against it, do many young people still drink and drive? The answer isn't something you can come up with sitting around in search of a line. You can only begin to discover it by researching the problem, its social and psychological dimensions. You've got to get out there and talk to some people and do some thinking.

Most don't-drink-and-drive advertising, sensibly enough, stresses the risk of death on the highway (see fig. 1.1). But suppose, in your research, you discover that it's far more likely people will lose their licenses than their lives by drinking and driving. Suppose you also discover that many teens, young and strong, consider themselves almost immortal and are largely unable to imagine their own deaths. They can, however, understand the value of driving—seeing it as an essential initiation into adulthood—and they can feel the weight of peer pressure. Knowing all this, you may want to make a different argument (see fig. 1.2).

Strategy versus execution

An ad really has two parts: *what* you're saying and *how* you're saying it. The "what" is your strategy—the plan of attack, the ad's big idea, its selling argument; the "how" is the execution of that strategy—the particular form it takes: the images, language, layouts, and media that you use. (Employing the battlefield distinction, some advertisers split these two into *strategy* and *tactics*.)

Looking at the preceding ads, one might say that the strategy of the first is: don't drink and drive because you may die. The strategy of the second is: don't drink and drive because you may live. Obviously these are fundamentally different propositions, different "whats," and each proposition could have been differently expressed, given a different "how," as well. Consumers respond to both the underlying selling idea and its particular expression. Notice that the

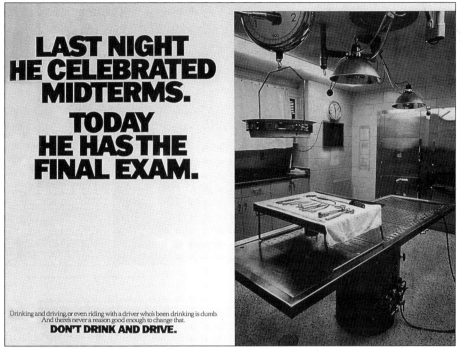

1.1. A reasonable advertising strategy for the teen-age drinking and driving problem.

1.2. Perhaps strategically even stronger, this ad directly understands its audience.

EVERY DAY, FEWER TEENAGERS DRINK AND DRIVE.

SAFE-RIDES

Instead of driving drunk, call us: 221-3800.

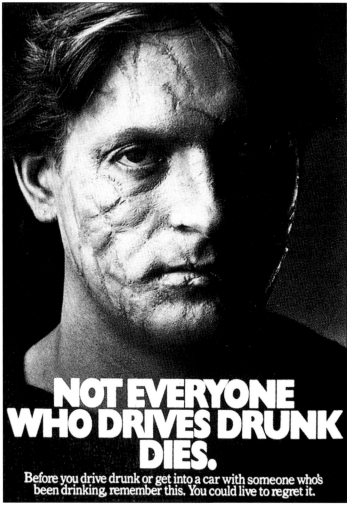

NOT EVERYONE WHO DRIVES DRUNK DIES.

Before you drive drunk or get into a car with someone who's been drinking, remember this. You could live to regret it.

1.3. The same two underlying strategies each receive a different execution. In generating ads you will frequently be asked not only to develop a strategy but also to express it in different ways.

two ads in figure 1.3, which look so different from the first two, really aren't. They express the same two ideas, but in new terms. They're different *executions* of the same two *strategies*.

When creating ads, you want to be smart at both strategy and execution. Often it's easy to admire the clever "creative" on an ad's surface, for example, the well-crafted, parallel headline on the kids-in-the-backseat ad (fig. 1.2), their wonderfully worried looks, Mom's irritation, the point of view of the camera—all of it—and think that those make the ad great. But what also makes the ad great is the idea behind it: what if you live?

How to create a strategy

To develop a strong strategy, you need to understand three things: the product, the consumer, and the marketplace.

1. The product. What are you selling, really? This can be something more and different than it might at first appear. It's certainly something about which you need to know more than you do right now.

2. The consumer. Who are you selling to, exactly? Have you located those people who are your best market? How well do you know them? The key to selling products is understanding people's relationships with them, what they want from them. What needs and motives does your client's product address? What problems does it solve?

3. The marketplace. How does your client's product (and its advertising) fit into the array around it? No sale occurs in a vacuum; there

> To do well what should not be done is to do badly.
> —Theodore Levitt,
> *The Marketing Imagination*

are probably other products like it, and the category has been advertised to consumers before. In short, they've seen it all and used it all, twice. How will your product stand out in the marketplace? Why should consumers choose it instead of a competing brand?

Those are all interesting questions—and all related: you can't locate your target market until you know what you're selling exactly, but you can't know what exactly you ought to promise until you locate a target market and decipher its needs. Nor can you create an effective strategy until you analyze the marketplace positions your client's competitors occupy and successfully differentiate your client's product from theirs.

Sorting your way through all this isn't easy, and each advertising situation will prove different from the one before it, too, so your job never reduces to a formula. Your goal is to understand the parts of the advertising scenario so well that you see how they all fit together—to know enough to write an ad that works, that talks to real people about real needs. You'd like to convince a teenager, perhaps for the first time, that "Don't drink and drive" isn't simply someone else's slogan. It's something that teenager truly believes—because of the advertising you created.

2 ▪ Researching Your Client's Product

One thing I try to do is know everything that is possible to know about a brand when I work on it. When you dig deep into a brand, really do a big archaeology on it, you find out why it was created in the first place, why they named it what they did, what the dreams of the founders were, why it comes in the kinds of packages it does, why the logo looks the way it does—you find truths and values that have probably gotten buried under creative trends through the years. So I'll do things like go back and look at old advertising they did decades ago, before bullshit crept into our business. This helps you discover the truth, and when you can build creative work around some kind of truth, it's much more powerful, and substantial.

—Jeff Weiss,
creative director, Amster Yard

In truth, advertising starts with consumers and what they want, but you will never be given the assignment simply to make some market segment happy. Instead, you will usually begin with a product and the assignment to help sell it. Thus, in practice, advertising problems start with your clients, who have a product—a good or service—with which they'd like help. You are called in initially to do something for a client's product.

Steep yourself in information

Become an expert in your client's product and its category. Get overinformed. I once knew a student who wanted to sell Aloe & Lanolin soap to her classmates as a course project, but it never occurred to her to find out what aloe and lanolin were, exactly, and what they were doing together in a bar of soap. Needless to say, her success was limited. Strive not to be that student.

Let this be your model instead. Before creating their legendary ad campaign for the Volkswagen Beetle, the creative team at Doyle Dane Bernbach first headed for the manufacturing plant in Wolfsburg, West Germany, to do their homework. Says William Bernbach: "We spent days talking to engineers, production men, executives, workers on the assembly line. We marched side by side with the molten metal that hardened into the engine, and kept going until every part was finally in place."[1]

And only through this effort did they find their selling proposition, the VW as an "honest" car—simple, functional, and incredibly well made. Whenever you see reprints of these classic VW ads, study them, not only because the ads are great, but because each ad shows so clearly the homework required to think it up. Read enough VW ads and two things will happen: (1) you'll learn a lot about the cars, and (2) you'll want one. Sufficient testimony to the power of that campaign (see fig. 2.1).

How to learn about your client's product

1. **Learn what's in it** and how it works, read the label, study the packaging. If possible, use it: wear it, eat it, drive it, bathe with it. Become its student. Try its competitors, too. Nothing replaces first-hand experience.

2. **Call the company's 800 number.** Go to its Web site. Get whatever you can from the company about its product. If it's possible to interview company people, interview them. Brochures abound, from both your client's brand and the competition. Study ads by everyone in the field. Build a file.

3. **Surf the Web and online databases.** Type key words into search engines and go where the results lead. But don't let sitting in front of the computer substitute for all other search engines. You have hands and feet, ears and

Volkswagen's unique construction keeps dampness out.

For years there have been rumors about floating Volkswagens. (The photographer claims this one stayed up for 42 minutes.) Why not?

The bottom of the Volkswagen isn't like ordinary car bottoms. A sheet of flat steel runs underneath the car, sealing the bottom fore and aft.

That's not done to make a bad boat out of it, just a better car. The sealed bottom protects a VW from water, dirt and salt. All the nasty things on the road that eventually eat up a car.

The top part of a Volkswagen is also very seaworthy. It's practically airtight. So airtight that it's hard to close the door without rolling down the window a bit.

But there's still one thing to keep in mind if you own a Volkswagen. Even if it could definitely float, it couldn't float indefinitely.

So drive around the big puddles. Especially if they're big enough to have a name.

2.1. Too many ads fail to find the drama in the product, "borrowing" interest from elsewhere instead. The original VW ads, however, made the car itself *consistently* interesting, a remarkable feat in a campaign that ran from 1959 to 1977.

eyes. Get outside and talk to people. Ask questions. Listen.

4. Ask local dealers about your client's brand and its competition. Ten minutes with a retailer can give you a lot of information about the types of buyers, the heavy users, the competitive advantages and disadvantages of the major brands, the whole playing field.

5. Find out what other people think. Ask them why they do or don't use the product, what they like and don't like about your client's brand and its competitors. Word of mouth,

actual information from real humans, is crucial, yet ad writers often fail to ask for it. Cultivate sources who understand their own consumer behavior, who can talk about shampoos for a while, or cell phones. Remember, consumers are ultimately your most valuable resource. Why do *they* wear cologne, how do *they* feel about Obsession or cKbe? Why do *they* choose or avoid Pringles? The answer is inside the consumer—who could be anyone you know—not at the end of an 800 number or online.

Daddy fought in the war.

The Motorola MicroTAC Ultra Lite™ comes from a long line of heroes. Like the original SCR 536 hand-held wireless radio, which cut our boys loose from the wires of war. Lives depended on us then. Busy lives depend on us now. Motorola. The best-selling, most-preferred cellular phones in the world.

MOTOROLA

2.2. You can't use facts like these until you find them. The moral? As David Ogilvy put it, "Do your homework."

6. Learn about the product category, too. If you're selling Centrum, find out about vitamins: drop into a bookstore and survey the health books, or search the Web for health information. A sentence like "Your body misses eight crucial vitamins every day" can apply to Centrum as easily as to any other brand, right? Not only can the category serve as a source of information for your client's brand, but you may end up selling the category rather than the brand (see "Generic Claim" in chapter 5). And no matter what, you need to know why consumers have the product itself in their lives, what it does for them, and how it does it.

7. Go to a library. Libraries have it all: encyclopedias (often a good first stop—how does soap work?), dictionaries (what's aloe? what's lanolin?), audio and video material,

bibliographies and indexes—from the *Readers' Guide to Periodical Literature* (useful in high school, useful now) to things like Business Periodicals Index, InfoTrac, ProQuest, and EBSCOhost—plus many other searchable databases otherwise unavailable to you.

And, of course, libraries have books—books on your subject (whose bibliographies often provide leads); books that, even if written a while ago, may still be definitive. Let's say you're researching a package design problem. Thomas Hine says in *The Total Package*'s bibliography, itself abundantly helpful, that "even though it's more than sixty-six years old . . . Richard B. Franken and Carroll B. Larabee's *Packages That Sell* probably remains the fundamental text on the development of the marketing dimensions of packaging."[2] How would you know about that book, or even Hine's book, if you let Google or Yahoo serve as your only research guide?

But best of all, libraries have real, live reference librarians—people with graduate degrees in knowing what's where, experts waiting to be called upon. Call upon them. I always do. They're terrific resources. Explain your project, say what work you've done, ask nicely for help, and watch them cut a path for you through the wilderness (see fig. 2.2).

Study the competition

Not everyone is buying your client's product. Find out what they're buying instead.

Two key issues

1. Who is your client's competition, exactly? Usually you assume it's competing brands. But it may not be other brands so much as other ways consumers spend their money to satisfy the same need—in other words, the indirect competitors. For example, Hallmark and American Greetings are direct competitors of each other, but they also face text messaging, voice mail, e-mail, phone calls, and even personal visits as indirect competitors. Each is a delivery system for feelings; they're all media for the consumer's "sentiment message." "When an advertiser dominates its category, as Hallmark does, an indirect competitor can be more formidable than a direct competitor."[3]

So ask yourself who the major players are,

both direct and indirect, with which your client's product competes. Assess their strengths and weaknesses. Where does your client's product fit in the array? And what competitive benefit does it offer that they don't (see fig. 2.3)?

2. What product category(ies) should your client's product compete in? This corollary of the first question can also be answered too quickly. If you're selling Wheaties, you may assume you're just competing with other cereals. But there are other categories you might want to compete in as well: Wheaties is a kind of vitamin; it's a snack food for the healthy-minded; it's a breakfast, not just a cereal. So remember to ask what product categories you can compete in and which ones are best. (For more on turning competitive position into the entire advertising strategy, see "Positioning" in chapter 5.)

2.3. Although there are two newspapers in San Francisco, the *Examiner* knows that its competition also includes TV. The *Oregonian* realizes that it competes with TV as a medium for retail advertising.

Maybe your second car shouldn't be a car.

Don't laugh.

It makes a lot more sense to hop on a Vespa than it does to climb into a 4000-lb. automobile to go half a mile for a 4-oz. pack of cigarettes.

To begin with, a Vespa can be parked. It'll give you between 125 and 150 miles to a gallon. Depending on how you drive. And using regular gas.

The Vespa is a reliable piece of machinery. Its engine has only three moving parts. There's not much that can rattle. (People have driven Vespas over 100,000 miles without major repairs.) And it's so simple to work on, a complete tune-up costs six dollars. It's air-cooled. There's no water, no anti-freeze.

The transmission is so well built that it's guaranteed for life.*

Vespa has unitized body construction. The whole thing is made from one piece. It's not bolted together. It can't rattle apart.

If you buy a Vespa your neighbors won't move out of the neighborhood. The Vespa is a motorscooter, not a motorcycle. There is no social stigma attached to driving one.

There are six Vespa models to choose from. You can buy one of them with the money you'd spend just to insure and fuel

the average second car for a year. And you can count on getting most of that money back should you ever decide to sell your Vespa. It won't depreciate nearly as fast as a car.

You may laugh at the Vespa today. But tomorrow when you're stuck in traffic and one scoots by, remember this.

The laugh is on you.

Vespa, Inc., 940 Commonwealth Avenue, Boston, Massachusetts. *Providing regular maintenance is performed in accordance with schedule outlined in the warranty. Warranty provides for replacement or repair "at importers' option" of all transmission parts at no cost to either parts or labor. Overseas delivery available. ©1964 Vespa, Inc.

Vespa

2.4. Not for nothing was McCabe, at 36, the youngest person ever inducted into the Copywriter's Hall of Fame. He can really assemble the case—with prose that's plain-spoken, specific, clear, and compelling. He makes you feel like buying a Vespa. A writer can't do better than that.

Ed McCabe once wrote an ad for Vespa motor scooters that showed one sitting in a garage beside a car, with this headline: "Maybe your second car shouldn't be a car" (fig. 2.4). He saw the wisdom in selling Vespa as a better car instead of a better bike. And the copywriter for the ad in figure 2.5 took the idea of competing product categories beyond the literal (beaches) to the abstract (vacations).

Identify what you are looking for in your research

If you let your research remain open-ended, it will go on forever, and you'll never get to the next step. It saves time to know what you're looking for and what you're not.

Tips to help you focus

1. Don't get hung up in corporate this and earnings that. You're looking for information about the product that makes it worth buying. It's not a lump of wet clay, so look for features, particularities, whatever makes it more than a commodity, and whatever distinguishes it from its competition. What's in it? What does it do? (My Quaker Oats canister tells me, loud and clear, that "Oatmeal helps remove cholesterol!" and with my numbers, I'm listening.) How is it made? Real slow? Real fast? At high temperatures? By whom? By European artisans? By the latest robotic wonders? Where is it made? Why there? Use the reporter's questions to help you generate material: who, what, when, where, why, and how.

2. What do people have against your client's product? What's its greatest liability? Why doesn't everyone use it? Maybe the nut your advertising needs to crack is objections people have to the brand. The classic Volkswagen campaign, for example, took one supposed deficit after another (small size, unchanging looks, putt-putt engine, ugliness, etc.) and turned each one into a virtue.

3. What's its greatest strength? Does it share that virtue with its competitors or own it itself? Is there an argument for this product category no one is claiming? Could you make that claim? Doing so, finding a "hole" out there in the marketplace, can be easier than you think—and a powerful way to differentiate your client's brand from everyone else's (see fig. 2.8).

4. How does your client's product fit into consumers' lives and culture? Is your product associated with any rites of passage, life transitions—like birth, graduation, marriage, retirement, and so on? Is it tied, or could it be, to major cultural issues—like self-improvement, health, environmental concerns, recommitment to education, emphasis on the family, and so on?

Remember: products are rarely simply themselves; they're also complex symbols, markers for larger psychological states, social roles, and cultural meanings. What yokes your client's product to consumers' lives?

Much of this information is divined, systematically analyzed, and then sold to advertisers by market research firms, but much is also available by simply paying attention to trends as they manifest themselves around you. Read newspapers and magazines, watch TV and movies, spend time on the Internet, listen to what's said by radio talk show callers and by people on the street. Everyone has pop culture antennae; the good ad writers keep theirs up.

Obviously I'm suggesting a lot of research here. You'll know by the nature of each project and its timeline how much you can realistically expect of yourself. Sometimes you'll have to do a quick study of your client's product and its competitors. Other times you'll be able to analyze more of the field. You can't be expected to do all this research all the time; but the more you do, the better. It will pay you back.

Translate features into benefits

Let's say you've done your homework. You now know all sorts of things about the product—its manufacture, ingredients, moving parts, founding father and mother, everything. But it's all inert data until you make it matter to consumers, and you do that by promising benefits, not just enunciating features.

Here's the distinction. Unless it's a commodity, like salt or sugar, whatever product you're selling undoubtedly has aspects that one might call features: a key ingredient, a selector switch that scans for songs, a self-cleaning button for the oven, a column by Anna Quindlen on the last page, three speeds to its motor, a lubricated strip above the blade, one-third the calories of the regular brand, no caffeine, extra caffeine, timed-release deodorant capsules, biodegradability, free online support, freeze-dried crystals, a hatchback, an angled brushing head, more dealers, and on and on. In other words, every product has certain parts, ingredients, things it can do, conditions associated with it, that taken together make it what it is, make it, in marketing professor Theodore Levitt's terms, not just a "generic product," the thing itself, but an "augmented product," a whole cluster of attributes that add value.

But features alone won't sell a product. They're just things hanging off a product. The real question is, what do consumers get out of them? Learn to ask, of any product fact or feature, "Who cares?" Can or does this matter to the consumer? What's the payoff? Link benefits to features. Complete the argument.

Using previous examples, you can see that a self-cleaning oven button means no more smelly scrubbing, stinging hands, backaches, and all-day labor.

Write about the product. In the greatest, soundest, most creative advertising, the theater revolves around the product. Ask yourself what makes the product "tick." How does it fit into people's lives? How does the competition fail or disappoint? What's its "personality" in the marketplace? Advertising that isn't really about the product is almost always self-indulgent crap.

—Cliff Freeman, quoted in
How to Put Your Book Together and Get a Job in Advertising

One-third fewer calories means people can have their cake and eat it, too—indulge themselves but still be attractively slim. A hatchback lets them load up their gear quickly and easily. Reading Anna Quindlen every other week means they'll smarten up fast and have insightful things to say to their friends. Freeze-dried crystals mean brewed-coffee taste without hassle. Timed-release deodorant capsules mean consumers won't be embarrassed by wetness and odor, appearing unflappable and cool to everyone. Online support means they can relax in their ignorance, feel good about their choice, and realize they're not alone with the complicated technology. No caffeine means they're taking care of themselves, not to mention being "safe" by following a trend. Now all these neutral features have been expressed as benefits, too, so consumers can see what's in it for them.

Remember this marketing maxim, simple but profound: people don't buy ¼-inch drill bits; they buy ¼-inch holes. As Theodore Levitt points out, people don't really buy gasoline either: "They cannot see it, taste it, feel it, appreciate it, or really test it. What they buy is the right to continue driving their cars."[4] When ad great Claude Hopkins was advertising patent medicines in the early 1900s, he realized that "people were not buying medicine, they were buying results," so he pioneered the idea of the druggist's signed guarantee.[5] This habit of mind—seeing products from the benefits end—seems obvious, but it's amazing how often ad writers overlook it when planning strategies and generating ads (see figs. 2.6 and 2.7).

MANY THINGS ARE FEATURES

All this focus on features may feel old school, and if you think of features in the most narrow, hardware-ish way, it is. But remember that a brand's image is a

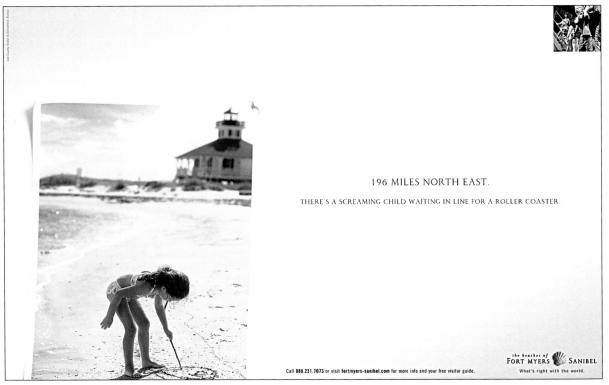

2.5. These Florida beaches realize they compete not just with other beaches but with other vacations.

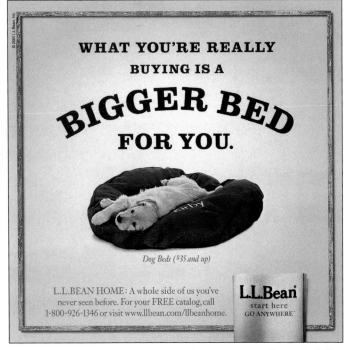

2.6. Who said the doggie bed was about the dog? Always look for the real consumer benefit of a product; it may not be what you think.

2.7. Most home workout equipment is sold with product features, tech-talk, and glistening abs, ignoring one obvious—and powerful—benefit people seek from home equipment: the right to stay home. As the subhead puts it, "No matter what the weather's like outside you can always get a great workout inside on a True treadmill."

2.8. Most credit lenders are eager to sell the supposedly limitless possibilities spending creates. This campaign instead focused on its limitations, finding an argument no one in the category was making: we're here to help you manage money better, not just spend it. A responsible credit lender; now there's a contradiction in terms. Good zig in a world of zags.

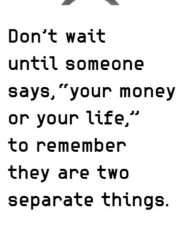

2.9. Avoid feature myopia. A feature doesn't have to be some physical part of your product, something mixed into or hanging off it; it can be any differentiating aspect of your brand's story. It can, for example, be a channel of distribution. Here the Wondergro line of lawn care products differentiates itself on the basis of being sold only in garden stores—by professionals, in other words, not by the hit-and-miss help found in giant retail outlets.

LOWLY TUBER BECOMES LUXURY VODKA.
A STORY OF REDEMPTION. For the humble Stobrawa potato, it is a glorious tale. In a tiny distillery in the countryside of Poland, the world's only luxury potato vodka is created. Chopin is handcrafted in the Old World way, according to a tradition that dates back five centuries, and distilled four times.

CHOPIN   THE WORLD'S ONLY LUXURY POTATO VODKA

2.10. Ads that have done their homework don't have to sound like it, the copywriter droning on beside the desk. This ad is selling a product feature, and a humble one at that, the potato. But the ad is intriguing and visually dynamic. It's not boring, and you shouldn't be either. Make the truth interesting. We'll listen.

feature, too, one that people will often pay plenty for (status benefits, quality benefits, etc.). The product's story, its history and cultural fit, is another feature. So, too, is a brand's tradition of customer service (Nordstrom comes to mind) or its emotional connection to people's lives (Pillsbury, Coca-Cola, and many more brands, yes?). As figure 2.9 shows, features don't have to be things. And, as figure 2.10 proves, features don't have to be exotic or unusual either.

Ernie Schenck, vice president and creative director at Hill Holiday, provides an excellent overview of what you're trying to do and why:

I think our job, particularly today, is first to be able to recognize a story—and then to be able to relate it in a meaningful way. And every

brand has a story. . . . I start out by looking at everything the client has, wading through a volume of information, most of which is completely useless. I'm talking about primary research, secondary research, everything. It's a pain to look through it. But if you do the due diligence, you will almost always unearth some wonderful nuggets of information that may begin to reveal the plot-line behind the brand.[6]

Translating features into benefits ultimately requires an understanding of consumer motives. What do people want from the material world? How many needs do they really have? Let's take a closer look at consumer psychology.

3 ▪ Understanding Consumer Behavior

If you want to build a ship, don't drum up people
together to collect wood and don't assign them
tasks and work, but rather teach them to long for
the endless immensity of the sea.
—Antoine de Saint-Exupéry,
The Wisdom of the Sands

Remember that marketing's central idea, as Theodore Levitt phrases it, is that "people buy products . . . in order to solve problems. Products are problem-solving tools."[1] Remember, too, that products may solve any problem from a physiological one all the way up to a psychological, social, or even spiritual one, and often several at once. So, for example, when people buy clothes at the Limited instead of at Wal-Mart, they are meeting the civilized need to cover themselves, certainly, but they aren't stopping there. They're also choosing to buy *insurance*—fashion insurance. People will pay more for these clothes because they want to reduce the perceived social risk of wearing the wrong ones.

Maslow's hierarchy of needs

The idea that a product can solve more than one problem at the same time owes much to the psychologist Abraham Maslow, who posited in human beings a "hierarchy of needs" ascending from the physiological to the psychological. He argued that people are driven to fulfill them all, although lower-level needs must be met before one can attempt to satisfy higher-level needs.[2] Here is his hierarchy:

  1. Physiological needs: hunger, thirst, warmth, pain avoidance, sexual release, and others
  2. Safety needs: housing, clothing, financial and physical security
  3. Love and belongingness needs: social acceptance and personal intimacy (Maslow argued that much of human frustration stemmed from inadequacy in this area, since lower-level needs had been met. People can

often say that they have eaten enough or own enough clothes, but who can say, "I am loved enough"? It isn't surprising, therefore, that the greatest number of consumer goods appeal to this level of need.)
  4. Esteem needs: feelings of adequacy and achievement, approval, prestige, social status
  5. Self-actualization needs: the need to understand, cognitively and aesthetically; the ultimate integration of the self and realization of one's highest inner potential

As is evident anytime you look at advertising, most products intersect Maslow's ladder at more than one point. Even as apparently simple an act as having friends over for pizza involves three levels of Maslow's hierarchy: physiological needs, love and belongingness needs, and esteem needs. People feed their bodies, bond with others emotionally, and perform some work on their social status; and they do it all by means of that innocent-seeming, double-cheese-and-pepperoni pizza.

Climb Maslow's ladder

Rarely do people buy products simply for their minimal satisfaction of the lowest-level need; therefore, as an ad writer you always want to think about climbing the ladder: in addition to a product's obvious solution to a need, what else is at stake? Always ask yourself, what is the *highest possible benefit* I can claim for this product? And realize that such ladder climbing is smart. In a culture as surfeited with competing material goods as America's, many products can satisfy lower-level needs, so consumers

A hearing aid can improve a lot more than your hearing.

⊜Starkey
Your hearing is our concern.

3.1. Smart advertising finds the strongest benefit, not simply the most obvious one. A hearing aid's highest possible benefit is more than just better audio, yes?

often differentiate among them on the basis of what else those products can do (see figs. 3.1 and 3.2).

For example, the durable slogan for Jif peanut butter ("Choosy moms choose Jif") sails right past the promise of satisfying the physiological need of hunger (everyone already understands that peanut butter fills stomach cavities) and promises to fill the higher-order needs of love, nurturance, and maternal competence. After all, those really are the psychological and emotional values at stake when a mother buys food for her children. Moreover, since peanut butter is a prepared food rather than some-

Search for some way to relate the tiny, constricted world clients live in to the larger, sunnier world people actually care about. Deodorants aren't about keeping dry, they're about being loved. Computers aren't about getting more work done, they're about power. Cars aren't about transportation. Food isn't about hunger. Drink isn't about thirst. And so on.

—Steve Hayden, president,
Ogilvy & Mather Worldwide

thing Mom made herself, since it's a convenience food, really, do you see that also embedded within that phrase is forgiveness for buying it, the assurance that such a food choice is more than convenience, or other than convenience? Buying Jif, far from being a labor-saving option, really reflects well on Mom. Do you see the promise there? Jif has climbed the ladder.

Nike doesn't just sell stylish, durable athletic gear. With phrases like "There is no finish line," "I can," and "Just do it," Nike sells the transcendence of sweat, self-actualization through the testing of the self. Rockport doesn't simply promise well-made shoes; it writes headlines like "Shoes that help you live longer" and discusses in the copy the health-enhancing virtues of walking. Even Rockport's simple campaign theme line "Be comfortable. Uncompromise. Start with your feet" relates the product to cultural trends (increased casualness in public places) while tying the benefit to issues larger than arch support.

Become sensitive to the problems being solved by a product; they are often more various and rise

PLEASE DONATE BLOOD.
DON'T LET SUPPLIES GET ANY LOWER.

THE BLOOD CENTER
OF SOUTHEASTERN WISCONSIN, INC.

3.2. Here giving blood is linked to a benefit even higher than helping another person: helping a whole country full of people.

3.3. The benefit of a successfully shipped package has to do less with the package than with the person or company that sends it. The maintenance or enhancement of that person or company's reputation and professional acumen is what's for sale, not package delivery itself.

3.4. DayOne sells products and support for new parents. What's the highest possible benefit? What's really for sale? The picture and headline ("The weight of the world— 8 lbs. 4 oz.") tell us everything we need to know.

3.5. They're not called "pets" for nothing: people nurture them. But they return the favor.

higher up the ladder than you might think. Usually consumers are looking not for a product that will do the least for them, but for one that will do the most (see fig. 3.3).

A shopping list of needs

Maslow's hierarchy is so brief that a more specific catalog of needs (and products associated with them) can be helpful. This list, not a hierarchy but a horizontal array, is from Robert Settle and Pamela Alreck's *Why They Buy: American Consumers Inside and Out.*[3]

1. Achievement: the need to perform difficult tasks, exercise one's skills
[Professional tools, sports equipment, any skill-providing service: computer training, physical training, college courses, and so on. The Army slogan "Be all you can be," Black & Decker's "How Things Get Done."]

2. Independence: the need to be autonomous, have options, be different
[Fashion makes this appeal; cars do, too. Hair care items "let you be you." Credit cards, alcohol, and cigarettes can be advertised this way; Virginia Slims cigarettes have linked themselves to women's rights with "You've come a long way, baby" and, more recently, "Find Your Voice." Saab's slogan urged consumers to "Find your own road."]

3. Exhibition: the need to gain public attention, show off, be noticed
[Clothing and fashion accessories, too. From big things like cars and homes to smaller items like hair styles, anything capable of asserting the self.]

4. Recognition: the need to be highly regarded by others, to be held up as a good example
[Many "badge" items symbolize this; so do getting a college degree, joining social organizations.]

5. Dominance: the need to exercise power over others, direct and supervise, have influence
[Any power item, from a big car or house to a pesticide or detergent that has punch. Oxy 10, a pimple cream targeted largely at teenagers, closed a TV ad with this line: "Exert control over *something.*"]

6. Affiliation: the need to be closely associated with others, the need for relationships
[Joining the army, joining anything, fills this need. Personal care items, breath mints, toothpaste, and the like facilitate closeness with others: "Aren't you glad you use Dial? Don't you wish everyone did?"]

7. Nurturance: the need to provide care for others, to have and protect (see fig. 3.4)
[Child care and pet care products; gardening; cooking and housekeeping, laundry; volunteer or charity work.]

8. Succorance: the need to receive help from others, be comforted, be encouraged and supported (see fig. 3.5)
[Anything that functions as a care-giver: personal services, especially those that work on the body; limousines, salons, spas, counseling services; anything that "pampers" us.]

9. Sexuality: the need to establish and develop one's sexual identity, be sexually attractive, give and receive sexual satisfaction
[All gendered products; colognes; fashion; dating accessories and entertainments.]

10. Stimulation: the need to stimulate the senses, pursue vigorous activity, engage the mind and body, stimulate the palate, be active (see figs. 3.6 and 3.7)
[Sporting goods, health clubs, restaurants, amusement parks, bubble baths, fabric softeners.]

11. Diversion: the need to relax, have fun, escape from routines, be entertained (see fig. 3.8.)
[Vacations, amusement parks, sports, etc.]

12. Novelty: the need to alter routine, be surprised, acquire new skills, have new and different experiences
[Travel, education, movies, books.]

13. Understanding: the need to comprehend, teach and learn, discover patterns, make connections
[Self-improvement courses, education, movies, books. Butler University's slogan is "Challenge your mind—change your world."]

14. Consistency: the need for order and cleanliness, to control uncertainty and avoid ambiguity, to make accurate predictions
[All cleaners, repair services, maintenance items; "matched" goods, organizers. The Holiday Inn slogan told travelers "The best surprise is no surprise." "Always Coca-Cola" suggests this brand's reassuring constancy in people's lives. The Container Store didn't think its surge

3.6. Some people like high-octane stimulation.

3.7. Other people do, too.

in sales after the terrorist attacks of 9/11 was a coincidence. According to its vice president of marketing, "Our customers want to get control, and when they can't control the world around them, they turn to things they can control."[4]

15. Security: the need to be free from fear, feel safe and protected, avoid accidents, acquire assets (see fig. 3.9)

[Insurance, burglar alarms, investments, all safety equipment. AC Delco's slogan encourages customers to specify its brand of auto parts: "If you're not asking for it, you're asking for it."]

Examining the list, you can see, for example, that many need–product connections can easily be made. Why buy a smoke alarm? Security. Why go to

3.8. A cluster of benefits: diversion, novelty, succorance, sexuality. A great headline, too.

3.9. A graphic visual metaphor and punning headline combine to make the case for motorcycle safety.

college? Understanding. Why buy household cleaners? Consistency.

But such easy connections can be simplistic. The smoke alarm, for instance, may also signal independence, especially for people living on their own for the first time. It may express affiliation if all their friends agree that no reasonable person should be without one. When parents put one in the baby's room, it becomes a form of nurturance. When people buy several and put them in many places, they might be expressing a need for consistency. Landlords might buy them simply to comply with property statutes; for these consumers, the alarms provide legal security. And all these people may be responding to more than one motive (see fig. 3.10).

When you're trying to sell a product and you begin listing benefits, from most important to least, you immediately ask, "Important to whom?" The list varies, depending on who's buying. Let's find out who is.

3.10. An ad that understands the multiple needs of the adolescent American male—achievement, independence, exhibition, recognition, affiliation, and stimulation—and shows how a Gibson guitar can help.

4 ▪ Analyzing the Marketplace

> There is no future for products everybody likes a little, only for products somebody likes a lot.
> —Laurel Cutler,
> VP-consumer affairs, Chrysler Corporation

The principle of market segmentation

> If you're not thinking segments, you're not thinking.
> —Theodore Levitt,
> *The Marketing Imagination*

Fewer and fewer products are sold today via a *total market approach*, that is, by creating one product and one argument for all humanity—"One Size Fits All" thinking, if you will. Sophisticated production techniques allow many product and packaging variations, so one size no longer need fit all. Plus, mass media have so splintered that broad-beaming an advertisement on major TV networks, for example, is often an inefficient and imprecise way to reach potential users. And given the heterogeneous lifestyles, media use, and consumption patterns in this country, a "mass audience" rarely exists.

So you will usually be selling via market segmentation strategies, that is, by creating separate selling arguments to separate segments or target markets of potential consumers, frequently with separate versions of the product.

Sometimes your advertising problem will present a fairly well-defined target market. For example, you'll be asked to write recruitment materials for a college, and you'll be able to gain a good sense of who might come simply by looking at the students already there. Or you'll be asked to create a brochure for a local soccer club or Macintosh users club, and you'll get to know them, too. Other times you'll be asked to sell a product with a less firmly established target market; part of your creative task then will be to locate and define a likely segment. You'll need to understand the target audience well enough to tailor an argument just for them.

Methods of segmentation

How do marketers find relatively homogeneous groups of people with similar product needs? There are many possible *segmentation variables*, those dimensions by which market segments can be defined, but you can think of all of them as grouping (and separating) people on the basis of either who they are or how they behave.[1]

DEMOGRAPHICS

Usually you begin by targeting product or category users. (For example, if you're selling running shoes, you target runners. If you're selling Wheaties, you target cereal eaters.) Then you further define the market through those physical attributes, including socioeconomic and cultural variables, commonly known as *demographics* and including such indexes as population size and shifts; gender and age; geographic location and mobility; income and expenditures; occupation and education; race, nationality, and religion; and marital status and family status.[2]

Every person is a sum of such parts, and if you think about yourself for a minute, you'll see that not only can you be so defined but lots of your buying behavior is a direct result of one or a combination of these characteristics. If, for example, you're a 20-year-old college student, think of the things you are interested in and buy as a consequence. If you live in San Diego instead of Minneapolis, consider how the geographical differences dictate everything from clothing to leisure activities to utilities use to food and so on. If you're a single, thirtysomething, working woman, look at how many of your product needs spring directly from such circumstances. The images in figure 4.1 indicate that, for example,

4.1. Two shopping magazines demonstrate the defining power of a demographic by talking differently about the same impulse. Many products not intimately related to sexual differences have been successfully "genderized," including cigarettes, shavers, deodorants, diapers, beverages, radio stations, and cable TV channels.

gender alone can determine not only what you sell but also how you sell it.

Marketers track demographics the way fishermen track schools of fish, and for the same reason. In fact, one marketing maxim, employing the same metaphor, says simply: "Fish where the fishing is good." With obvious relationships to consumer behavior, demographic data do indeed tell marketers where to drop their lines by indicating what the buying patterns are, how they're concentrated, and where they're headed. Consider age. Each age brings with it certain needs, tastes, preferences, role-related behavior, and disposable income, all of which help determine what is bought.[3] Levi's Dockers, for example, were created because marketers realized that the Baby Boomers, that large cohort of consumers born between 1946 and 1964, had outgrown their jeans, both literally and metaphorically: they needed more room and wore jeans less often but could find nothing to fill the need. Dockers—mid-priced, casual, stylish-but-jeans-inspired—understood the aging of the boomers and spawned a whole new category of men's fashion as a result.[4]

PSYCHOGRAPHICS

As important as they are, however, demographics alone often prove insufficient as a way of locating target markets and of explaining and predicting consumer behavior. A demographic segment may include various consumer patterns; various demographic segments may contain the same consumer pattern. Runners, for example, share certain product choices, yet they cut across many demographic segments. A 40-year-old single male with an income of $75,000 may be a plumber, a college professor, or an airline pilot, each with an obviously different lifestyle and consumption pattern. The "green revolution," the environmental concern that has affected so many attitudes toward product use, can't be measured by demographic indexes at all. People haven't changed quantitatively; they've changed qualitatively, in their attitudes.

Thus to demographics must be added *psychographics*—people's attitudes, opinions, and habits; their personality traits, lifestyles, and social class. Think of psychographics as the opposite of demographics: not the outside of one's life, but the inside. And think just how much those insides have been changing over the years—the continual redefinition of women, men, and sex roles in this society; the rise of alternate lifestyles (and people's changing attitudes toward them); the psychological effects of single parenting and latch-key child-hoods; the "post-literate" but visually sophisticated mindset of many young people; the rising health consciousness of the past decade; the demand for convenience across almost all product categories—the list is both endless and ever-evolving. You can see how much of consumer behavior is tied up with

4.2. Demographics and psychographics combined: these ads target the upscale gray market (many of them "empty nesters"), understand what that market is thinking, and tie recreation vehicles to the lifestyle change.

4.3. A very clever way to announce the opening of the "ultimate" Boston Market. This campaign whimsically suggests that the food's so good people will have to find new uses for all that soon-to-be-desolate kitchen stuff.

these factors. Since people express their values and realize their lifestyles with the things they buy, employing psychographics helps define target markets, create profiles of targeted consumers, and determine advertising strategies themselves (see fig. 4.2).

BUYING BEHAVIOR

You can also separate consumers into groups by how they think about and use products themselves—by how people behave with them, if you will.[5] The major behavioral indexes are discussed below.

Occasions

When people buy or use something can be a means of market segmentation. Think of popular holidays—Mother's Day, Father's Day, Valentine's Day, Christmas, and so on. Each gift-giving holiday becomes a way to segment a market. Rites of passage do, too. People give computers to high school graduates, rings at weddings, gifts for birthdays, anniversaries, and the like. Even certain times of day or year require purchases: a camera and film for a vacation, snacks for late at night (Wendy's: "Eat Great, Even Late!"), coffee in the morning ("The best part of waking up is Folgers in your cup"). Retailers hold grand openings, anniversary sales, going out of business sales, you name it. Events—the New York City Marathon, for example—are opportunities for sponsorship and advertising (banner along the route: "Five boroughs. Two caplets. Tylenol"). There are many, many ways you can sell something by tying it to an occasion (see figs. 4.3 and 4.4).

Benefits sought

What people seek in a product varies, and you can create market segments by appealing to those varying needs. Toothpaste marketing is a classic case of benefit segmentation: if people want fresh breath, they buy Close-Up; if they want fewer cavities, Crest; white teeth, Ultra Brite; and so forth. Ask yourself what benefits consumers seek from your client's product, and create target markets accordingly. Low price may be a benefit some people seek. Or good service.

Usage rate

If you consider your own buying habits, you may notice that you are always running out of milk but

4.4. L.L.Bean presents itself as one solution to a busy gift-giving season.

rarely replenish the six cans of pop at the back of the refrigerator; that you have the latest audiophile gear, but your most complicated kitchen appliance is the can opener; that you buy a new car every three years but would never own a motorcycle. In brief, of all the products out there, you buy only a small number; and within that small number, you consume a lot of some things but a lot less of many others. In short, you're a heavy user of some products, a light-to-moderate user of others, and a non-user of far more products.

So is everyone—a truth that leads to targeting these various consumption levels, segmenting markets on the basis of usage rate or user status. Are your target customers non-users of a product, ex-users, light users, first-time users, moderate users, heavy users? People in each segment tend to be similar. Sell one way to a light user, another way to a heavy user. Many strategies target the heavy users for the obvious reason that those people account for the bulk of sales in a product category. In fact, a marketing rule-of-thumb, the "80/20 rule," says that in many categories 20 percent of the market consumes 80 percent of that product: roughly 80 percent of all the beer is consumed by 20 percent of all the beer drinkers, 80 percent of all the ketchup is consumed by 20 percent of the ketchup users, and so on.

Although such percentages vary, for many categories there is a heavy user who can be profiled, then targeted. By seeking to locate and understand those consumers, marketers hope to fish where the fishing is really good. But even good spots can be too heavily fished, so marketers often target the light-to-moderate user (and occasionally the ex-user or non-user) since those markets, frequently ignored, have less competition. Carving out a larger percentage of a smaller segment can often be more profitable than getting only a small percentage of a larger one.

Loyalty status
Find out who the brand-loyal users are. What unites them? What separates them from others?

Analyzing the Marketplace / 35

SOMEWHERE ON AN AIRPLANE A MAN IS TRYING TO RIP OPEN A SMALL BAG OF PEANUTS.

Give us life at ground level, rolling along the endless highway on a Harley-Davidson. 100% depressurized. Just sunlight on chrome. The voice of a V-Twin ripping the open air. And elbow room, stretching all the way to the horizon. Maybe you too think this is the way life ought to be lived. Time to spread some wings. 1-800-443-2153 or www.harley-davidson.com. **The Legend Rolls On.**

4.5. The ad isn't positioning one way to travel against another so much as it's ridiculing non-bikers. It invites Harley-Davidson loyalists (and aspirants) to bond over the freedom of the road. A wonderful headline, don't you think? It makes flying seem so small-minded, such a cramped, pathetic idea.

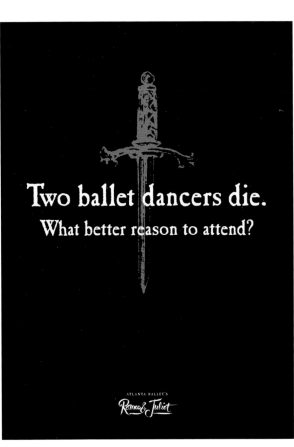

4.6. Targeting people who don't normally attend the ballet by making a joke they'll appreciate. And the joke's wit suggests that the evening might be more fun than they thought.

What unites those loyal to another brand or to no brand? Consider creating appeals to each. (See fig. 4.5 for an ad that appeals to members of the club.)

Readiness stage
Are your target consumers ready to buy, unaware of the brand or product category, informed, interested, what? Intersect them, wherever they are (see fig. 4.6).

Attitude toward product
Perhaps people's attitudes, from negative to positive, toward the product or brand divide clearly enough that different ones can be targeted. For example, in introducing Silk soymilk to a broader audience, its advertisers had to figure out consumers' "stuck points," the attitudes toward soymilk that were holding them back. One was a sense that soymilk just couldn't taste good, so an ad in the campaign had this headline: "First time tasters rave, 'It doesn't suck.'" (For another ad in that campaign, see fig. 4.7.)

Segmenting markets is rarely a clear-cut choice among demographics, psychographics, or the behavioral indexes; rather, these indexes are combined to target and profile a product's likeliest consumers. For example, the Dockers marketing example mentioned earlier combined the age/gender demographic (25- to 40-year-old men) with psychographics (the mindset—casual and jeans-oriented) and benefit sought (comfort) to determine the right advertising message.

What can you do?
Short of taking a course in market research, subscribing to a market research firm's data, or becoming a market researcher yourself, you may assume that there's no realistic way to generate and combine psychographic, demographic, and buying behavior information. And to some extent you're right. But no matter how sophisticated such research becomes, it still remains simply the *assertion* of buying categories by people thinking about consumers; it's not revealed, unalterable, inscrutable Truth. So you, too, can think about who's out there buying your client's product and how many kinds of "whos" there might be.

First let's look at a real-world example. Chiat/Day/Mojo, Nissan's ad agency, used psychographic segments of new-car buyers created by a market research firm to help it devise strategies.[6] The study postulated six consumer categories on the basis of

Our marketing experts have advised us to use the triple double dog dare.

All natural, lactose free, high in protein, with a surprisingly good taste. *Don't be so stubborn.*

4.7. Getting people over that first speed bump.

people's attitudes toward cars and the "driving experience."

Gearheads, the true car enthusiasts, actually work on cars and are mostly male, blue collar. They are the most likely to believe that the car they drive says a lot about them. They love sports cars, both domestic and Japanese.

Epicures, the largest group, like fully equipped, comfortable cars, are looking for style and elegance, and represent the second-highest percentage of women and the highest household incomes, $100,000 or more. They especially like convertibles.

Purists, the youngest group, are skeptical and not brand loyal but like driving and love sports cars. They represent the high concentrations of laborers and Asian Americans.

Functionalists are conservative homeowners, often with children, who want sensible, fuel-efficient transportation. They buy small to mid-sized domestic cars.

Road-Haters, tied with the epicures as the largest group, are safety conscious, strongly prefer large

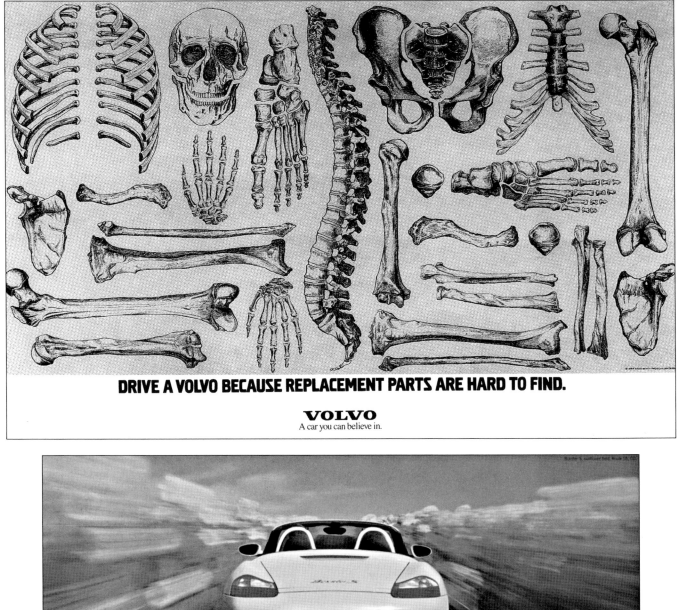

DRIVE A VOLVO BECAUSE REPLACEMENT PARTS ARE HARD TO FIND.

VOLVO
A car you can believe in.

What a dog feels
when the leash breaks.

Instant freedom, courtesy of the Boxster S. The 250 horsepower boxer engine launches
you forward with its distinctive growl. Any memory of life on a leash evaporates in the wind
rushing overhead. It's time to run free. Contact us at 1-800-PORSCHE or porsche.com

PORSCHE

4.8. Volvo targets road-haters; Porsche, epicures.

domestic cars, don't enjoy driving, and represent the highest share of women, the highest ages, and the lowest incomes.

Negatives are uninterested in cars, regarding them as necessary evils, hassles. They're the most educated, with large incomes, and frequently buy small foreign cars.

You can see that these categories really are just assertions (who knows for certain how many kinds of new-car buyers there really are?). But they combine psychographics and demographics in ways that seem to jibe with your intuitive sense of who might be out there (see fig. 4.8). You can also see that if you're Nissan this is helpful material. You can target as many segments as you feel you have cars for, and you can create advertising that talks about those cars in ways that fit the needs of the targets. (You can also use this material to change the kinds of cars you make, another virtue of good research.)

SPEAK THE AUDIENCE'S LANGUAGE

> To know whom to write for is to know how to write.
>
> —Virginia Woolf

Consider the following ads and note how well they know whom they're written for—how well they understand and locate, by their language and thought, highly specific market segments. This one, which appeared in London newspapers in 1900, was written by polar explorer Sir Ernest Shackleton:

> Men Wanted for Hazardous Journey. Small wages, bitter cold, long months of complete darkness, constant danger, safe return doubtful. Honor and recognition in case of success.

Response was overwhelming and immediate. The ad worked because it understood exactly what certain men wanted to hear, and said it to them clearly, simply, and powerfully.[7]

Another ad, written ninety years later, was placed in men's magazines. It, too, understands what a certain market segment wants to hear and says it to them. Notice how precisely a particular person is evoked—the appeal combines demographics (male, thirty-plus, upscale, urban) with psychographics (a particular lifestyle motive for running). The ad, a spread for Nike, shows a small figure running in downtown San Francisco, with these words as both headline and copy:

> He's fat and he's soft and he's wearing your clothes and he's getting too old and he was born on your birthday and you're afraid that if you stop running, he'll catch up with you.

See figures 4.9 through 4.12 for more ads that understand who they're talking to.

THINK LIKE THE MARKET SEGMENT

> If you can't turn yourself into your customer, you probably shouldn't be in the ad writing business at all.
>
> —Leo Burnett,
> founder, Leo Burnett agency

It's easier to sell a product if you actually know someone who is part of its target audience. If, for example, you're selling golf equipment and you've played the game and know golfers, then you can become them in your mind while making ads.

One difficulty occurs when you must imagine an audience with which you have little experience: a different subculture or ethnic group, any audience a long way from you—maybe you're an undergraduate in New York City writing ads that sell farm equipment, or someone who's never taken more than a snapshot selling photography gear to pros. What to do? If possible, locate and interview someone who is a part of the target group. Find the magazines of that profession and read them. Study the ads to see what the issues are, what the selling arguments are, how the language works, what the slang is. You cannot write a good ad for a target audience until you become a surrogate member of it; and if you aren't born into it, then you must join it through empathy and effort. You must think and talk and want like your audience.

Another difficulty arises with business-to-business advertising: not only must you imagine two audiences, but neither one of them is a person. For example, you're asked to write an ad from a home construction firm to an architectural firm seeking to convince the latter that the former is the builder to choose. Even in this instance, however, the trick is to forget the firms and to simply become two people: a guy who builds houses talking to a guy who designs them. (Business-to-business advertising is examined more completely in chapter 12.)

IDLE HANDS ARE TROUBLE. HANDS STUCK IN MELTED MARSHMALLOW, LESS SO.

CUB SCOUT ENROLLMENT IS HERE. WWW.JOINCUBS.COM

4.9. Think like a parent, and you'll get more Cub Scouts. Another ad read, "Ever gaze at your child and wonder: Shouldn't he have more grass stains on him?"

4.10. People identify with their cities. Why not invite Milwaukeeans to share, with a smile, part of their city's heritage?

In the church started by a man who had six wives, forgiveness goes without saying.

The Episcopal Church believes that just as we all make mistakes, we can all be forgiven. Come and join us in the joy of worship and fellowship soon.
The Episcopal Church

Where women stand in the Episcopal Church.

If you believe that men and women should share equally in the sacraments and service of Christianity, join us where God's calling can be answered by anyone.
The Episcopal Church

You can't meet God's gift to women in a singles' bar.

If the singles life sometimes leaves you feeling alone and empty, remember that God's gift to all women and men is Jesus Christ. Come join us in worship this Sunday in the Episcopal Church.
The Episcopal Church

4.11. An aggressive campaign for the Episcopal Church realized that more than one kind of person was missing from the pews, for more than one reason. Ads targeted specific segments of potential churchgoers by addressing various lifestyles and needs.

What market segmentation means to you

Segmenting the market clarifies things. You understand what motivates each targeted segment of consumers, what they go to the product for, and what language they speak. If, however, you never decide on target markets and instead try to sell to everyone in a language that offends no one—the "8 to 80" perplex—if you never place a particular person before your mind's eye when creating ads, then diffusion and blandness will undo you.

So never content yourself with addressing fuzzy somebodies at best or demographic nobodies at worst, thinking, for example, that you are sufficiently precise if you say that your ad is "aimed at women 25–45." (Imagine for a moment the variety within those demographics. It could vary all the way from the young woman sitting beside you in a class to your mom.)

Instead, always try to locate a particular person in your mind's eye: your brother, your grandmother, that camera buff you know. Can you make that person laugh? Can you get inside with the right talk and the right imagery? Try.

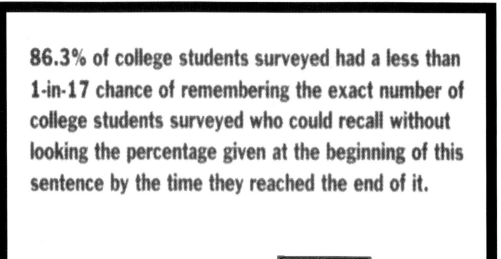

4.12. Ever stayed up too late for an exam and found your mind swimming and your eyes blurry? Celestial Seasonings quietly sells Sleepytime tea by bonding with college students. In this ad, a product that might have been sold as "relaxing" is wisely given a sharper focus. A series of such ads, each matching a tea with a target audience, would be stronger than any number of more generic ads. People look up when their names are called.

5 ▪ Defining Strategic Approaches

> Start with strategy. We try to begin with a strategy that feels different, that immediately defines the client and sets them apart. If the strategy isn't doing that job, the creative probably won't do it either. Your gut usually tells you when you've found a good strategy—it seems obvious, even though it wasn't obvious before. Like, "Why didn't I think of that before," or "Why isn't anybody else doing that?" Then you start to get a little nervous that somebody's probably working on that strategy right now. That's a good feeling, it usually means you're onto something that's right.
>
> —Mike Shine, copywriter and creative director, Butler Shine & Stern

If I were to say—in three words—what all good ads do, I'd say: "Dramatize the benefit." Advertisers differ, however, in what they consider the benefit in need of dramatizing—sometimes it's a product's feature or a marketplace position, other times a problem solved or a state of mind achieved.

Also, since ads sell a product to a consumer, ad writers can choose to emphasize one or the other. Thus, you can think of advertising approaches as residing on a continuum from product-oriented strategies, on the one hand, to consumer-oriented ones on the other, from hard product to soft lifestyle. You could also say that the approaches range from rational to emotional—product-oriented arguments frequently appealing to a sense of reason, the consumer-oriented approaches often stressing the emotional qualities of life with the product.

How many kinds of strategic approaches there are depends on who's counting and how. Here's my count; others, of course, will differ.

Product-oriented

1. Generic claim: sell the product category, not the brand.

2. Product feature: sell a product feature; appeal to reason.

3. Unique selling proposition: sell a benefit unique to the brand.

4. Positioning: establish a distinct and desirable market niche.

Consumer-oriented

5. Brand image: create and sell a personality for the brand.

6. Lifestyle: associate the product with a way of life.

7. Attitude: associate the product with a state of mind.

When you artificially separate the flow of advertising, all categories—including these—are false, their distinctions neat on paper but messier in reality. Many ads borrow from several of these categories; other great ads can't be lodged in any of them. When you're making ads, use the idea of categories, but don't be bound by it. Don't worry over which you're using so much as this: Is what you're doing working?

Product-oriented strategies

First, let's examine strategies that emphasize the thing for sale rather than the person who might buy it.

GENERIC CLAIM

Selling one of the principal benefits a given product category delivers—fast headache relief for aspirin

Celibacy isn't always a choice.

Designer eyewear 40-60% off everyday. FOR EYES

5.1. These brands make generic claims—the small car promises economy, the optical retailer offers good-looking glasses—but they do so energetically. The strength of the execution (rather than the singularity of the strategy) is what makes these ads distinctive.

Why gas stations sell food.

Civic Hatchback
HONDA

and other pain relievers, water-borne relaxation for cruise lines, clean clothes for laundry products, and so on—is probably the most widely used advertising strategy. Many ads simply make a generic claim, associate the brand with that claim, then count on the cumulative power of advertising and association, as well as the memorability of a strong execution (see fig. 5.1) to link the principal benefit with that brand. They do this even though competitors can (and do) make the same argument and deliver the same benefit.

Selling the product category, not the brand, makes even better sense if your client's product has a dominant share in a market. Your client's main competitor is consumers themselves—their levels of usage—more than other brands. As marketing consultants Jack Trout and Al Ries advise, "When you own the pie, you should try to enlarge the pie rather than try to increase the size of your slice."[1] Arm & Hammer thus needs to sell the idea of baking soda, not its brand. Likewise, Campbell's doesn't need to sell its brand but the generic product; the

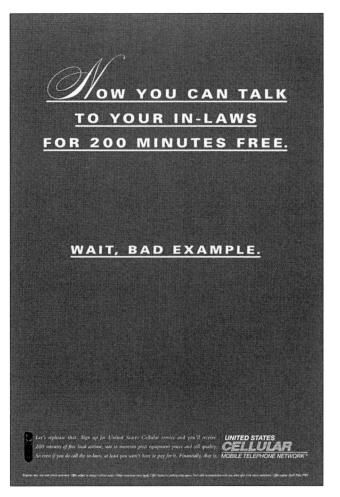

5.2. Pioneering ads for cellular phones, like the traffic jam ad from 1985, made the generic claim. As the market grew and became competitive, ads focused on differentials, such as better service or lower rates, as did the "bad example" ad from 1995.

Imagine dangling a bowling ball from the earpiece.

The lengths to which we go to ensure the lasting quality of Costa Del Mar sunglasses are legendary.

But there is certainly nothing more impressive (some might say outlandish) than our metal frame stress test.

This consists of attaching a *twenty-pound free weight* to the temple of every fiftieth pair of frames.

If they can survive this, we feel fairly confident that your American-made Costa Del Mar sunglasses will live up to their weighty responsibility as a lasting investment.

CostaDelMar

If your store doesn't carry them, patronize better stores.

Why half the time spent making our glasses is spent polishing them.

Cheap sunglass frames may be painted or coated in some fashion. This finish invariably wears off with use. By contrast, American-made Costa Del Mar sunglasses are *polished* to a natural sheen by tumbling the frames in *teakwood chips* for six days.

To some, this may seem a bit extreme. But then, when you spend the other half of your time making the finest lenses available, wouldn't it be a shame to skimp on the frames that surround them?

CostaDelMar

If your store doesn't carry them, patronize better stores.

5.3. If you've built a better product, tell people about it, explain your competitive advantages. In this campaign great headlines dramatize distinctive and relevant product features, and great copy makes the case.

Most cheap sunglasses — and an appalling number of expensive ones — are made with nylon frames. The nature of this material is that it has a "memory."

By contrast, American-made Costa Del Mar frames are made of top quality *Zyl*

(cellulose acetate). When you twist Zyl, it doesn't fight back. Which means, unless your ears are somewhere on your elbows, your Costa Del Mars will retain your perfect fit. CostaDelMar

If your store doesn't carry them, patronize better stores.

For the name of a better store nearest you, or to order direct, call 800-221-0484. In Florida 800-447-3700.

Why a well-made pair of sunglasses has no memory.

Campbell's slogan "Soup is good food" encouraged consumers simply to eat more soup.

New products (like digital video recorders and HDTV) also needed at first to sell the basic argument (why buy a DVR? why get HDTV?) before worrying about brand differentiation (see fig. 5.2).

PRODUCT FEATURE

Ask yourself why people buy your client's product.

If their choice is largely rational, a sifting among product distinctions (most hardware, large and small; durable goods; high-ticket items), and your client's product truly has distinctions that matter, then sell them. Focus, not on generic product benefits, but on competitive ones. In this situation you appeal to the logical choice based on sensible differences among brands. Consider the ads in figure 5.3. Gary Knutson, creative director at Howard, Merrell

& Partners, explains the campaign: "Every other manufacturer was selling sunglasses as fashion statements. We simply zigged when everyone was zagging, and spelled out product features that made Costa Del Mar sunglasses superior."[2]

This strategy can work in competitive markets, where you're fighting to distinguish your client's product from others, and it can work whenever *why* people buy is at least partly a rational decision. You can emphasize either the product's virtue or the consumer's problem being solved—or both, as does this headline for an Acura coupe underneath a picture of the car in action: "Could your heart benefit from the use of another 24 valves?"

UNIQUE SELLING PROPOSITION

If you can fill in the following sentence for your client's brand, then you're making a Unique Selling Proposition: "You should buy a ____ because it's the only one that _____." You're telling consumers that if they want this feature/benefit, the only place they can get it is from your brand.

Rosser Reeves, an American advertiser of the 1950s, built his career on the idea that the best way to sell things was by making what he called a "Unique Selling Proposition" (USP), a specific promise of benefit unique to the product, one that the competition either did not or could not claim. So, for example, M&Ms "melt in your mouth, not in your hands," an argument implying that its competitors failed to do so. This singling out of some specific aspect of the product and then basing an ad campaign on it was predicated on the buying public's willingness to believe that products do indeed differ from one another, that a given brand can deliver something that others can't (see fig. 5.4).

For decades Folger's emphasized that its coffee was "mountain grown." All coffee is mountain grown, but Folger's said it first, thus appearing to make an argument unique to itself and owning territory in consumers' brains as a consequence. (This first use of a generic feature by a brand is sometimes called a *preemptive claim* instead of a USP. You are preempting its use by competitors even though they too could have made the same claim, had they thought of it first.)

Although it's often true that technological parity now makes it difficult to create and maintain a hardware differential, products whose selling argument is a USP are still out there. Apple, for example, has always emphasized hardware/software

uniqueness in selling its computers and digital products, from the very first personal computer to Cube, iMac, iPod, iTunes, and beyond. The argument is that only an Apple is an Apple.

Nonetheless, product-oriented USP advertising has given way over the decades to softer, brand-image, style- and feelings-oriented advertising. People are still willing to believe that brands are different from one another, but the differences have shifted from those of technology and hardware to ones of emotion and relationship. In fact, John Hegarty of London's Bartle Bogle Hegarty thinks trends have moved past the USP to, first, the "Emotional Selling Proposition," where *how* people felt about a brand was what made it unique (see fig. 5.5) to the "Irrational Selling Proposition," from the 1990s onward, where only fun, odd, often absurdist campaigns registered with ad-drenched consumers (think of the ads for Lee Jeans featuring the Buddy Lee doll, for example, or of the funny, ironic, behind-the-scenes sportsworld created by ESPN's advertising).[3]

POSITIONING

> The true nature of marketing today involves the conflict between corporations, not the satisfying of human needs and wants.
>
> —Al Trout and Jack Ries, *Marketing Warfare*

The advertising world owes *positioning* to Trout and Ries, who developed the concept in a series of articles and later a book.[4] Simply stated, positioning is the perception consumers have of a product, not unto itself, but relative to its competition. Products are "positioned" in consumers' minds, each being given an evaluation, a definition, a niche, in the product inventories they maintain. Consumers condense their estimate of each product into one simple (and often permanent) perception and create hierarchies of similar products.

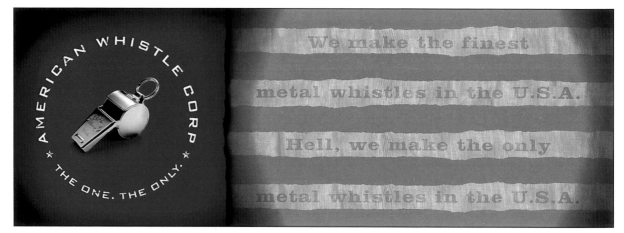

5.4. USP advertising: as the slogan says, this is the one, the only, metal whistle.

LET'S PUT AWAY
THE MIDDLE FINGER.

Let's lay off the horn.
Let's be considerate of cyclists.
Let's volunteer jumper cables.
Let's pay a stranger's toll.
And for crying out loud,
let's remember to turn off those blinkers.

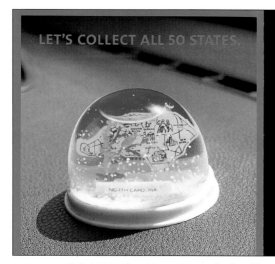

LET'S COLLECT ALL 50 STATES.

Motoring is about mileage. City miles. Highway miles. It's all the same. A MINI with a lot of mileage is more interesting than a MINI with only a few miles on it. And it's easy to put on the miles considering the MINI gets some sweet, sweet gas mileage. So, don't be afraid of a seasoned odometer. Consider it an experience-o-meter. It says you've been places and you've done things. It's a scrapbook bursting at the seams. And there's nothing sadder than a four-year-old photo album with six pictures in it.

When you see other MINI owners, try not to rub it in if you have more miles than they do. They're trying. Maybe they've been busy at work or something. And don't be embarrassed if you meet someone with more miles on their MINI. You'll get there. If you find that you're not hitting the road as much as you'd like, don't feel guilty. Just being in a MINI means you're motoring more than the next guy.

5.5. Mini advertising presents both a Unique Selling Proposition and Hegarty's Emotional Selling Proposition. Minis are unique partly because of hardware but also, and just as important, because of the emotional connection they invite people to make with them. People can buy a lot of small cars, but they'd only feel quirky, cool, and ready to say "Let's motor" in a Mini.

For example, among detergents, people consider Tide all-American, all-purpose; Cheer is all-temperature; Dreft is soft, for babies' things; Dash is the budget brand; Fab combines a softener with the cleaner; Bold is the enzymes cleaner; and so on. To be successful, a brand must carve out for itself an identity that's not only distinct (a handle by which people can recognize it) but also viable (one for which they'll buy it).

The power of positioning

Positioning is a marketing idea so strong that entire campaigns can be based on it. People probably remember 7-Up as "the Uncola," a pure example of the power of positioning; they were asked to buy it for what it wasn't. Pepsi's slogan "The Choice of a New Generation" sought to reposition Coca-Cola as the drink of old folks, while Coke's "The Real Thing" and "Coke Is It" campaigns tried to position it as the only authentic cola. (Many slogans and campaign theme lines are simply crystallized position statements. See "Write Slogans and Theme Lines" in chapter 14.)

Positioning strategies are essential when products are new, since those products occupy no place whatsoever in consumers' minds. How you position them has much to do with their success. If your client's is simply a "me-too" product, then its chances for survival may be poor. Roughly 20,000 new products are introduced in America every year, and 90 percent of them fail: a killing field.[5] Discovering and then expressing a distinct, competitive position thus becomes a major goal of your advertising. Positioning can also determine advertising strategy when your client's product is not the category leader. After all, there is nowhere to go but up. If the product is a strong #2 or #3, say, you may want to go right after the leader. The key is finding a weakness inherent in the leader's strength (see figs. 5.6 and 5.7). As Trout and Ries argue, "What the leader owns is a position in the mind of the prospect. To win the battle of the mind, you must take away the leader's position before you can substitute your own. It's not enough for you to succeed; others must fail. Specifically, the leader."[6]

Key positioning questions

    What position does your client's product now
        occupy?
    What positions do the competitors' products
        occupy?

    What new position does the client want to
        occupy? Or how do you want to modify
        its current position?
    What strategy should your advertising adopt
        as a consequence?

While many campaigns are based on positioning, its greatest value to you may be as an *idea*, an indispensable index by which to gauge the product and its relationship to the competition. You may never make positioning a dominant advertising strategy, but you should never be ignorant of the product's place in consumers' minds. How they regard it, especially relative to other similar products, is essential information. No product is position-less.

Consumer-oriented strategies

Instead of focusing on the thing you're selling in your ads, you may want to go beyond hardware to what surrounds it. There can be a lot for sale out there.

BRAND IMAGE

Image means personality. Products, like people, have personalities, and they can make or break them in the market place. The personality of a product is an amalgam of many things—its name, its packaging, its price, the style of its advertising, and above all, the nature of the product itself. Every advertisement should be thought of as a contribution to the brand image.
    —David Ogilvy, *Ogilvy on Advertising*

David Ogilvy is generally credited with developing the idea of brand-image advertising, and each of his great campaigns from the 1950s—Rolls Royce, Schweppes, Hathaway shirts, and others—established a consistent style and sensibility that, once begun, were maintained. Brand-image advertising is not the selling of specific product features, elements intrinsic to the object itself, but instead the selling of

5.6. *Sporting News* takes on the market leader, *Sports Illustrated*, whose definition of sports can be pretty broad.

5.7. Ace positions itself against the big-box megastores by going after their strength. What's good about the big boxes—a million things—is also what's bad—a million things. Good for selection, bad for feet.

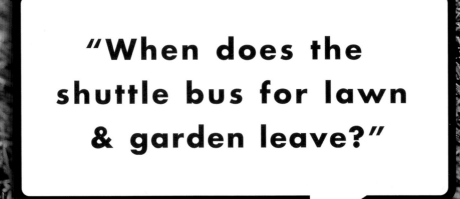

the object's aura, its personality, those aspects extrinsic to it that make up its (self-created) image.

All ads, regardless of strategy, contribute to a brand's image, so in this sense all advertising is brand-image advertising. If a brand has no image, then it's got a bad ad agency. Thus, discussing the *strategy* of brand-image advertising becomes tricky, since image is always at issue. But in this instance let's use the term to mean a strategy focused on the personality of a brand. When people look at that product's advertising, they realize that they're being asked to buy into a personality, not an argument. That's the distinction.

What, for example, differentiates Reebok from Nike, Coca-Cola from Pepsi, BMW from Lexus? Primarily their advertising symbol systems. Each makes a good product; none is so advanced that its technical merit alone distances it from its competition. In consumers' rational minds, they realize that as an object, each is substantially equivalent to its major competitor(s). Since the product is intrinsically similar, the extrinsic brand image of the product, communicated through its advertising (often called advertising's "added value"), becomes the meaning customers seek. The differentiated systems of language and design in which the products reside are what customers buy. And they are happy to do so (see figs. 5.8 and 5.9).

Ogilvy makes this comment:

> Take whiskey. Why do some people choose Jack Daniel's, while others choose Grand Dad or Taylor? Have they tried all three and compared the taste? Don't make me laugh. The reality is that these three brands have different images which appeal to different kinds of people. It isn't the whiskey they choose, it's the image. The brand image is 90 percent of what the distiller has to sell.[7]

And so it is with many products: most of what they have to sell is symbolic. You should consider this strategy when your client's product is in a competitive, parity situation or when the product is almost a commodity: cigarettes, beer, liquor, cologne, soap, and so on (for which a unique feature or rational argument is often hard to find). Brand-image advertising is also a good idea for *badge products*, those items whose names are visible, whose identities are socially obvious (clothes, cars, etc.), unlike socially invisible products (canned goods hidden in cup-

5.8. I've never held a Milwaukee tool, but the visual and headline ("Nobody ever got a blister building a Web site") have already convinced me that no job's too tough for it.

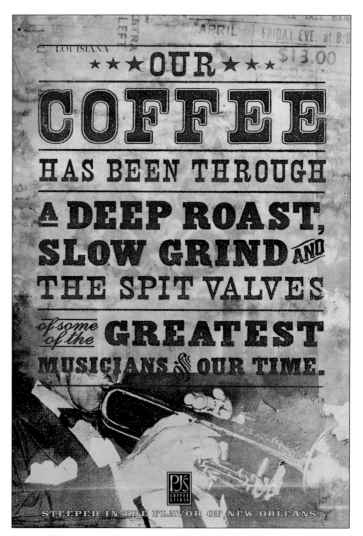

5.9. Coffee may be like liquor: a lot of what people are tasting is in their heads. Looking at this ad, I can taste a coffee that's rich, deep, and steeped in New Orleans tradition. Where am I getting these ideas? Brand image.

boards, detergents stored in the laundry room, etc.). Other products, invisible themselves, that contribute to people's social esteem—personal care items, for instance—can also be sold via brand image.

If you think that's a long list, you're right. Brand-image advertising pervades so many product categories and has become so ubiquitous that in many ways it has won the how-to-advertise war. Lee Clow, chairman of TBWA\Chiat\Day, explains why:

> You have to connect with consumers. Brands are like people, and the personalities you create for brands, the likability, the "I like spending time with those guys," has to open the door before anyone will visit your Web site. They'll ultimately want the informational side of [your message], but you have to make them like you first, before they want to spend time with you and hear what you think about this, that and the other thing.[8]

How to create brand-image advertising

1. Study the image advertising created for other brands, such as Nike, Mini, and Apple. What do you think of these brands, and what in their advertising has led you to think that?

2. Ask, what is the product or brand? What's a Volvo? What's a Timex? and so on. See what answer you get. Either create ads that express that personality, or reshape the personality to fit the answer you seek.

3. Regard the product as a person; write up a profile of it as though it were a person, and study that. Dan Wieden, co-founder of Wieden+ Kennedy, Nike's principal ad agency, calls Nike "complex, contradictory and genuine, like an interesting person, which is why people respond to it."[9] (For more on brand personality, see the discussion of voice in chapter 8, since the sense of personality comes so strongly from the voice of the ads.)

4. Pay attention (as much as a copywriter can) **to the design and typography of the cam-**

paign, how the ads look and feel. Design and type are also powers behind brand images. Style is substance with brand-image advertising.

LIFESTYLE

> Brands have become so similar to one another that the real leverage in the advertising is no longer the content of the product but the placement of the product in the consumer's life.
>
> —Barbara S. Feigin,
> research director, Grey Advertising

Closely related to brand-image advertising is another approach that emphasizes, not product hardware, but consumer states of being—an approach one might call *lifestyle advertising*. Rather than creating an image of the brand itself, it creates an image of the consumer, making him or her, in effect, the product. The viewer is shown a desirable state of being, to which the product is appended.

Lifestyle advertising is what it sounds like: ads show a desirable way of living and simply insert the product into it. Such advertising expresses the highest possible benefit because rather than arguing a narrow product advantage, it implies a large personal improvement. The lifestyle shown is one the viewers desire and can have, or begin to, if they buy the product that seems to be its indispensable accessory (see figs. 5.10 and 5.11).

Remember: the idea is that the target audience doesn't so much see the product (in fact, many such ads barely show it at all) as they see what it must be like to own it. When creating this kind of advertising, don't regard the product as some piece of hardware with features and USPs, some thing over there. Regard it as an indispensable accessory to a way of being; and then use imagery that you think communicates this atmosphere—these psychological benefits, this alternate reality, if you will, that can be the audience's if it uses the product.

ATTITUDE

Attitude advertising is advertising in which tone of voice is so dominant that it becomes what's for sale. Usually the attitude is the brand's—part of its personality, the "tone of voice" part—and it can be so distinctive that it runs the advertising. Nike may have initiated this attitude-is-everything approach when it began the "Just do it" campaign in the mid-

Free. Like wild horses,
like geese bound for Canada.
Leave food for the cat.

Drive the 180hp Jetta 1.8T. **Drivers wanted.**

Swipe the debit card.
Pump the gas, buy the jerky,
close the door and go.

Drive the 180hp GTI 1.8T. **Drivers wanted.**

5.10. Lifestyle advertising. In these ads the product accompanies a way of life that the target audience aspires to. By seeming indispensable to such a lifestyle, the brand becomes an incremental way of achieving it.

1980s. Assuming responsibility for consumers' physical—and by implication, spiritual—health, Nike raised the pitch of its admonitions. Bold type and bold people looked up from the page or from their workouts and scolded folks for being their usual, sloppy selves. "Just do it," the ads warned, and as one of the players added, "And it wouldn't hurt to stop eating like a pig, either." "Ouch. Yes, ma'am," people seemed to say, as they sprinted out the back door wearing Nikes.

But attitude advertising doesn't have to be finger-in-the-face aggressive. Think of Mini's "Let's motor" campaign, which is driven by a sweet but spunky, sociable but iconoclastic voice. Every ad brings this same attitude to life on the road and invites consumers to share it by buying a Mini. Consider, for example, the headline and part of the copy for a magazine ad: "Small thought #7: How is it that dogs can stick their heads out of moving cars? Have you ever tried that? It hurts. Hurts bad. . . . But for some reason, dogs can take it. And they love it. But humans get to steer. So it all evens out." This attitude—a sense of pleasure in the small things and

fun behind the wheel, a sweet blend of whimsy and adventure—is the essence of Mini's advertising. Consumers read their way from one ad to another, always encouraged to share the mindset. That's finally what's for sale: a great big box of attitude, with a lovely little box of car inside.

ABC created an all-type print campaign that aimed to distinguish its TV network from all the others by expressing an ironic attitude toward people's too-heavy TV use. Tongue-in-cheek ads recognized and then "celebrated" the TV-centric, couchified life. Here are three of the ads:

If TV's so bad for you, why is there one in every hospital room?

Before TV, two World Wars. After TV, zero.

Don't just sit there. Okay, just sit there.

Sometimes, though, brands adopt the audience's point of view. The attitude is the consumer's rather than the brand's. Attitude ads become a corollary of lifestyle advertising, perhaps even its next develop-

Every man should have blown a job he wanted; kept a job he hated; been in a wreck; to a funeral; sat shiva; should know how to cook a meal without opening a freezer; how to iron a woman's shirt; should be able to visit his parents and not arrive with laundry; leave with money; should have made peace with baldness; been troubled by the God issue; briefly sported a goatee; lied about his height; wondered if he was gay; tried meditating; held a gun; built a fire; should understand that clothes make the man look good, they don't make the man. BUTCH BLUM Clothes for every man.

1408 Fifth Avenue, Seattle, Washington. (206) 622-5760

5.11. Lifestyle as deathstyle. This ad takes a man's last trip with his buddies and uses it to sum up the meaning of life. Clothes are mentioned only at the end—Butch Blum is a Seattle clothier—and then only to dismiss them. Great copy. Powerful work.

ment: the symbolic simplification of a complete narrative into its one purest emotion. A long-running Miller High Life beer campaign has used headlines that sound like the attitude of a middle-aged, unpretentious beer drinker. Here are four of them:

Who cares what's in a hot dog.

Would the man who invented artificial turf care to step outside?

No callus too thick.

Can someone please tell me why baldness is regarded as a problem?

Often it's hard to say whether the attitude is coming from the brand or from consumers because the brand seems to be agreeing with their inner speech. Their attitude is its attitude is their attitude. As essayist and social critic George W. S. Trow put it, "The progress of the advertisement is toward the destruction of distance between the product and the person who might consume the product."[10]

Regardless of whether you're considering attitude as a part of brand image, consumer lifestyle, or both, it can be central to the ads you create. Ask if an emotion or attitude is part of what's for sale. Maybe it's the brand's attitude toward its competitors or toward the culture or toward users or nonusers of the product. A clever student ad from Brainco for Godiva Premium Ice Cream, an upscale product, says simply, "Waiting for a sale? How amusing," with the slogan "Cold. But rich." Now there's an ice cream with attitude.

Or maybe the attitude in question is one people have toward the product category or about your client's brand or about the social circumstances that surround using that product. Create ads whose tone of voice, whose mindset, becomes the argument. A recent campaign for Timberland sold outdoor gear by opposing it to the indoor life that consumes most office workers. Headlines sounding like Zen epigrams pointed out the desiccated life of the corporate indoors. One ad showed an EXIT sign in a hallway, with the headline "This is not a sign. It is a calling." Another ad showed an open elevator and said, "The elevator. Yet another box within a box designed to take you to a box." On a stark photograph of an empty, fluorescent-lit meeting room: "Frustrations grow best in artificial light." The implication? A spiritually-centered life awaits, if one simply develops the right attitude. (For an example of a brand's attitude springing right up from the ground, see figure 5.12.)

Alive, a weekly city paper, wanted to position itself as the source of information for what to do and where to do it (slogan: "Music, art and culture in Columbus"). So it ran a bus card campaign with headlines like these: "You in the Mini, yes. You in the mini-van, not so much" and "You on the Vespa, yes. You on the crotch-rocket, not so much." *Alive* didn't just claim it was an arbiter of the social scene. It proved it through its attitude.

Why has attitude advertising become so crucial? For the same reason that its cousin, brand-image advertising, has. Jeff DeJoseph, executive vice president of brand planning at J. Walter Thompson, explains:

> [Because] in a whole variety of categories there's nothing to say about the product. The actual competitive differences are ever so slight. Many brands have parity status. And consumers are bombarded with exponentially more messages. So there's no reason to select a brand other than how you affiliate with it, how you feel about it. It's not the fact of the brand, it's the emotion you attach to the beer or the car or the jeans.[11]

Strategies as a continuum

When you're creating ads, it's not a case of either-or: either you use this kind of strategy or you use that

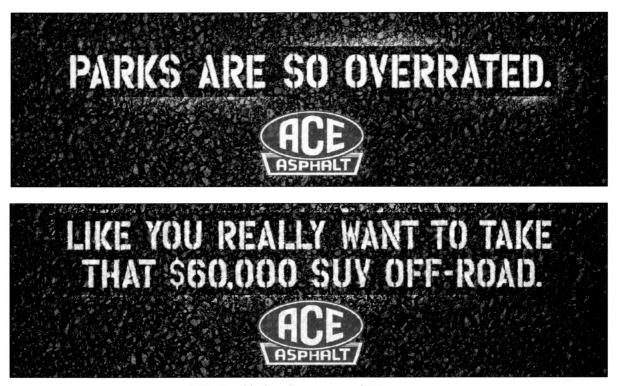

5.12. Can blacktop have an attitude? It can now.

one; either you sell product features or you create a feelings-oriented brand-image campaign. These categories are really more a continuum than a rigid set of mutually exclusive approaches. In fact, given the unending discussion about whether people buy with their heads or their hearts, it's best to neglect neither reason nor emotion. Focus on one, but include the other. As Rosser Reeves put it, "the best theoretical objective is to surround the claim with the feeling."[12]

Also remember that although you may be working on only a small part of a large campaign or creating only a few ads for your portfolio, in the real world ads are parts of campaigns and function in concert to accomplish more than one aim. Some ads will establish the campaign theme so that other ads, operating within that theme, can be product specific. Ads can, and usually do, blend strategies. These categories are yours to use. They are suggestions for thinking—not binding, separate entities.

Take what you've learned and mix thoroughly

To create great advertising, you must examine product, competition, consumer behavior, and target markets. But don't simply weave your way through them impressionistically. Combine them into a plan of action, a strategic document in which you summarize the research and decide what your ads must accomplish. Write a creative brief. Let's see what needs to be in it.

6 ▪ Developing the Creative Brief

> With all the noise, infinite brand touch points and multiple marketing partners working for a common client, it's critical that creative briefs be exactly that: brief. Without a crisp, elegant statement to guide us and keep us honest, none of us stands a chance of pulling off what we get paid to do. If the next brief you see contains more than one idea or has to be explained to the team working on it, kill it. Or it'll kill you later.
> —John Colasanti, president and managing partner, Carmichael Lynch

Setting the objective

It's easy to see the virtue of analyzing consumer behavior, defining target markets, understanding your client's product, and examining possible strategies; but it's easy to forget that a precise objective is as important as anything else. Some advertising problems may sharply define your objective, others will be looser, and, if you're working on ads for your portfolio, you'll have no objective whatsoever until you give yourself one.

A hearty endorsement of the product—"This product is good, so buy it now"—might feel sufficiently precise. But unless you're creating reminder advertising, whose purpose may simply be to wave hello to the consumer, your advertising objective should be as specific as possible—utterance, not gesture. Otherwise you'll create ads whose effectiveness can't be determined, partly because you've never asked what they ought to be doing. Advertising is too expensive for even well-intentioned fuzziness.

So what's a good objective? That's obvious: one that solves your advertising problem. What's your advertising problem? That's often not so obvious, but it is something your research should suggest. Information about consumer behavior, target market, product, and position in the marketplace—all the issues this text has been discussing—should be coming together to indicate what your advertising needs to do.

Maybe your client's product is new, so you need to introduce it, generate awareness. Maybe the product isn't new, but it's got new, more convenient packaging or better flavor, so communicating that becomes your objective. Perhaps the product is on the downhill slope of its product life cycle, and you're reversing its direction by proposing new uses, as Arm & Hammer did for its baking soda—encouraging consumers to put it in the refrigerator, sprinkle it on the carpet, use it on insect bites, on their toothbrush, in the washer, in the cat litter, and so on. Maybe you're trying to expand product consumption among heavy users, as was the purpose of the long-running campaign "Orange Juice. It's not just for breakfast anymore." Or you want to change attitudes about your client's brand or product category (see figs. 6.1 and 6.2). Perhaps the client faces heavy competition, so you must communicate product superiority—by announcing a unique feature or creating a differential via a distinct brand image. Maybe you're targeting new markets, so you must create ads that speak their language and bind your client's product to their needs.

Who can say what your objective should be? That comes only from intelligent, creative analysis of everything in the product's force field. It's complicated, but you need to become simple and single-mind-

> There is nothing worse than a sharp image of a fuzzy concept.
>
> —Ansel Adams, photographer

We fell. We got up. End of apology.

6.1. When Schwinn's product quality went south, the company needed to admit it. Casting the apology into tough talk and bike metaphor gave Schwinn an attitude that suggested it really had fixed its bikes.

ed; distill all that into one advertising objective. Just what, exactly, do you want to communicate? What one thing do you want the consumer to believe, or understand, or feel, or do about the product? Unless you focus on a specific objective, your ads will suffer from blurriness. Be an arrow, not an ink blot. Think of the words of Norman Berry, executive vice president of Ogilvy & Mather: "Vague strategies inhibit. Precise strategies liberate."[1]

Developing the creative brief

In its shortest form, all your creative brief needs is to provide the answers to these three basic questions:

What benefit are you promising, what's your selling argument?
Who are you making it to?
Why should they believe you?

And you can put all that in a sentence or two:

Ads will target current orange juice drinkers and persuade them that orange juice is good any time of day or night; proof will be that it's nutritious, thirst quenching, and energy-giving, all benefits needed at various times in the day.

Ads will target environmentally conscious users of household cleaners and persuade them that Murphy's Oil Soap cleans thorough-

ly without damaging the environment. Support will be that it contains no harsh detergents or alkalis: it's 100 percent pure vegetable oil.

Ads will target upscale women, ages 18 to 34, and persuade them that Limited Express clothing will help make them successful, professionally and socially. Support will be the creation of a brand personality: fashion-forward, self-confident, hip.

Typically, however, ad agencies flesh this out into a couple of pages, and so can you. Creative briefs often cover these areas:

Key Fact	These combine to
Advertising Problem	tell you what your
Advertising Objective	ads need to do.
Target Consumer	These focus
Competition	your approach.
Key Consumer Benefit	
Support	

The following sections explore each area.

KEY FACT

Bill Westbrook, when he was corporate creative director at Earle Palmer Brown, began each of his creative briefs with "a single-minded statement that sorts out from all the information about product, market, competition, etc., the element that is the most relevant to advertising."[2] Many advertising strategists concur. Begin your strategic thinking by looking for the key fact about your client's product. Why? Because it will cast the light by which to see the advertising problem you must solve.

But often the key fact is less obvious, or there are lots of key facts, so finding the advertising problem they point to is tricky. The creative brief can help you think things through.

ADVERTISING PROBLEM

Once you have identified that key fact, what is it telling you? What is the product's biggest consumer-related problem? Let's say you're trying to get people, especially young people, to stop smoking. One key fact is that telling people that cigarettes are bad, which stop-smoking advertising has done for years, doesn't work. People know cigarettes are harmful, and still they smoke. Teenagers, especially, find authoritarian injunctions counterproductive. Telling them not to do something is often encouragement enough to do it. So the insight, from Arnold

Worldwide and Crispin Porter+Bogusky, was to give young people another authority figure against whom to rebel: Big Tobacco. The argument of the Truth campaign became, then, not "Stop smoking" but "Quit being a sap." Cigarettes aren't the enemy as much as are tobacco's corporate honchos who play people for suckers by telling them lies. In other words, the strategy is to make Big Tobacco the bad guy, not cigarettes or parents.

A related insight is that if cigarette brands are cool, Truth better be cool, too.[3] And so it is. Crazyworld, one of many creative ideas from the Truth campaign, posits a carnival gone mad, where up is down and wrong is right, as a symbol of the "logic" of tobacco advertising. Another creation, Shards O' Glass, a faux company satirizing cigarette manufacturers, claims on its Web site, "Our goal is to be the

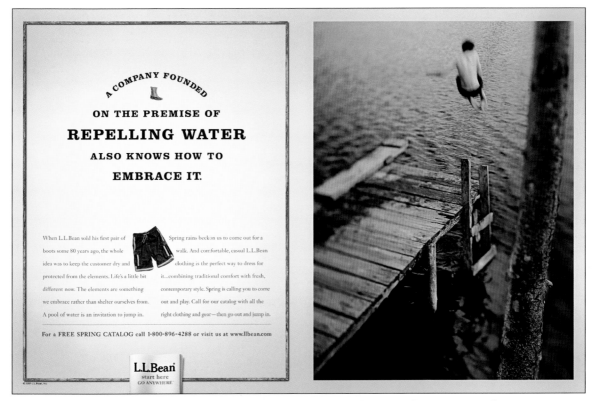

6.2. L.L.Bean, known for its winter-worthy, no-nonsense clothing and gear, wants to be known for other seasons, too. Good use of opposition in the headline.

most responsible, effective and respected developer of glass shard consumer products intended for adults. Our Shards O' Glass Freeze Pops are the nation's top-selling frozen treats containing glass shards. Little wonder, considering all we put into them! . . . And remember, Shards O' Glass Freeze Pops are for adults only."

ADVERTISING OBJECTIVE

Given the problem, what should your objective be? What effect do you want to have on the consumer? An advertising objective is really a communication objective: what you want people to understand, believe, or feel about the product. (You can't set marketing tasks for yourself—like improving sales by 20 percent—since these can be realized only by the entire marketing effort operating in an economic climate, not by advertising alone.)

For example, American Standard, makers of toilets and sinks, faced this problem: a marketplace misperception was limiting sales. "We had to make this product seem not-so-standard. A lot of people felt American Standard was fine for airport restrooms, but not for 'my house.' It wasn't considered special," explains Kerry Casey, Carmichael Lynch's executive creative director.[4] The advertising objective became to persuade consumers that American Standard cared about bathrooms—their bathrooms. The ads Carmichael Lynch created were witty and beautiful and featured great-looking bathroom fixtures, all to change that marketplace perception of the brand (see fig. 6.3).

TARGET AUDIENCE

To whom do you want to communicate this message? Which product users will you target? Define the target audience more specifically than simply demographically, just with numbers. What about psychographics—lifestyle and attitudes? Can you create a profile of the consumer you're addressing?

COMPETITION

Where does your client's product fit in the marketplace? How is the product perceived now, and how do you want it to be perceived? What product category should it compete in? Who are its competitors, both direct and indirect? Assess their strengths and weaknesses.

KEY CONSUMER BENEFIT

If the objective is what you want to happen, the benefit sees it from the target audience's point of view. What benefit does the product deliver; what problem will it solve?

SUPPORT

Now, prove it. If you promise a benefit, what's your evidence? Support that claim.

Sometimes creative briefs also address two other areas. They include a tone statement, explaining the feel the ad writer envisions for the campaign. Whimsical, no-nonsense, aggressively competitive, off the wall? Voice and tone are crucial. What's best for the product, target audience, and advertising problem? Creative briefs may also identify mandatories and limitations. For example, Westbrook includes in his creative strategy "any restrictions or client data which are necessary to a clear understanding of creative direction including legal cautions, carry-over of a successful slogan, items of line to feature, type of casting acceptable and corporate tags."[5] Usually you cannot simply start over with a clean slate but must deal with the advertising and brand image already in place. Taking the advertising in the direction you want it to go without rupturing current consumer perceptions in the process, making the transition toward your goals a seamless one, is often your real-world task.

Say all this in one page. Try. Remember that the essence of your creative brief is simply:

> What benefit are you proposing?
> To whom?
> Why should they believe you?

The categories above suggest areas to cover, but there's no one way to write a brief, except thoughtfully. The San Francisco advertising agency Black Rocket, for example, uses these categories in its creative briefs:

1. The Business Problem
2. The Target
3. The Insight
4. The Marketable Truth
5. The Particulars (Budget, Timing, Required information)

Goodby, Silverstein & Partners uses these:

1. Why are we advertising at all?
2. What is the advertising trying to do?
3. Who are we talking to?

4. What do we know about them that will help us?
5. What is the main thought we need to communicate?
6. What is the best way of achieving this?
7. How do we know we're saying the right things in the right way?
8. Executional guidelines.[6]

The following creative brief, written for a diamond ad campaign, demonstrates a slightly different way of organizing its approach:

CREATIVE BRIEF

Client: Diamonds Direct

What is the business objective?
To source a greater share of business from local competitive jewelers—both big box retailers and specialty stores—in shopping malls.

How can advertising help accomplish this objective?
By demonstrating that Diamonds Direct is a prestigious jeweler that sells quality engagement rings at a reasonable price.

Who is the target consumer?
Men who are getting married for the first time. Age: 23–32

Buying an engagement ring is one of the larger purchases a man will make. His future wife, her family and friends will evaluate him based on the choice he makes. This leads to a great deal of fear that he will make a mistake. At this stage of life most men do not have a great deal of disposable income, so they do not want to pay too much. Getting a good deal will also mean he will have more money available to purchase a larger, higher quality stone, which will in turn impress his mate. The fear of paying too much for a ring is potent, in some cases more potent than the fear of choosing the wrong ring.

Men will typically talk to friends and family, research diamond quality and contemporary ring designs, and, having settled on a type of ring they want to buy, will then factor in cost as part of their decision-making process. A premium quality diamond jeweler that promises the right ring for less than its competitors would be a welcome ally in the process that men navigate when purchasing an engagement ring.

What do we want them to know about us?
That Diamonds Direct has high quality engagement rings at a price you're prepared to pay.

Why will they believe this is true?
Diamonds Direct is not part of a large retail chain located in a shopping mall so they can sell their product with less mark-up than their competitors.

Figure 6.4 shows two of the ads created for this campaign. Christopher Cole, its art director, says, "Mark [copywriter Mark Wegwerth] and I focused on talking to men from a man's point of view. Up to that point most ads for engagement rings would talk to men, but from the woman's point of view. Both Mark and I had purchased engagement rings within a year of making these ads, so we were very much in the frame of mind of the target audience."[8]

Final advice

Sometimes creative people mistakenly think that the brief is at best a perfunctory outline, a simple condensation of the obvious, and at worst a straitjacket against good ideas. But neither is true. The genuine complexities of the marketplace are what make this strategic document so essential, and they're also why thinking one through requires intelligence and marketing savvy.

> The quality of the solution depends entirely on how well you state the problem.
> —Craig Frazier, illustrator/designer

6.3. Personifying the bathroom made American Standard very much at home in many customers' houses.

6.4. Funny, simple, and painfully true. Other headlines in the campaign: "Asking her used to be the hard part" and "Maybe commitment isn't what men are afraid of."

PART TWO

EXECUTION

> *The truth isn't the truth until people believe you; and they can't believe you if they don't know what you're saying; and they can't know what you're saying if they don't listen to you; and they won't listen to you if you're not interesting. And you won't be interesting unless you say things freshly, originally, imaginatively.*
>
> —William Bernbach,
> founding partner, Doyle Dane Bernbach

You've done your homework: you now know your client's brand inside out, the strengths and weaknesses of the competition, and where everybody fits in the marketplace. You've studied the target consumers, too—their wants and needs—and translated product features into meaningful benefits. You've examined the kinds of strategies available to you and formulated your own. You know what argument you're making, to whom, and why. In short, you're as armed and loaded as you're ever going to get. Now it's time to put that hard-earned creative brief into play. It's time to create eye-popping, drop-dead ads. How to do so?

7 ▪ Headlines and Visuals
Thinking in Words and Pictures

Nobody reads advertising. People read what
interests them; and sometimes it's an ad.
—Howard Gossage,
Is There Any Hope for Advertising?

Remember that basically advertising is a relationship between language and imagery: words are tied to pictures. There are complications and exceptions, of course. In TV and video a soundtrack accompanies a series of images. In direct mail the words frequently dominate, even exclude, the visuals. And in radio there are no visuals at all (except in listeners' heads, where there can be plenty). But fundamentally the rhetoric of advertising involves some relationship between showing and saying: show people a picture, then say something about it. Or say something, then show a picture about it.

Achieve synergy, not redundancy

Try to create a relationship—tight, almost molecular—between words and pictures. The word *synergy* has been applied to the desired effect between what you say and what you show.[1] (When two or more elements combine to achieve a total effect greater than the sum of their individual effects, they are synergistic; so too are great headline/visual combinations.) Each ad in figure 7.1 shows how its two halves—headline and image—can depend so utterly on each other that neither makes sense by itself, and their combined impact is stronger than a simple totaling of effects.

In baiting a trap with cheese, always leave room for the mouse.

—Howard Gossage,
quoting the short story writer Saki

You can't always write an ad in which word and image depend that completely on each other. But you can avoid the Dumb Ad, which shows something and then says the same thing. Such redundancy flattens ads, makes them boring and too clear, and gives consumers nothing to do but bear up under the repetition. People don't want to see an ad that says "Giant savings!" and shows a giant-sized product. But if it says "Giant savings!" and shows a little, bitty picture of the product, then things get more interesting, don't they? That's the key principle. Create some tension between word and image.

So get in the habit of asking, "If I say thus and such, what will I show? If I show thus and such, what will I say?" And never content yourself with merely repeating in words what you show with visuals. Following this rule isn't easy, but you'll know it when you do. William Butler Yeats talked about the sound a poem makes when it finishes: like a lid clicking shut on a perfectly made box.[2] Your ad should make a similar sound when you get just the right fit between headline and visual.

Let the consumer do some of the work

One way to hear box lids shut is to let the consumer do some of the work. The problem with Dumb Ads is that their redundancy belabors the point. Smart ads leave room for consumers to do something, and in the moment when they confront this not-quite-instantaneously-clear ad, they become involved. In figure 7.2, for example, readers look at an apparently incomprehensible headline but then quickly enough resolve it. This little do-it-yourself moment is a kind of pleasure. Readers are being

Or buy a Volkswagen.

DON'T VOTE.

THINGS ARE PERFECT JUST THE WAY THEY ARE.

7.1. Quintessential examples of synergy in a headline/visual. In both ads, the headline and visual require each other to make sense—and that very synergy delivers the message more forcefully than text alone or image alone ever could.

respected for their intelligence and given a chance to put it into play. They snap the lid shut themselves.

Combine overstatement and understatement

One way to create synergy between headline and visual is by combining understatement with overstatement. If your visual is wild and crazy or obviously excessive, then back off verbally. And vice versa. In other words, don't shout twice. This juxtaposition of loud and soft, big and little, really snaps that box lid shut (see fig. 7.3). And it works as well in TV as it does in print—run one kind of soundtrack over another kind of imagery. If the car is undergoing a visual torture test, speak quietly about the "modest testing procedure" or play "Singin' in the Rain."

OVERSTATEMENT

Consumers have been hyped so much ("Greatest offer ever!" "Unbelievable performance!" "Specta-

cular savings!") that such exaggeration no longer works, if it ever did. But intentional overstatement (hyperbole) can work; it can "prove" the product benefit without your having to prove it, get a laugh or a smile in the process, and create enough ripple on the page or the screen to get consumers' attention.

A law firm wanted to position itself as eager to work for small clients. With the line "No case too small," what to show? How about one of those tags from comforters, blankets, and mattresses—you know, the ones that say, "UNDER PENALTY OF LAW THIS TAG NOT TO BE REMOVED"? That became the whole ad: the torn tag and the line "No case too small." (Notice how quiet that headline is.) The ad is funny and persuasive, at least of the law firm's claim to take on small cases. It "proved" the point, without ever getting into the land of belief—or, these days, disbelief.

How to overstate? Find your product's benefit and over-exaggerate it. What's the strongest thing

AHOPONABARSTOOLB

7.2. Leaving room for the mouse: Acela, Amtrak's high-speed rail service, cleverly announces one benefit of getting from point A to point B on the train. The ad puzzles for a moment, and in that moment the reader is caught.

WELCOME TO NEW YORK.

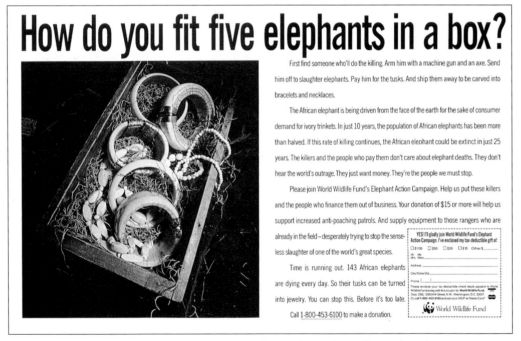

How do you fit five elephants in a box?

First find someone who'll do the killing. Arm him with a machine gun and an axe. Send him off to slaughter elephants. Pay him for the tusks. And ship them away to be carved into bracelets and necklaces.

The African elephant is being driven from the face of the earth for the sake of consumer demand for ivory trinkets. In just 10 years, the population of African elephants has been more than halved. If this rate of killing continues, the African elephant could be extinct in just 25 years. The killers and the people who pay them don't care about elephant deaths. They don't hear the world's outrage. They just want money. They're the people we must stop.

Please join World Wildlife Fund's Elephant Action Campaign. Help us put these killers and the people who finance them out of business. Your donation of $15 or more will help us support increased anti-poaching patrols. And supply equipment to those rangers who are already in the field – desperately trying to stop the sense- less slaughter of one of the world's great species.

Time is running out. 143 African elephants are dying every day. So their tusks can be turned into jewelry. You can stop this. Before it's too late. Call 1-800-453-6100 to make a donation.

7.3 Strong ironic relationships between headline and visual: one funny, the other tragic.

you can think of, especially out of category? Or find its ideal user and exaggerate him or her. Or find a hyperbolic image or headline for the worst possible consequence of not using the product. Pick the point you want to make and then just blow it out the top. Exaggerate that claim to ludicrous extremes. Put your claim or benefit in a "It's so . . . that . . ." or "If it were any more . . . , it would . . ." format, and voila!—there's your hyperbole. You can run the exaggeration in your headline or in your image. And once you've shouted, back off in the other half of the ad.

Usually, if not always, you're making a joke and sharing a wink with the consumers. They don't

66 / Execution

7.4. Exaggeration becomes a kind of truth telling.

"believe" the claim literally—they're not being asked to—and that's why it works (see figs. 7.4 and 7.5).

UNDERSTATEMENT

Don't over-exaggerate things; under-exaggerate them. Say or show less than the situation calls for. Consider this example from real life: after a tornado leveled a town, one family spray-painted a sign on the garage door of what was left of their house: "Just another weekend with the grandkids." That's the saving sense of humor in intentional understatement. Do the same thing with your ad: write a dry line that kicks.

How to do it? Give yourself a wild visual and then ask, "What's the quietest comment I could make about it?" Or if you write an outlandish headline, then undercut it with the visual.

If you start with a visual about which there appears to be only one thing to say, consider saying something else (see fig. 7.6). For example, if you're selling dental floss or toothpaste, you may show an old guy with no teeth. But then what to say? The obvious choices would be things like "Do you want to be this guy?" or "Don't let this happen to you!" But they're too obvious. What else could you say? "Relax. Baby food tastes better than it used to." "Hey, think of the time you'll save not chewing." Or "Smile. No more dental bills." And so forth. If, on the other hand, you use a visual of a smiling person with beautiful teeth (probably the visual cliché of the toothpaste genre), provide an alternative meaning: "Too bad he didn't use Crest." And explain in the copy that his teeth only look okay.

Learn to look at any visual and say not the expected thing, but something off to the side, especially something that intersects your client's product or brand.

For more on comic misdirection and the art of the headline, see chapter 14, How to Write a Headline.

7.5. Whimsical hyperbole: a bottled water becomes its own hors d'oeuvre.

Emphasize one idea per ad

Always pick one selling idea and let it dominate the ad. Even though you'll often be tempted, don't try to say several things at once. Your readers or viewers will simply get confused, and you'll dissipate the power of one thought driven home. Advertiser Dick Wasserman puts it this way: "It's natural . . . to want to boast about every last one of a product's benefits. This impulse must be resisted. Making an ad or commercial try to say more than one simple thing at a time is like inviting two people to give a lost driver directions at the same time."[3] A Vancouver advertising agency, Rethink, provides another helpful metaphor with its "Ping Pong Ball Theory":

> It's simple. If we were to throw one ping pong ball at you across a table, you'd probably catch it. If we were to throw five balls at the same time, you probably wouldn't catch any of them. Most advertising messages have at least five ping pong balls. We strive to keep our messages single-focused, with just one ping pong ball per ad. This means there's a far greater likelihood that our message will be seen and absorbed.[4]

You *can* sell more than one idea at a time, *if* you make them feel like one idea, if you roll them together in the carpet. In the following headline the copywriter connects two different selling ideas—the car is sporty yet sensible—with a psychological metaphor, making two arguments seem like one:

> A sports car for both sides of your brain. The half that's seventeen, and the half that's retired and living in Miami. (Subaru SVX)

For years Miller Lite beer promoted itself via the slogan "Tastes great, less filling," attempting in that phrase to say two things at once. Secret deodorant created a theme line that has driven the brand for over forty years: "Strong enough for a man, but made for a woman." Two ideas again, but rolled together nicely.

The questions are these: do consumers hear you (or are you just making noise)? And do they believe you (or are you claiming too much to be credible)?

How to write a headline

If I had a foolproof checklist for how to write a headline, I'd retire to Tahiti immediately with the money I'd make. Who knows how you write one besides just basically think it up? This book will give you techniques and advice, but ultimately you're alone inside your own head. As I mentioned earlier, once a visual does arrive, you should write the headline in response to or in consideration of that image—and try to complement it, not repeat it. So what you show is always part of how you think one up.

One way to jump-start yourself is to write down in a plain and straightforward way your advertising strategy, the promise you plan to make to the consumer—the benefit(s) of the product, the problem(s) it solves. What's your selling argument? Say it as many ways as you can. This is your starting point, conceptually. These arguments are *what* you want to say; they're probably not *how* you want to say it yet.

You can be wrong at this level (that is, by choosing the wrong strategy), but if you're making the right appeal, then the problem with most of your sentences is that they're not stoppers—they're too flat, too bald, too blah. No one will be compelled to consider them. So take each one and try to say it another way; spin it out sideways, heat it up. Get that idea in readers' faces more, push it, be slangy, take some chances. Wrestle that reasonable idea out of its middle-of-the-roadness and into the ditch. Ogilvy & Mather's Steve Hayden gives this advice: "To me, the secret of advertising is to make an irrational presentation of a rational argument."[5]

The benefit has to be on strategy, but its *expression* has to be a little twisted, lateralized, non-clichéd, or made more specific, more interesting. The dead clichés are usually right there in the middle, the first things you think up. Keep going. With this technique you must still supply the necessary wit and ingenuity, of course, but at least you have given yourself a method of operating and clarified your task.

TWO EXAMPLES

The following headlines are solid selling arguments wrestled into the ditch. Watermark Water Centers, a California pure water bottler, wanted to warn consumers that most of them were drinking water contaminated with one or another impurity. It was a "Hey, did you know your water's bad?" kind of argument. Research indicated that 90 percent of Californians could be said to have a water problem. Final headline over a glass of water: "9 out of 10 people in California have a drinking problem." That's the same idea as the original strategy, but now it's phrased energetically enough to stop anyone who reads it. It's a solid idea made clever.

Another example: Kaufman and Broad home-builders advertised that its homes were so well made that customers were invited to walk through unfinished houses to see for themselves. The eventual headline, with a visual of an unwalled, half-finished house: "Walk through our homes naked." Again, the strategy has been played with and made clever enough, unusual enough, to stop the reader.

Remember: always try to express the selling promise as a consumer benefit; see it from the consumer's point of view. For example, in a contest for a membership to Scandinavian health spas, the big headline was "Win Yourself a Brand New Body." The smaller subhead explained, "Enter for a Free 1-Year Membership." That's the way to say it. Why sell just a membership when you can express the benefit so much more powerfully? In this case the big promise dominated, as it should, with the subhead clarifying the offer.

As you discover when you work on advertising problems, you often lose the selling idea in the act of trying to express it creatively. There's a continual struggle between being on-strategy and being clever. Each wants to pull you away from the other. Your job as a thinker and problem solver is to keep both in mind, to spin the strategy without losing hold of it. As though to indicate this truth, the two most common rejections of your ideas will be "I don't get it" and "I've seen it before." In other words, it's either too weird or too obvious. That's why the great ones don't come easy.

VISUAL ADVICE

Although you're free to show almost anything, of course, it never hurts to consult a list of suggestions. The following list captures the most frequently used visual approaches:

1. Demonstrate the product in use: if it's got some motion or drama, show it (see fig. 7.7). Show it being spread on something, being worn, getting things clean, or otherwise being demonstrated.

2. Show the product itself, unwrapped or still in its package: great importance rests, in this case, on what you say about the product.

One technique is to be metaphorical: talk about the product in terms of something else; express its benefit via language usually associated with something else (see fig. 7.7 again) For a discussion of this popular, powerful headline approach, see chapter 20, Verbal Metaphor.

3. Present a close-up of some critical part of the product: the springs on Nike Shox, the three stripes in Aqua-Fresh toothpaste, and so on. This is a sensible strategy for any feature-oriented approach (see fig. 7.8).

4. Emphasize a visually interesting aspect of the product story that you discover in your research: the unusual plant it's made in, the founding city or founding father or mother, the valley where it's grown, a piece of historical data that captures the consumer's mind and eye.

5. Emphasize not the product but a person connected to it: this person may be a celebrity, an authority figure or expert, someone from history, a pop culture icon, even an invented character like Tony the Tiger or the Keebler elves (see fig. 7.9 and chapter 16, Testimonials).

6. Highlight the benefit of using the product: the people pleasures rather than the thing itself. In other words, show the payoff, the result, of using the product. Or show the negative consequences of *not* using the product (see fig. 7.10), usually less clichéd (and therefore more interesting).

7. Go a step further and show the lifestyle the product helps create: beyond the white teeth and smiles there is a desired lifestyle. Show this state of mind, this attitude or way of being that the product engenders. (Or, again, show the *un*happy state of mind of the *non*user.) This is a good visual technique for brand-image/lifestyle advertising.

8. Use split-screen imagery: before and after; a comparison with the competition, or among versions of the product itself, or with something unexpected (see chapter 17, "Two-Fers").

9. Show not the product but some modification of it, a transformation or metamorphosis that is visually arresting and communicates the selling idea (see fig. 7.11). Or go further and show a metaphor for the product or service, something dissimilar that stands for its benefit. (For further discussion of these techniques, see chapter 19, Metaphor.)

10. Remove rather than add: crop the image,

7.6. The headline states the last thought that would occur to most people seeing the ad. But because it states the first thought of the ad's speaker, it demonstrates the monomaniac's true belief—and readers find themselves impressed by his conviction. The joke makes its point.

7.7. Conveying the motion and drama of the product—in this case, white-water rafting. The headline is a terrific example of verbal metaphor, talking about the product in language people associate with other contexts. Another headline in the series: "Water gives life. Occasionally it takes some back."

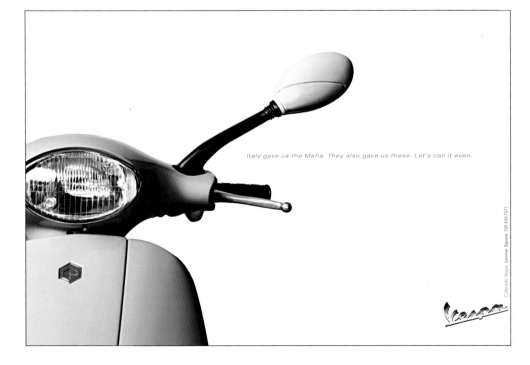

7.8. A Vespa campaign showed cropped shots of the scooter, emphasizing its Italian styling heritage. Great headline, too. Other headlines in the campaign: "Never have to help your friends move again" and "If you don't like my driving, stay off the sidewalk."

He's got user-friendly products.

He's got freezer-space solutions.

He's got nothing on besides
a toque and a handkerchief.

Whatever your needs are, the Doughboy can help. Take, for example, Pillsbury's new Scoop Easy drop biscuit dough. It saves you time and labor. You just scoop, drop and bake. Best of all, the result looks and tastes just like it was made from scratch. And because Scoop Easy has a five-day refrigerated shelf life, it frees up valuable freezer space. To find out what the Doughboy can do for you, call 1-800-767-5404.

There's a lot the Doughboy can do. Pillsbury

7.9. Pillsbury wanted to expand its presence in the food service industry, so it literally walked the Doughboy into a big freezer as a way of saying the company belonged there.

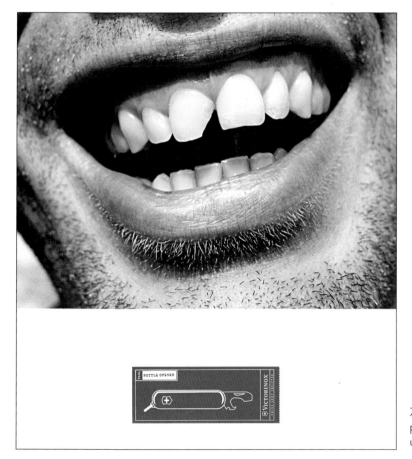

7.10. Demonstrate the benefit of using a product by illustrating the liability of *not* using it.

UNTIL THE WORLD'S THIS SAFE, WEAR A HELMET.

BRAIN INJURY ASSOCIATION OF AMERICA
www.biausa.org

7.11. Metamorphosing the landscape is a visually dramatic way of showing the need for protection.

show only part of the product, boil a complicated narrative down to its simplest aspect—reduce, reduce, reduce. That Vespa ad (fig. 7.8) crops a motor scooter. The poster in figure 7.12 crops a play.

11. Show nothing: use all type instead.

12. "Walk away from the product": while it makes sense to start visual thinking with either the product or its happy user, you can land in Clichéville that way and never get out. Try to walk away from the product—go toward things associated with it, or consequences of it, or conditions that lead to it (see fig. 7.13).

HEADLINE ADVICE

The best headline ideas will arise out of your own approach, both strategic and visual. Nevertheless, try these suggestions:

1. Consider command headlines. You generate commands by using the imperative form of the verb, with "you" understood: "Join the army"; "Visit the zoo." Commands make readers pay attention because someone is verbally pointing a finger, demanding a response (see

fig. 7.14). So don't say, "People should discover the Bahamas" or "Discovering the Bahamas." Say, "Discover the Bahamas." Nike didn't say, "Just doing it," did they?

2. Be aware that questions have an obvious rhetorical power: "Are your feet happy?" "Have you looked at your wife lately?" They come up from the page, out of the radio, or off the screen in a way a statement doesn't, getting in the consumer's face, making the consumer deal with them. When you want a response from someone in conversation, you ask a question. Hey, you haven't fallen asleep reading this, have you? (See? It works here, too.)

3. Add "how" or "why" to a headline to increase its pull and bond it to the visual.

blah:
> We put side-impact airbags in our Volvos.
> (visual of open airbag)

better:
> Why we put side-impact airbags in our
> Volvos.
> (visual of a loving, happy moment between
> husband and wife)

"How" and "why" also draw consumers into the ad by promising inside knowledge:

How to tell whether your house has termites.
Why you should spend $150,000 on a DePauw education.

4. Let the consumer know, in one way or another, "This ad's for you." Ad legend David Ogilvy once wrote, in his elegance, that a print ad's "headline is 'the ticket on the meat.' Use it to flag down the readers who are prospects for the kind of product you are advertising. If you are selling a remedy for bladder weakness, display the words BLADDER WEAKNESS in your headline. . . . If you want mothers to read your advertisement, display MOTHERS in your headline. And so on."[6]

Writing in 1963, Ogilvy now sounds dogmatic and dated, but he's still correct. The message does not have to be in the headline, however, nor must it be as literal-minded and obvious as Ogilvy implies. In the decades since then, people have become sophisticated consumers of public messages. Lots of elements besides the ad's language can be the ticket on the meat. In print it might be the images themselves, the typography, or the design of the page; on TV it might be the editing rhythms or the soundtrack; in radio the sense of humor or just the tone of voice. But it's got to be there. I only look up when someone flags me down, when someone calls my name, and so do you.

5. Decide whether you need to shout. Other traditional advice has been to name the brand in the headline (or use great big product shots or large logotypes to identify the ad's commercial point). This is another "rule" that's not always wise, necessary, or graceful. How prominently—visually or verbally—to emphasize the product's name in the ad should be approached

7.12. This ad looks like anything but what it's for. An apparent photo of a hospital hallway, it both crops the play and updates it, moving it out of time and place. Hip humor brings Shakespeare closer to the audience.

7.13. More interesting, and more suggestive, than looking at a fish, don't you think?

situation by situation. You want to sell the product, but shouting is not often the best way.

6. Consider how long the headline needs to be. As long as it needs to be to say itself, not one word longer. The tendency is to keep headlines short, although it's always possible to find a great, long one. The classic is, of course, Ogilvy's seventeen-worder for Rolls-Royce:

> At 60 miles an hour the loudest noise in this new Rolls-Royce comes from the electric clock.

Since that headline was written in 1958, you may argue that people won't read that many words anymore. But here's a headline written in 1997 for Portland's newspaper, *The Oregonian*:

> Run your ad on TV and people will head for the bathroom. Run your ad in *The Oregonian* and they'll bring it with them.

Here's another, written in 1997 for Adidas swimwear. It accompanies a photo of a woman, swimming laps:

> One selfish lover, three late trains, two disastrous meetings, one irate boss, two large bills. The weight I lose in the pool.

The real trick is to say what you want to, *then* tighten it. Don't limit your ideas by presupposing that you must have teensy ones or be terse. For example, a tongue-in-cheek headline for a minor league hockey team, the Columbus Chill, could have been written this way:

> If you assault someone in America, you'll get five years in prison. But if you assault someone in hockey, you'll only get five minutes. So is this a great game or what?

The actual headline, however, said the same

7.14. A command form of the verb, not to mention a terrific way to dramatize the product's benefit.

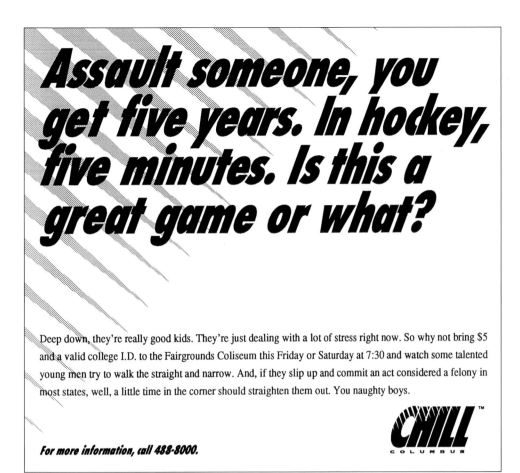

Assault someone, you get five years. In hockey, five minutes. Is this a great game or what?

Deep down, they're really good kids. They're just dealing with a lot of stress right now. So why not bring $5 and a valid college I.D. to the Fairgrounds Coliseum this Friday or Saturday at 7:30 and watch some talented young men try to walk the straight and narrow. And, if they slip up and commit an act considered a felony in most states, well, a little time in the corner should straighten them out. You naughty boys.

CHILL ™
COLUMBUS

For more information, call 488-8000.

7.15. An all-type ad with a tightly written headline.

thing without wasting a word (see fig. 7.15). Feel how much stronger it is?

7. Use both internal and end punctuation on headlines. Most ad writers use periods to close headlines (and often slogans), even when they aren't complete sentences. Periods add a sense of certainty and authority to the fragment or phrase.

8. Use subheads frequently. Learn to finish headlines, usually, with more straightforward subheads or underlines. Give yourself enough display type (the major language in the large point sizes) to communicate completely to readers. "Oh, they'll get it when they read the copy" is almost never a good excuse for an ambiguous, teaser headline or a headline/subhead combination that still doesn't make enough sense. An ad should work both fast and slow; that is, a scanner should get something from it—at least the selling idea—and a true reader should get more—the complete story.

8 • Body Copy I
Establishing Voice

> In your natural way of producing words there is a
> sound, a texture, a rhythm—a voice—which is the
> main source of power in your writing.
> —Peter Elbow, *Writing without Teachers*

The importance of ethos, persona, voice

Body copy is really part of something larger—the rhetoric of the entire ad or campaign—and it's important to examine that before discussing copy itself. The literary critic M. H. Abrams, discussing Aristotle's theories of rhetoric, said this: "An orator establishes in the course of his oration an *ethos*—a personal character which itself functions as a means of persuasion; for if the personal image he projects is that of a man of rectitude, intelligence, and goodwill, the audience is instinctively inclined to give credence to him and to his arguments."[1]

Advertising is a form of public speechmaking, and whenever people consume ads, they confront a speaker delivering a persuasive message. Even if the ad has no literal spokesperson, it always has a consciousness, and people's response to this frequently invisible but everywhere apparent speaker becomes central to the ad's success: consumers are never just buying a product, they're buying an *ethos*, too. Do they like this person or don't they? Are they interested in this sensibility or aren't they? Do they want to bring this person home with them or not?[2]

In talking about this sensibility behind the product, I am, of course, talking about the product's brand image, the personality behind the brand. You've all noticed how an advertising agency creates a persona for a corporation and its products and then maintains it through the years. (*Persona*, Latin for the mask once worn by classical actors, is another good word to use for this sense of self created by the ads—the speaker or personality implied by the language and imagery.)

For example, Volkswagen's classic ads from 1959 through the 1970s, created by Doyle Dane Bernbach (DDB), seemed to have a self-deprecating, funny, modest-but-self-assured persona—people almost felt as though they'd enjoy having lunch and some laughs with the VW person, whoever he was. People also felt that the mind behind the car was the car's argument for itself: rational, practical, intelligent, whimsical, but ultimately serious.

In 1998 with VW's introduction of the New Beetle, Arnold Communications faced a tough challenge: re-invoke that original Beetle persona while moving it forward. Arnold needed to remind Baby Boomers how much they'd loved their Bug, but the agency didn't want younger audiences to dismiss the New Beetle as a Geezermobile. Sell nostalgia but be contemporary about it, that was the task—and live up to the greatness of the original DDB campaign in the process.

The original Beetle persona had to reappear, as though back from an extended vacation and as hip as ever. "It's tonal. You can't mess up on voice," said art director Alan Pafenbach, one of the campaign's leaders.[3] The new advertising took the graphic simplicity of the original campaign (sans serif typography and lots of white space) and intensified it: there was no copy in the print work, just a snappy headline, and no visual context for the car, just its silhouette in white space. Arnold Communications reprised the original witty voice while updating it to address improvements to the car and changes to the culture since the 1960s. And the car now had an additional benefit for sale: not just utility and reason, but nostalgia (see fig. 8.1). The ugly car had long since become cute. Terrific, headline-driven print ads cited improvements while making gentle fun of the original Beetle's weaknesses:

> Comes with wonderful new features. Like heat.

> The engine's in the front, but its heart's in the same place.

Or invoked Baby Boomers' nostalgia:

> If you were really good in a past life, you come back as something better.

> If you sold your soul in the '80s, here's your chance to buy it back.

But spoke to younger generations, too:

> Digitally remastered.

> Is it possible to go backwards and forwards at the same time?

TV spots did cool stuff like show a silver Beetle zipping and bouncing in white space inside the TV frame, with this closing line: "Reverse engineered from UFOs." (Music soundtracks from German alt-rock bands added a contemporary feel to the voice.)

The ads invoked the past but spoke in the present tense. They looked back and leaned forward at the same time.

In short, the advertisers for both Volkswagen Beetles created a personality by which consumers could identify the brand and relate it to themselves. All great brands not only create a strong image for themselves but also manage it, modifying its characteristics to match changing circumstance and purpose. The New Beetle has the same personality as the old one, it's just been updated for new times and new audiences.

According to David Martin, founder of The Martin Agency and a strong proponent of sustaining successful brand images, "Personality is a buoy, not a dead weight. Great brands are built over a long period of time with advertising that is faithful to product personality. . . . Brand personality is permanent. Lose it and lose the franchise."[4]

How to think about image and voice

Since you inevitably create a product's "self" when you write copy, brand image is always at stake: you add to or subtract from it with every word. To make sure that this "self" you're creating works, think about these issues:

1. What image of the brand already exists?
2. Is it the right one for your client's product? Does it fit your client's target market? Your client's competitive position in the marketplace? The times?
3. What modifications, if any, do you want to make to it?

Once you've settled on the appropriate brand image, then consider these issues:

4. What voice is the best expression of this image?
5. How will you use this voice to communicate the objectives of the ads you're making? In other words, how would the brand's persona make this specific selling argument? How would he or she say it?

So, before you ever write a word of body copy, you need to determine—or to understand, if someone else has determined—these larger concerns of product personality, the overall voice and stance of the advertising. Not until they are resolved can you write effective copy. Once you start to write body copy, however, you'll make a pleasant discovery: you already know how, for the simple reason that you've already done it.

How body copy is like freshman composition

You probably took a college composition course in which you wrote essays. Body copy is really nothing more than English Composition 1: nonfiction prose written to support an argument. The ad's headline and visual advance the argument, and the body copy justifies it. Although well-written body copy does differ from the prose of a well-written essay (and I'll discuss those differences soon), the similarities far outweigh the differences. Good writing is good writing. Period.

If you apply what you learned in freshman composition to your copywriting, you'll be fine. Let's recall those principles of good prose your English professor taught you:

1. Voice: The writing has a natural, authentic sound, free of clichés.

8.1. The voice of the New Beetle.

2. Details: The writing is full of specifics; it's particular, not vague.

3. Style: Form matches content: the prose is not overwritten. It's stylistically graceful, with strong, clear sentences and well-chosen language.

4. Thesis: The writing has one central, unifying idea. It hangs together.

5. Organization and structure: The writing develops this idea in some order; has a beginning, middle, and end; and coheres throughout.

That's a familiar list, isn't it? The first item on the list—voice—is so important that I'll spend this chapter analyzing it and save the others for the next chapter.

Voice

As I suggested earlier, the voice in a product's advertising should flow from the overall strategy; *voice* is the brand's image as expressed in language. For the voice of a specific ad, look to your headline/visual concept. If the headline relies on wit, then the copy had better share the same clever persona. If the headline is brash and assertive, then the voice in the copy ticking off the selling points should be just as aggressive.

Voice is so crucial to writing that in a sense it's everything. As you remember from freshman composition, all good writing has a sound—the human,

expressive rhythm that animates it. Good writing sounds like someone particular uttered or thought it. If your language has no sound or rhythm, it's dead, and so is your ad.

But voice is difficult to talk about for several reasons. For one thing, you can't point to it exactly. It's just there, *among* all the words. For another, it's made up of myriad things: the words you choose, the sentences you write, the amount and kind of detail you use, what you're talking about, what your point is, how you organize the writing, who you're talking to. Almost every choice you make as a writer plays a part in creating the voice of the copy—the sense readers get, when they read it, of living speech. Throughout this discussion of good writing, remember that I'm always talking about voice, too.

ANALYZE THE VOICES OF ADS

Let's look closely at some copy to see if it's possible to isolate the characteristics that make up a voice, the parts that combine to create a reader's intuitive sense of the speaker. Consider, for example, this copy for an ad for Nike's water socks (fig. 8.2):

Headline:
  Hawaiian shirts for your feet.

Copy:
  So, you're hanging ten in Maui or you're just stepping into your hot tub. Fine. You'll need a few things. First, you'll need a solid rubber

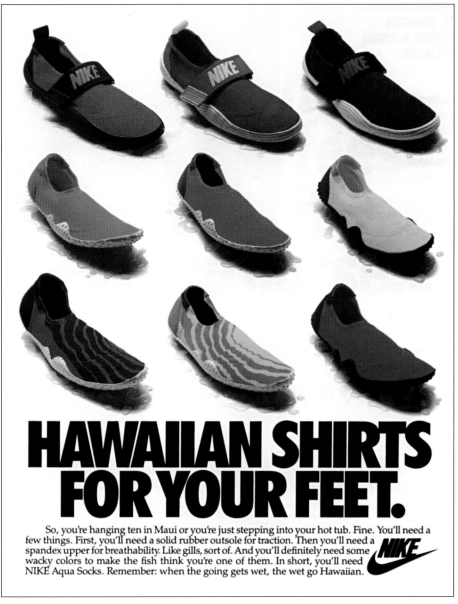

So, you're hanging ten in Maui or you're just stepping into your hot tub. Fine. You'll need a few things. First, you'll need a solid rubber outsole for traction. Then you'll need a spandex upper for breathability. Like gills, sort of. And you'll definitely need some wacky colors to make the fish think you're one of them. In short, you'll need NIKE Aqua Socks. Remember: when the going gets wet, the wet go Hawaiian.

8.2. Nike's distinctive voice—hip, flippant, but authoritative—perfectly matches product with target audience.

outsole for traction. Then you'll need a spandex upper for breathability. Like gills, sort of. And you'll definitely need some wacky colors to make the fish think you're one of them. In short, you'll need NIKE Aqua Socks. Remember: when the going gets wet, the wet go Hawaiian.

How to characterize this voice? It's hip and flippant, but it's got some steel, too. The tone is authoritative, telling readers what to do, what's cool, but doing so with jokes. It's clearly a variant of the Nike voice ("Just do it") that consumers have been hearing for years.

How do I know all this? The authoritative tone comes from the repetition of the near command, "you'll need," which doesn't allow room for disagreement; but the voice lightens that tone by mixing in whimsical allusions ("to make the fish think you're one of them," and so on). Also, the language contains slang ("hanging ten," "sort of," "wacky"), contractions ("you're," "you'll"), and sentence fragments ("Fine." "Like gills, sort of."), all of which produce a very informal, almost chummy tone. By

CIVILIZATION IS ADVANCING AT A STATELY 18 KNOTS.

Long before reaching your destination, you will experience a sense of having arrived. Such is life aboard our newest ship, the intimate *Royal Viking Queen*, and her larger, more stately companion, the elegant *Royal Viking Sun*.

Here, all that has made sailing Royal Viking Line so wondrous over the years is heightened as never before. Consider mingling with learned experts in World Affairs. Or collecting secrets of aquatic life from the Cousteau Society.

Elsewhere, guest chefs the likes of the renowned Paul Bocuse will provide exquisite nourishment for areas found somewhat south of the mind.

We do not wish to prod, but if this appeals to your sense of adventure, **ROYAL VIKING LINE**

there is no better time to experience it all than now, as we depart for 165 charmed ports including the storied waters of Europe. Your travel agent has particulars, or call 1 (800) 457-8599. We look forward to seeing you on board.

8.3. A more sophisticated voice works well for a more expensive product and an older, more urbane target audience.

beginning in the middle of a thought ("So"), the copy implies an already formed relationship; it seems to know the reader. The closing, clever twist on the cliché adds to the sense of a witty hipster. Finally, the diction (word choice) is unpretentious, so the voice is that of a peer—a fun but knowledgeable older brother, perhaps. Altogether, a perfectly created voice, given the advertisers' sense of this product, the Nike audience, and the Nike campaign theme. Here, as elsewhere, they're telling consumers *how* to just do it.

By contrast, look at the ad for the Royal Viking Line (fig. 8.3). Consider some of the copy:

Headline:
   Civilization is advancing at a stately 18 knots.

Copy:
   Long before reaching your destination, you will experience a sense of having arrived. Such is life aboard our newest ship, the intimate *Royal Viking Queen*, and her larger, more stately companion, the elegant *Royal Viking Sun*.
   Here, all that has made sailing Royal Viking Line so wondrous over the years is heightened as never before. Consider mingling with learned experts in World Affairs. Or collecting secrets of aquatic life from the Cousteau Society. Elsewhere, guest chefs the likes of the renowned Paul Bocuse will provide exquisite nourishment for areas found somewhere south of the mind.

The copy obviously implies an older, more genteel speaker and audience. The implied distance between the two is greater also. This is not chumminess. How can you tell? The sentences are more sophisticated, and so are the words. There are almost no fragments and no slang, no contractions. With adjectives like "wondrous," "exquisite," and "renowned," the copy is more intent on evoking a mood, an upscale one at that. Each element, from the self-congratulatory paradox of the opening sentence to the unusual details (the Cousteau Society, chef Paul Bocuse), helps accentuate the copy's "we are the best" attitude. The tone is self-assured, precise, authoritative but at the reader's service. It sounds like this cruise might cost quite a bit, but consumers would have a fabulous time. The voice perfectly embodies the kind of experience Royal Viking is selling.

You can simply *hear* how each piece of copy creates its own unique persona, can't you? Explaining the differing effects requires analysis, but clearly the right speaker is presenting each product, and each voice rings true. That's the goal: to sound like a real person, not an edifice of polished prose. As Elmore Leonard says, "If it sounds like writing, I rewrite it."[5] Here's how copywriter Steve Hayden, vice-chairman of Ogilvy & Mather Worldwide, puts it:

I look for body copy that's written with care, for copy that strikes the imagination. I look for phrases like, "Most people come back from vacation with little more to show for it than tiny bars of stolen soap." You know, how did that get into the ad? But it's that occasional application of wit that lets you know you're still alive. I look for surprises that say there's a human being behind this, as opposed to a corporation. And I look for that ability to project a human quality. To communicate one-on-one.[6]

Two points. You don't create copy by analyzing it; you create copy by throwing yourself into a voice. But you do improve copy by analyzing it, and that requires a sensitivity on your part to what aspects of the language are creating what effects. Become a good critic of voices. It will help you rewrite your own.

WRITE IN THE FIRST AND SECOND PERSON

To write well, you must become the sound of someone talking—not literally your own self, but the self of the seller: the corporation or the person talking to consumers in the ad. If you just write logical, institutional prose that *assembles* the case for a product, prose without someone inside it, then you're missing the essence of good writing. It must project a personality, a living voice, and that's always an "I," whether your copy uses one or not. As Thoreau said, "We commonly do not remember that it is, after all, always the first person that is speaking."[7] He wasn't talking about ad copy, but he could have been.

So prefer the first person ("I" and "we") and the second person ("you") to the third person ("it," "they"). Don't say what "they're" doing at Nike for people and "their" problems. Say what "we're" doing at Nike for "you" and "your" problems. How will "our" products serve "your" needs? Copy that

pulls the reader close this way is much more intimate and effective than stiff, third-person prose. Try to sound like speech, or at least very warm thought.

The two preceding examples of ad copy use "you" and imply "we." (The Royal Viking's "her" is, of course, the feminine pronoun sometimes used for ships. Use of this pronoun not only tells readers that each ship has a distinct personality but also adds a touch of formality—a good idea, given the cruise line's upscale product.)

DECIDE WHO'S TALKING

Who are you going to be in this ad? There are several possibilities:

1. Be the company. Usually you'll assume the company's voice and make nice. Sometimes you'll sound best-friendly, other times more distantly pleased-to-be-having-a-conversation friendly. But whether you throw your arm over the consumer's shoulder or not, you usually try to be sociable. After all, if you want to talk people into something, being friendly is a reasonable approach. (Both the Nike and Royal Viking ads adopt the company's point of view and make nice.)

But you don't have to smile. As I've illustrated elsewhere, Nike can be stern, telling people things they should do, acting as their self-improvement conscience, their tough-love coach. Many public service ads (for and against causes or issues) shame readers with pointed, impatient tones, wagging their finger at human sloth, selfishness, or stupidity. Ads for products can also surprise by getting right in the reader's face (fig. 8.4) or by inviting the reader to get in someone else's face (fig. 8.5). So you don't have to wear a big grin and say a big howdy to sell something.

2. Be the consumer. Don't address your readers, *become* them. Climb inside their heads and see things their way instead of making nice corporate talk. What are they saying and thinking about life around them and the products in it? What shape are they in? How can your client's products help them out and help them get their feelings out? And remember, consumers come in many variants: the heavy user, reluctant user, ex-user, nonuser (see figs. 8.6 and 8.7). There are all kinds of potential, former, or current audiences whose inner voices are waiting for

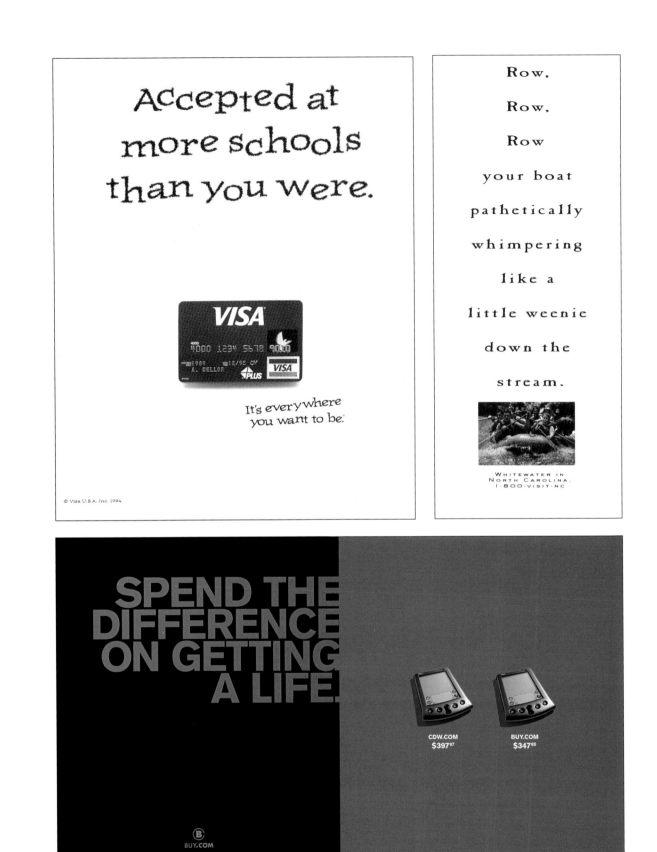

8.4. Selling people things by insulting them.

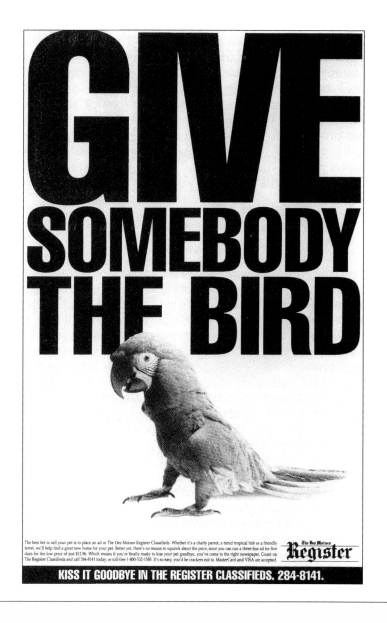

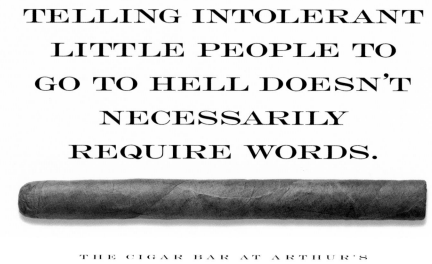

8.5. Selling people things by inviting them to insult others.

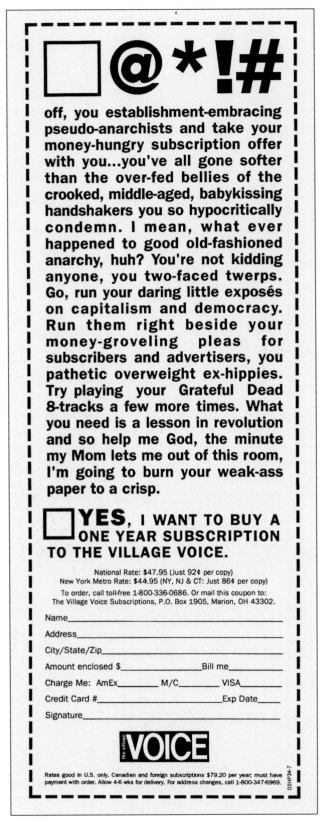

8.6. The voice of the extreme non-user; his vitriol inversely and hilariously suggests the value someone might find in the *Village Voice.*

---

you to use. Jack Supple, managing partner and president of Carmichael Lynch, offers good advice:

> Don't say it; be it. You need to become one with your target audience. Use their voice. Talk as the target talks. If you're talking about Harley-Davidson, be a Harley person. If you're talking to Schwinn riders, you better be a Schwinn rider. . . . It's like this: In the end you're telling one of your best friends about another one of your best friends.[8]

3. Be both the consumer and the company. In a lot of ads it's hard to say who, exactly, is speaking. The headline or voice-over could be something consumers are saying to themselves, but it just as easily could be the company reading their minds and agreeing with them. Not a bad place to locate the voice of your ad. How can consumers disagree with themselves? And how can they ignore this product, especially if it's saying what they're thinking right out loud as they pass by its ad (see fig. 8.8)?

4. Be the voice of some other player in the scenario. It's easy to assume that an ad's voice has to be either the company's or the consumer's. After all, they're the two most obvious players in the drama. But consider supporting players, too—from people (friends, parents, or children of the consumer; passers-by) to props (the product itself, a competing product, or any of the various elements in the scenario). If you're selling running shoes, for example, think about the dog accompanying the runner; the sidewalk on which she runs; the weather in which she runs; the cars, trucks, and mud puddles she avoids; her legs; her feet; even her shoelaces. Every selling situation has lots of potential participants. Any of them could become the voice of the ad, and many memorable ads owe their originality to just such an unusual point of view (see fig. 8.9).

How to decide which voice to use? Let your strategy help you decide: what's the best way to express your selling argument? If you're selling shoes that feel good, maybe you should let feet do the talking. If you're selling shoes as part of a lifestyle, the way Reebok was (fig. 8.7), overhearing their owner makes sense. If you're selling shoes as well-made

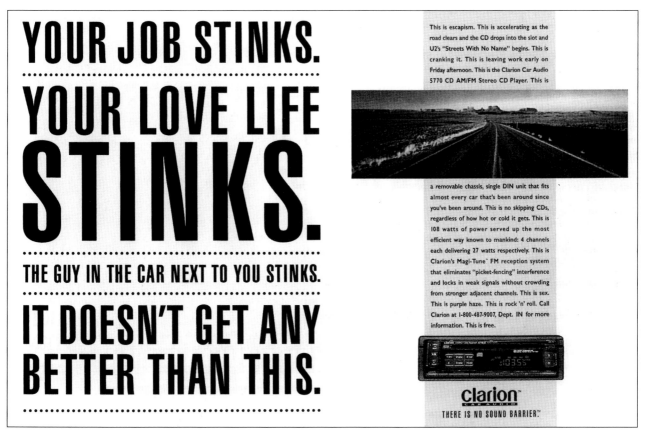

There's a story in every Boks.

BO
KS
Reebok

8.29.92

Another summer spent bagging groceries, scanning bar codes, dusting canned goods...When the manager asked if I'd be back next summer, I couldn't keep a straight face.

R.A.

Men's
Recker

Call 1-800-843-4444 for the store nearest you.

8.7. An example of an ad whose voice is the consumer's, not the corporation's. A lifestyle and attitude are for sale; the implication is that the shoes either accompany them or help make them possible.

YOUR JOB STINKS.
YOUR LOVE LIFE STINKS.
THE GUY IN THE CAR NEXT TO YOU STINKS.
IT DOESN'T GET ANY BETTER THAN THIS.

This is escapism. This is accelerating as the road clears and the CD drops into the slot and U2's "Streets With No Name" begins. This is cranking it. This is leaving work early on Friday afternoon. This is the Clarion Car Audio 5770 CD AM/FM Stereo CD Player. This is a removable chassis, single DIN unit that fits almost every car that's been around since you've been around. This is no skipping CDs, regardless of how hot or cold it gets. This is 108 watts of power served up the most efficient way known to mankind: 4 channels each delivering 27 watts respectively. This is Clarion's Magi-Tune™ FM reception system that eliminates "picket-fencing" interference and locks in weak signals without crowding from stronger adjacent channels. This is sex. This is purple haze. This is rock 'n' roll. Call Clarion at 1-800-487-9007, Dept. IN for more information. This is free.

clarion
CAR AUDIO
THERE IS NO SOUND BARRIER.™

8.8. Attitude and lifestyle ads frequently adopt the consumer's point of view. They don't address the consumer; they *become* the consumer. People are, in effect, overhearing themselves. Company and consumer have merged.

> *All* interesting attitudes are complex.
> —Walker Gibson, *Persona*

things, interview the shoemaker and see if his voice can run the ad. As writer Tracy Kidder says: "Choosing a point of view is a matter of finding the best place to stand, from which to tell a story. The process shouldn't be determined by theory, but driven by immersion in the material itself."[9]

DECIDE HOW THAT PERSON IS TALKING ABOUT THE PRODUCT

Most ads sound like they're in love with what they're selling. But this can easily be overdone: the features are said to be great, the product marvelous, and the offer nothing short of astounding. Hype (unearned overstatement) is a real turn-off—unless you wink about it. Experiment with other relationships toward your client's product: undersell it, oversell it (with that wink), be flippant, be modest, make fun of it, wonder why people would buy it, point out its limitations. An unusual attitude about what you're selling can get you past the clichés and unbelievability inherent in adoration of product.

An ironically overstated or understated attitude toward the product lets you say more than one thing at a time, provides readers or viewers the richness of more than one meaning, and gives them a little work to do; you leave room for them to get involved.

Irony occurs when there's a difference between what you say and what you mean. Everyone uses irony (and its cousin, sarcasm). People will watch a LeBron James 360-degree slam dunk and say, "Not too bad." They'll sit in gridlock on the freeway and say, "I love this city." Why do people like these comments better than obvious, literal ones? Because they express a more complicated attitude toward the subject and the person speaking; such comments create more than one meaning simultaneously, and they can create of the speaker someone smart enough to be of two minds about a single

Rain meets suede.
Rain kisses suede.
Suede is unimpressed.
Rain moves on.

Eddie Bauer
SINCE 1920

Introducing Seattle Suede. Washable.
Life in the Pacific Northwest inspired us to develop a suede jacket that can withstand a driving mist, a torrential downpour, a tsunami, flood or twister. In other words, an average day in your wash cycle.

8.9. Rain and suede are personified, the coat's feature (washable suede) being dramatized by the encounter between the two. Neither the consumer nor the company is speaking here. Who is? Hard to say. The weatherman as romancer?

8.10. An example of the attention-getting power and persuasiveness of a voice that understates rather than overstates its endorsement of the product.

topic. With LeBron people are saying "great shot," but they're also implying that he's so good he should do that, and they're preserving their own cool by acting unfazed. They're getting extra mileage out of one comment. Thus the value of irony: richness.

In an age inundated with hype, you're wise to think about your copy's attitude toward its product. Can you find an attitude more interesting than "This product is fabulous. Buy it now and be the happiest person alive."? I bet you can (see fig. 8.10).

Remember, too, that with most advertising you're creating a relationship between words and pictures. So, just like the ironic comment about LeBron's basketball shot, you can make ironic comments about your ad's images. You create a more complex voice—and your attitude toward the selling argument becomes subtler—when the image is *more* than the usual, the comment *less* so (or vice versa). Although this chapter has been focusing on the words in an ad, remember that an ad's voice is really the entire rhetorical package: language+ image. The whole ad has a voice, and you can use all the ad's elements to create it (see fig. 8.11).

KEEP YOUR VOICE FREE OF CLICHÉS

The best voices sound distinct, singular. One way they do so is by avoiding clichés, whether they be particular to advertising or general to the language. You probably remember from your freshman writ-

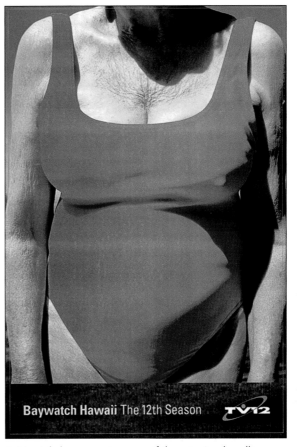

Baywatch Hawaii The 12th Season

8.11. Ads have a voice even if there isn't a headline. How to comment on yet a twelfth season of *Baywatch*? Why not use a visual that humorously overstates the implications?

There are no hammers. There are no nails. But that's okay. There's no lumber, either.

Look at it this way: at least you won't need a building permit. What you will need is plenty of determination.

Foresight. The ability to look beyond very real hardships and obstacles and discern a greater good: that of

empowering others, of helping them become self-reliant. It might mean

teaching people how to raise new shelters. Or how to raze old ones.

In every case, it will mean replenishing the most important resource a

person can have: their dignity. And you thought construction wasn't

a noble profession. **Peace Corps.** The toughest job you'll ever love.

8.12. Sometimes it helps to avoid clichéd approaches to "cause" advertising—earnest pleas to idealism—by creating instead a voice that seems to smile through the apocalypse.

ing course that *clichés*—overused words, expressions, and ideas—are bad: they flatten the prose, numb the reader, and make your voice sound like borrowed clothes look. They are you at your least individual, least interesting, most plagiaristic. So if you find yourself writing a phrase that sounds too familiar, too slick, especially one that tumbles out too fast, cross it off and look for another way to say the same thing.

One problem with copywriting, however, is that the language that defines advertising's territory, the phrases that constitute its meanings, are themselves clichés: "buy now and save," "new and improved," "state of the art," "now with even more cleaning power," "take advantage of this special offer," "for a limited time," "be the first to," "introducing a revolutionary way to," "complete satisfaction or your money back," and so on.

Of course, advertisers *do* want people to buy now and save, they *do* promise more power in this new formula, they *are* introducing a new product. But the language with which these arguments are made is itself so clichéd and corrupted that what ad writers have to say and how they say it have merged into one big cliché in many consumers' minds. Indeed, advertising may have more and more overused clichés than any other field. Consumers see advertising all the time, too, which only accelerates the speed at which fresh language decays into cliché.

It's a content and a form teetering on bankruptcy. The fact that as an advertiser or copywriter you must go in there one more time, make the same argument but make it with enough originality to escape the dead zone of consumer disbelief—this is the great challenge of advertising writing.

How to avoid clichés

Writing well when there are *so* many clichés around almost seems to require a new dictionary. And to the extent that your voice is un-adlike, to the extent that you can sound not like an ad but like a person, an *interesting* person, so much the better. However, sometimes you can avoid a cliché simply by inverting or otherwise modifying its expression. Lots of headlines and clever lines of copy result from twisting a cliché, as Nike did with "when the going gets tough, the tough get going": "when the going gets wet, the wet go Hawaiian" (fig. 8.2). So don't shun clichés outright; but be certain that if you do work with one, you tweak or twist it.

My best advice is the same as what's given in freshman comp courses: recognize and replace clichés in your own writing, and read, read, read good prose (in this case, body copy). Copywriters know how many land mines are buried in the fields they must traverse; read the good writers to see how they get across.

For example, the copy for a Peace Corps ad could have sounded like this:

Become a Peace Corps volunteer and help those less fortunate than yourself. Bring your energy to an underprivileged nation and watch it bloom where there was desert. Bring smiles to the people as you teach them how to use modern methods of agriculture, develop healthier sanitation, and find hope in the future. Become your own best self by helping people help themselves.

By contrast, figure 8.12 presents a Peace Corps ad that knows about the clichés of volunteerism. So it features something else instead: ironic commentary about just how impossible the job may be. The attitude here is the hook: not overstated idealism but wise-guy cynicism (the first line of copy: "Look at it this way, at least you won't need a building permit."). Thus the voice is richer than that of most ads because it's more complicated, of two minds: the Peace Corps experience may be both rewarding *and* nightmarish. There is wisdom in this voice, and it wins readers over by transcending clichés.

FIND YOUR VOICE

> The larger one's repertoire of selves, the more wisely one can choose an effective voice in a given situation.
>
> —Walker Gibson, *Persona*

The two best ways to learn to write better are, simply enough, to read and write. As I mentioned earlier, study the good copywriters like a fiend. Depending on where you live, you may not be exposed to consistently top-shelf copywriting. Especially in the smaller markets, local radio, TV, and newspaper advertising can be mediocre, and a good deal of work is missing altogether. So reading the advertising annuals (and looking at ads in newspapers like the *New York Times* and *USA Today*) becomes doubly important. Read the brochure copy in the design annuals. Study the copy in the advertising annuals. Subscribe to as many sources of the good stuff as you can afford; seek out the rest in your library. (I highly recommend *Communication Arts, Lurzer's Int'l Archive, Graphis, Creativity,* and *Print* magazines; *The One Show* (from the One Club for Art & Copy); the British *D&AD Annual, The Art Directors Annual,* and the magazine of student work, *CMYK. Adweek, Brandweek,* and *Advertising Age* cover well the business side of advertising—trends, themes, issues.)

Don't limit your reading to copywriting. The American voice—in all its variety—is the one you need to hear in your inner ear. Read Carl Hiaasen, Ian Frazier, Bia Lowe, George Saunders, Susan Orlean, Dave Barry, Adam Gopnik, Sarah Vowell, David Sedaris. Read *Time* or *Newsweek, Rolling Stone,* the *New York Times, Outside,* the *New Yorker.* Open Studs Terkel's books and hear people talk. Assimilate American speech, from formal and literary down to funky and street-smart, because all copy comes out of these voices. You re-create the American vernacular when you write copy, becoming the people's voice, their human sound. The rhythms and words you need are out there in print (as well as in music, movies, bumper stickers, and everywhere else). Stock up.

Stylistically, the closest cousin to advertising copy is journalism, so attend especially to the voices of good journalists. Consider, for example, this little bit of Bob Greene, writing an obituary for the wrestler Buddy "Nature Boy" Rogers:

> Nature Boy had the greatest speaking voice. He sounded like confidence squared. He walked with a strut even when he walked with a cane. Two strokes last month killed him. The last time I was in south Florida, I took him and his wife to dinner at an Italian restaurant called Casa Bella. He seemed to have a little trouble reading the menu. Maybe his eyes were going bad. I didn't mention it. Some things you just don't do.[10]

Greene's diction (word choice) is common, so he sounds real; he puts in details, so readers see things; and his sentences are straight-line American vernacular, subject+verb+object, so they make reading easy. Readers simply follow someone talking out loud. There's an authenticity to it. You wouldn't want to sell a Cadillac with this voice, but there are plenty of no-nonsense products for which it would work. (And all you've got to do is open a copy of *Architectural Digest* to hear how you'd sell a Cadillac.)

Also you've got to write regularly yourself to get better; exercise that writing muscle. No one gets much better just by watching. Try to write every day. Begin copy assignments with freewriting (rapid, uncensored stream-of-consciousness writing). As E. M. Forster said, "How do I know what I think until I see what I say?"[11] You've got to get the words out there before you can do anything with them. Quick freewritings push you past writer's block and begin to show you what you have to say.

Remember: the essence of good advertising language is its human sound. Your first job is to get the consumer's attention, and your next job is to convince him or her that this corporate announcement aimed at thousands, if not millions, is really a nudge of the elbow from one friend to another.

9 · Body Copy II
Writing Well

Many copywriters labor for endless hours to create and hone the headline and concept for an ad, only to dash off the body copy as an afterthought. This is a disservice to both the advertiser and the consumer. Seldom can a sale be closed, or a significant change in attitude be brought about, by a headline alone. A well-crafted, literate, and persuasive selling argument is at least as crucial to the ultimate success of an ad as any other element.

—Rod Kilpatrick, copywriter, Fallon McElligott

Voice is critical to writing well, but it's not alone. Let's examine the other items from your English professor's list of principles:

1. Voice.

2. Details: The writing is full of specifics; it's particular, not vague.

3. Thesis: The writing has one central, unifying idea. It hangs together.

4. Organization and structure: The central idea is developed in some order; there is a beginning, middle, and end, and the writing coheres throughout.

5. Style: Form matches content: The prose is not overwritten. It's stylistically graceful, with strong, clear sentences and well-chosen language.

Detail, detail, detail

While no "rules" of writing are absolutely and always true, this one comes close: good writing is concrete and specific; bad writing is abstract and general. Do you remember your freshman composition instructor always asking for more detail? You needed to point to things, put them in your writing, so that your audience knew what you were talking about. You had to hang your ideas on something besides thin air. This obligation to support generalities with specifics holds true in body copy. A well-chosen detail is more persuasive than a multitude of vague claims of superiority. Consider the advice of ad great Claude Hopkins: "The weight of an argument may often be multiplied by making it specific. Say that a tungsten lamp gives more light than a carbon and you leave some doubt. Say that it gives three and one-third times the light and people realize that you have made tests and comparisons."[1]

What are the best ways to generate detail? Read on.

DRAW FROM YOUR RESEARCH

What works when you're researching your client's product also works when you're writing it up. Go back through the facts you discovered on the company and product—awards and honors won; the most intricate but essential part in the machine; the most distant place from which the company procures a part, or the farthest-flung user of the product; where, when, and how the CEO fell in love with the company's product; who he or she studied under; examples of corporate dedication. (Do the chefs grow their own herbs right outside the kitchen? Is the water recycled through filters every twenty minutes? Do the engineers—as Ogilvy discovered when researching Rolls-Royce—listen for axle whine with a stethoscope?) Look for particularities that you might use in the copy.

Deciding which details to use depends on the purpose and scope of the copy you're writing. If it's a brochure, a lot of details might be useful; if it's a single ad, the headline/visual concept will obviously narrow and direct your writing. Focus on the details that support the ad's concept; save the rest for other ads. Regardless of which details you end up using, however, the point is always the same: specifics give density to your copy—weight, realism, and reader interest. They make whatever story you're telling more believable.

Just as copywriters look to the classic VW campaign from Doyle Dane Bernbach for other advertising virtues, they also see that it was a very specific campaign, citing fact after fact in its continuing argument for the Bug:

Headline:
After we paint the car we paint the paint.

Visual:
A VW bug body shell, freshly painted

Copy:
You should see what we do to a Volkswagen
    even before we paint it.
We bathe it in steam, we bathe it in alkali, we
    bathe it in phosphate. Then we bathe it in a
    neutralizing solution.
If it got any cleaner, there wouldn't be much left
    to paint.
Then we dunk the whole thing into a vat of slate
    gray primer until every square inch of metal
    is covered. Inside and out.
Only one domestic car maker does this. And his
    cars sell for 3 or 4 times as much as a Volk-
    swagen.
(We think the best way to make an economy car
    is expensively.)
After the dunking, we bake it and sand it by
    hand.
Then we paint it.
Then we bake it again, and sand it again by hand.
Then we paint it again.
And bake it again.
And sand it again by hand.
So after 3 times, you'd think we wouldn't bother
    to paint it again and bake it again. Right?
Wrong.

Some people think that product specs just don't cut it in copy anymore because all products are so similar as to make the specs irrelevant. But remember: detail can be of all sorts. Consider the follow-

ing copy from an ad for Barney's New York, a clothing retailer. The campaign used the end of summer as impetus for buying fall clothes. The ad's visual was a full-bleed photo of an empty lifeguard chair at the beach, with the headline "SPF 0." The details in this copy aren't about clothing; they're about summer. And look at how specifically the copy remembers:

Blonde hair darkens.
Visine sales plummet.
Lifeguard whistles fall silent.
The signs are obvious.
Summer is over.
Once again baby oil is for babies.
Pool men take up roofing.
And towels migrate to bathrooms.
Slowly, the healthy glow is fading.
A milky luminescence returns.
But all is not lost.

You can still look good without a tan.

Come see the new Fall Collection. Barney's New
    York

You don't have to be writing huge chunks of copy to use detail, either. Even with a copy crawl, a little ant-line of words, you can say something rather than nothing. A trade ad for Wren, makers of housings and accessories for closed-circuit television, showed a surveillance camera with the headline "Giving you that creepy feeling of being watched since 1982" and this brief, but helpful, copy:

For fifteen years we've been making surveil-
    lance domes, globes, and camera mounts. That
    means saved inventory. Protected employees.
    And the occasional uneasy glance over a shoul-
    der. Call 1-800-881-2249 to learn more.

Most first-draft copy is too vague, too thin. Readers just hear a pleasant, buzzing noise. Give them the rest of the story, whatever that story is, however quickly you have to tell it. Make their trip into your copy worth the trouble. Readers should know more after reading it than they did before. Rewrite it until they do.

USE PARTICULAR LANGUAGE
"Detail, detail, detail" doesn't simply mean bringing

in facts. It also means being specific, not general, throughout the language. Find the best word, not just the most available one. Not "good" chocolate if "seductive" chocolate does more. Not "fabric" if it's "wool." Don't write "every zipper is well made" if instead you can write, as Timberland did for one of its coats, "every zipper is milled and tumbled smooth so as to not injure the leather."

Don't float above your subject; get down into its texture.

FIND THE RIGHT CONNOTATIONS

Connotation counts as much as denotation. You might remember from freshman composition that the *denotation* of a word is its strict dictionary definition, and its *connotations* are the shades of meaning that surround it. Thus "smile," "grin," and "smirk" all denote the same thing, but each has a different shade of meaning, a different connotation. There are no synonyms. "Childish" and "childlike" denote the same state, but which would you rather be called?

The Timberland copywriters could have said the zipper was "manufactured," but wisely they added the sense of old-time, small-company methods with the word "milled." They could have said it was polished with "abrasives," but "tumbled smooth" sounds so much better I'd almost like it done to me. Both choices supply the right connotations to the same denotative facts.

Developing this feeling for words, turning them over in your mind before using them, is central to writing good copy. A few bad words can break the spell you're trying to cast. The pressure on word choice in the compressed space of body copy makes it similar to poetry—a high-wire act, grace along a narrow line.

CREATE IMAGES

An *image* is anything that appeals to one or another of the senses: sight, touch, taste, hearing, smell. Good writing puts the reader somewhere, and it does so largely through imagery. That's why "russet" is better than "potato" (the reader *sees* more), "sandpaper" is better than "rough"(he *touches* more), and "simmer" beats "cook" (she *hears* and *smells* more). Appeals to the senses are also conduits to the emotions. The more your readers see, touch, and so on, the more they feel. Images reach them.

Read the Mitsubishi TV ad in figure 9.1. The creative problem was how to *show* in print the power of large-screen video. You can't really do that in print because you don't have the size and you don't have movement. So why not create an all-copy ad that shows, through its vivid language, what dramatic pictures are like? One axiom of good writing is "Show, don't tell." Look at how well this copy does that: things aren't referred to or labeled ("great," "terrible," "exciting"); they're brought right in. Readers experience them; readers have been shown, not told.

CONSIDER METAPHORS

Whenever you talk about one thing in terms of something dissimilar, you're using *metaphor*, and this is often a good idea—it makes what you're saying more clear and more vivid. Look, for example, at the metaphor in the Porsche ad's headline in figure 9.2. And the copy develops the comparison between horse and car: "Since its introduction in 1974, the Porsche 911 Turbo has given birth to an entire generation of hopeful imitators. None of them even came close. Considering these bloodlines. . . ." The metaphor becomes a kind of detail; readers see the car *as* a thoroughbred, which is more vivid than "widely imitated," "quality craftsmanship," or other nonmetaphorical equivalents would have been.

The danger with metaphors? Without thinking, you can add other metaphors to the current one and create *mixed metaphors*, which are visual incongruities: "If he goes to the well one more time, he's going to get burned." That sort of thing. So comparing the Porsche to something else while also thinking of it as a horse—for example, saying "it's a piece of sculpture"—would be a mistake; readers' minds prefer one picture system at a time. Also with any metaphor you're taking a chance: maybe it's too weird, too cute, too clichéd, or—if overextended—too irritating. How many more times do you want the Porsche copywriter to mention horses in the ad? Not many, right?

Thesis

Copy is not a bunch of one-liners. It's not an Eddie Izzard or Steven Wright routine full of clever twists, catchy phrases, bizarre non sequiturs. (In this regard it differs from headlines, which often are like something out of a stand-up comedian's act.)

Just as an essay develops one main idea, or *thesis*, so too does copy. It follows from the ad's approach or thesis. Once you've figured out the ad's concept, you'll know what kind of copy to produce, and probably how much. Getting the copy right won't be easy—writing well is always hard—but you'll know what ought to be there. If you're selling children's toys because they help kids learn, then emphasize the educational, imaginative benefits of the toys. If, however, you're selling durability, then talk about rugged plastic and tough wheels, the indestructible little heart of these toys. Even though copy can be the place where you cite additional selling points—that's part of its function, after all—copy should have a dominant idea running through it, and that idea comes from the ad's concept.

Write your sentences in a straight line. Ask of each one, "Does this follow the thesis?" If not, is there a good reason, or have you just digressed? Look back at that VW copy; it was all about the paint job and nothing else.

Organization and Structure

> "Begin at the beginning," the King said, very gravely, "and go on till you come to the end: then stop."
>
> —Lewis Carroll,
> *Alice's Adventures in Wonderland*

Like an essay, good copy has a beginning, a middle, and an end. Don't keep resaying the thesis; develop it.

BEGINNING

Think of the first line of body copy as the next sentence after the headline. That's why people read copy—to finish what the headline/visual started—so give them what they expect. What's the next thought after that headline? Say it. Follow directly from your lead. And pull hard. You either draw people into the copy with a strong beginning—or you lose them.

MIDDLE

The middle is where you put the selling facts; after all, people don't want more jokes, more one-liners at the headline level. They've gone to the copy for the fine print, as it were; they want details. Put them right here. Even though you may cite additional selling points, keep the ad's concept in mind; don't drop it altogether in the copy. Use its dominant idea as occasional language or imagery. Pull the ad's concept through the copy—not only to make the copy cohere with itself but to unify it with the ad's Big Idea.

Notice in the ad for L.L.Bean (fig. 9.3) how a "satisfy the customer" argument is made throughout the copy. Its point is single-minded and sustained: founder L.L.Bean's experience with his first boot taught him a lesson the company still observes. His story becomes its story, and readers leave the copy convinced of one thing: that L.L.Bean stands behind anything it sells.

END

The close is the place where you put the call to action. Much national brand advertising doesn't ask consumers to do anything more than consider the product. But retail ads (and increasingly all advertising) encourage a more active response: "Act now. Sale ends May 21," "Call our 800 number or visit our Web site for more information." The L.L.Bean ad invites customers to do exactly that: call the 800 number or visit the Web site to get a free fall catalog. Whatever you want the consumer to do, put it here, in the closing.

THINK OF COPY AS A THREE-PART STRUCTURE

Body copy should end rather than just stop. You want to create a sense of completion, a journey begun and satisfyingly concluded. One way to do this is to think of the headline, the first line of body copy, and the last line of body copy as a trinity—a unified, frequently clever, almost syllogistic summary of the selling idea. (It's handy, by the way, to think of two "last lines": the last line of your argument and what's often literally the last line—the call to action.)

Here's the three-part pattern in the L.L.Bean ad:

Headline:
   The first boot he made lasted 2 weeks. The lesson it taught him has endured 89 years.

First line of copy:
   Some lessons in life stay with you for a long time.

Last line of copy:
   Today, you'll find the apparel and gear in our fall catalog considerably updated from those times. You'll also find the philosophy behind it unchanged.

You don't have to write copy this way, but it can be effective. Such symmetry is itself a kind of per-

The sound of a single bullet buzzed straight past my ear.

I didn't have to look at the rear-view mirror to know that Dubrov was back on our tail. Our only avenue of escape was through the street market up ahead.

The brightly colored patchwork of stalls rushed up to meet us as Johnson put his foot to the floor. A crate of watermelons exploded wetly against the car, the pink juice streaming across the windscreen.

I stole a quick glance in the mirror. Dubrov's gleaming black limo was getting closer by the second.

It was then that I sensed the first hints of acrid smoke. The stink of a grinding, dying engine.

Our car was going to go, and with it, all our chances.

And as the billowing smoke began to tear at my nostrils and burn my eyes, I realized that it was something much, much worse than an overheated engine. It was my

chicken pot pie burning in the kitchen, the charred, inedible victim of my engrossment in Mitsubishi's Home Theater with Dolby Surround Sound.

9.1. Demonstrating the vivid, involving power of language itself, this ad uses virtually no pictures in the ad—just copy. But readers see, hear, touch, taste, and smell a lot, don't they?

Imagine the stud fees we'd get if it was a race horse.

Since its introduction in 1974, the Porsche 911 Turbo has given birth to an entire generation of hopeful imitators. None of them even came close.

Considering these bloodlines, it should be no surprise that the new Porsche 911 Turbo is already being hailed as the next benchmark of contemporary supercars.

Made in extremely limited numbers, it combines the remarkable refinement of the new

generation Carrera 2 with the blistering performance of a 316-horsepower turbocharged engine, all wrapped in a legendary muscular body that has steadfastly defied imitation.

We invite you to come see it, along with our entire family of new Porsches.

After all, if this is the head of the family, imagine how beautiful the offspring are.

9.2. The power of metaphor.

THE FIRST BOOT HE MADE

LASTED 2 WEEKS.
THE LESSON IT
TAUGHT HIM HAS ENDURED
89 YEARS.

Some lessons in life stay with you for a long time. Our founder L.L.Bean learned one in 1911 that's still with us today. In September of that year, L.L. made and sold his first 100 pairs of the Maine Hunting Shoe. When the rubber on the boot failed, he accepted 90 pairs back and promptly refunded all money. The experience taught his company something we still remember. We must always work to satisfy the customer. Today, you'll find the apparel and gear in our fall catalog considerably updated from those times. You'll also find the philosophy behind it unchanged.

Get your FREE FALL CATALOG. Call 1-800-221-4211 or visit www.llbean.com

L.L.Bean
start here
GO ANYWHERE

9.3. Copy sustains the headline's concept while delivering the specifics that complete it.

suasiveness: the argument is reiterated but not repeated; the case *feels* closed.

ESTABLISH COHERENCE

So far I've been saying that copy should have one central idea that everything hangs from; it should be unified. But it should also appear unified, which means it must cohere. In addition to hooking up with the Big Idea, the copy's words, phrases, sentences, and ideas must hook up with each other. One writer called good prose a "nest of hooks," and that's a fine image by which to understand coherence. You shouldn't be able to pull any sentence out of the copy without bringing others with it (or without tearing a hole in the copy's sense). Everything should depend on everything else. Thus the relationship of the parts to the parts (*coherence*) is as important as the relationship of the parts to the whole (*unity*).

How to accomplish this? Lots of ways, but transitions are essential. They link one element to another: "first," "second," "another," "and," "but," "so," "however," "above," "under," "last," "therefore," and so on. Pronouns deftly stitch one part to another,

too: "The driver walked away from his car unhurt. *Its* airbag saved *his* life." Prepositional phrases, subordinate clauses, and other bits of language tie your meanings together for readers: "*In today's world*, who's safe? *As you know*, the police . . ." The repetition of a word or idea brings coherence, as does the repetition in parallel structures: "If a car is safe, its passengers are safe."

Put transitions up front in sentences so readers know where they're going. In other words, let the transitions steer them through your sentence, as, for example, "in other words" just did. As you write each sentence, keep the previous sentence in mind. Write every line *in response* to the one before it. Keep stitching sentences together (or go back later and do so).

Style

> Have something to say, and say it as clearly as you can. That is the only secret of style.
> —Matthew Arnold, poet and critic

Copywriters shouldn't sound the same any more than essayists or poets should. But this does not mean that all approaches to style are equal. Nor does it mean that style cannot be taught or that it has no rules. Here are some stylistic fundamentals that good writers observe, no matter what they're writing:

1. Tighten and sharpen ruthlessly; never waste words.
2. Write with nouns and verbs, not adjectives and adverbs.
3. Write grammatically straightforward sentences.
4. Use concrete subjects and verbs. Avoid nominalization.
5. Prefer the loose style.

Most stylistic advice boils down to one rule: keep it simple. Use words and sentences no bigger than necessary to deliver the meaning (that is, never write to impress; write to say what you mean). Match form to content, language to idea.

In ways I hope to show you, all the preceding rules are interrelated; they're almost four ways of talking about the same problem.

TIGHTEN AND SHARPEN

Don't waste words. One thing you can always hear in great copy is all the words its writer *didn't* use, all the words left out, pruned away. Great copy is lean and like an arrow: it goes where it intends, no waste or wobble. Art directors (and readers) are in no mood for rambling discourses that leisurely visit the selling points.

As a guideline, write your copy to the best of your ability—and then cut it in half. While you probably can't eliminate 50 percent without cutting into muscle tissue, you'll be surprised by how much fat can go. When you strip your prose to its leanest, you'll notice a happy consequence: your voice sounds better—sharper, smarter, more persuasive. One benefit of cutting drafts is that you improve their sound. The VW copy quoted earlier serves as an example; it is so simple and unadorned, pure clear function, just like the car. William Strunk,

> You want to write a sentence as clean as a bone. That's the goal.
> —James Baldwin, novelist and essayist

coauthor of *The Elements of Style*, offers a good perspective on writing concisely: "Omit needless words. Vigorous writing is concise. A sentence should contain no unnecessary words, a paragraph no unnecessary sentences, for the same reason that a drawing should have no unnecessary lines and a machine no unnecessary parts. This requires not that the writer make all his sentences short, or that he avoid all detail and treat his subjects only in outline, but that every word tell."[2]

To tighten your work, reread it and ask of every word or phrase, "Do I need this?"

1. Have I said the same thing elsewhere in the sentence?
2. Is there a word I can substitute for a phrase? (For example, "it will not be very long before" can become "soon.")
3. Am I redundant? ("red in color," "visible to the eye," "new innovation," "final result," and so on)
4. Am I pompous, using more and bigger words than I need to?
5. Am I using the passive voice unnecessarily? ("After the car is painted, the paint is painted" is both wordy and impersonal. Wisely VW wrote, "After we paint the car, we paint the paint.")
6. Do I make meaningless distinctions? ("Are you the sort of person who likes the sport of golf?" reduces to "Do you like golf?")
7. How many of my words are just along for the ride, words that look like they're doing something but aren't? ("Honesty with people is a rare human quality that very few individuals possess" says no more than "Honesty is rare," which isn't saying much in the first place.)

You can eliminate a lot of wordiness simply by taking a pencil to it or hitting the delete key. You'll have to recast other sentences to tighten them. But either way, tightening is wondrous: watch the sentences get quicker, the writing start standing up.

Scrutinize your sentences, too. How many of them can go? Are you using two sentences to deliver an idea you could express in one? With body copy, check out your first few sentences. Are you taking too long to get started, just clearing your throat? Maybe your real first sentence is the third one. Mine often is.

Another piece of advice about editing yourself:

the longer you can let a draft "cool," the more you can see the cracks in it. As time passes (an hour, a day, a month), the writing becomes less yours and more someone else's. Eventually it's just words on a page; you can hear and see them objectively. Editing can really get something done then. Try it.

WRITE WITH NOUNS AND VERBS, NOT ADJECTIVES AND ADVERBS

At first this seems to counter common sense: if copywriters are to be "descriptive" and "specific" in their body copy, what better way than by adding adjectives and adverbs? Don't they bring specificity to nouns and verbs? Yes they do, and copywriters need adjectives and adverbs. But it's possible to overindulge, clogging up the flow of sentences with modifiers at every turn.

Nouns and verbs are the two big powers. They run sentences, and you should let them run yours. Strong writers, whose work "flows," write with concrete nouns and verbs. They keep it simple and don't let too much modification stall the movement or muddy up the meaning:

> On the day before Thanksgiving, toward the end of the afternoon, having motored all day, I arrived home, and lit a fire in the living room. The birch logs took hold briskly. About three minutes later, not to be outdone, the chimney itself caught fire.[3]
>
> —E. B. White

> A weasel is wild. Who knows what he thinks? He sleeps in his underground den, his tail draped over his nose. Sometimes he lives in his den for two days without leaving. Outside, he stalks rabbits, mice, muskrats, and birds, killing more bodies than he can eat warm, and often dragging his carcasses home.[4]
>
> —Annie Dillard

> You don't buy a car. The bank buys a car. Of course, if you had bought a Volvo two or three years ago, you'd have something today. You'd have a two or three year old Volvo. Which isn't bad to have. Because where three years is the beginning of the end for some cars, it's only the beginning for a Volvo.
>
> —Ed McCabe, Volvo copy

> In 1941 millions of Jews were looking for ways to escape Nazi death camps. Gandhi recommended suicide. The movie *Gandhi* por-

trays the Mahatma as a saint. But an original article in the July *Reader's Digest* shows the advice of a saint can be hard to live by.
>
> —John A. Young, Jr., *Reader's Digest* copy

It would be easy to screw up any of these by throwing in adjectives and adverbs:

> On the <u>cold</u>, <u>snowy</u> day before <u>another</u> <u>turkey-filled</u> Thanksgiving, toward the end of the <u>long</u> afternoon, having <u>happily</u> motored all day, I arrived home <u>at last</u>, and <u>quickly</u> lit a <u>warm</u> fire in the <u>cozy</u> living room. The <u>very dry</u> birch logs took hold briskly. About three minutes later, not to be <u>vastly</u> outdone, the <u>red hearthstone</u> chimney itself <u>roaringly</u> caught fire.
>
> —E. B. White, ruined

Most copywriters would laugh at this exaggeration, except they realize how often they approximate it in their own writing. Find good nouns and verbs and then leave them alone.

More about verbs

In his timeless book *Diary of an Ad Man*, James Webb Young speaks with the voice of experience: "Don't praise the product. Just tell what it does, and how it does it, so that the reader will say: 'I must try that.' In short, go light on the adjectives and heavy on the verbs."[5]

Verbs hustle, weep, surprise, beam, tear, sear, shimmer, and shine; they can stick a finger right in your eye, split your heart open, or collapse into something you'd wedge in your hip pocket. Verbs (and verbals—words derived from verbs, like gerunds and participles) are the only words that *do* anything. Without them nothing happens, and with only general ones ("make," "do," "come," "go," "have"), not enough happens. So use strong verbs, and use them to express the action of an idea. That one Timberland sentence cited earlier offers "milled," "tumbled," and "injure." A lot happens.

That determinedly simple VW paint-job copy offers basic but vigorous verbs—"paint," "bathe," "dunk," "bake," "sand"—and they're repeated until readers almost see the sweat of the workers.

Is-ness

Track down and replace excessive "is-ness" in your writing: too many uses of "to be" as the *main verb* ("is," "are," "were," "will be," "has been," and so on). "To be" is an odorless, colorless, actionless verb—just an equals sign, really. It's the weakest verb. If it's running the sentence by itself, you risk the word pile: a sentence with a bunch of upright things in it, all tottering into one another but not going anywhere.

Remember that "to be" often functions as an auxiliary verb, a helper, and that's fine. Thus the sentence "I am smiling because my hair is shining" really has two active verbs ("smile" and "shine"), so it moves, however quietly. "I am here but you are there and it is sad," that's is-ness. Try "I wilt here because you bloom there." See?

You can't eliminate "to be," nor do you want to. (I've been using it a lot in these sentences decrying its use.) Copywriters just rely on it too much. Verbs make sentences move; they animate the universe of things. Always examine your verbs to see if you've got your motor running.

WRITE GRAMMATICALLY STRAIGHT-FORWARD SENTENCES

This is perhaps the trickiest challenge. Your sentences are your most complicated stylistic element. They're you. Everyone can locate a better verb and delete unnecessary words, but restructuring language use is a larger matter. Nevertheless, my advice so far has centered on simplicity, and all of it is interrelated. If you find the right verb, you'll avoid is-ness. If you keep from overdosing on adjectives and adverbs, your writing will be tighter and sharper. It'll move and be readable. Now let's take this same idea of simplicity and apply it to sentences.

If writing good sentences has one first principle, this is it: "State who's doing what in the subject of your sentence, and state what that who is doing in your verb."[6] This sounds easy and obvious, but it isn't. Remember that a sentence, any sentence, is simply a way to say that some thing *does* something. Make sure that this thing (the real agent of action) is also your grammatical subject. And make sure that the real action is also the main verb. Lots of times copywriters put the true agent of action

elsewhere than in the grammatical subject, and they stick the real action elsewhere than in the main verb. In other words, they hide what the sentence is saying, and they end up with a fuzzy style that nobody likes.

> The sensation of driving the Miata is pure enjoyment.

A bad sentence. Why? Its grammatical subject is "sensation," its main verb "is." Is the real meaning of this sentence "sensation is"? No. The real meaning is that people will enjoy driving the car. You've hidden the true subject and verb. The real agent of action is either "you" or "driving," and the real action is "to enjoy" or to have sensation. So if that's the real meaning, then put it into the grammatical subject and main verb:

> Enjoy driving the Miata.
> Driving the Miata will thrill you.
> Recharge your senses in a Miata.

Although the last example is the freshest, any of these is better than the original one. Now the agent of action and the action run the sentence; they're not hidden. If one of your sentences feels "blah," you may have the wrong noun and verb in charge. Ask yourself, "What's the real do-er in my sentence, and what's the real action?" Then get those two things, the real subject and verb, in their grammatically correct spots:

> *Bad:*
> A unique approach to outdoor gear by North Face has resulted in clothing that can be worn in any climate.

"approach has resulted"? "clothing can be worn"? Are those the crucial meanings? Of course not.

> *Better:*
> North Face designs its gear so you can tackle any climate.

"North Face designs" and "you can tackle" carry your meaning more directly.

AVOID NOMINALIZATION

Copywriters often fail to match agents with subjects, actions with verbs because of something called nominalization. *Nominalization* involves making nouns out of verbs, and it's the way I killed that Miata sentence previously. "Sensation" is a noun, but it comes from the verb "sense." Likewise, "enjoyment" comes from "enjoy." Somehow or other, copywriters learn to sound formal and pretentious and educated by writing in a style that's heavily nominalized:

> A determination of financial conditions facilitates re-evaluation of mortgage arrangements.

Do you mean that people should rethink their mortgage because rates have improved? Say so.

Much writing is dead because people fall in love with the pompous and the obscure. A nominalized style is like a crypt that entombs living speech. Let your nouns name real things, and turn your verbs loose. Don't lock them up in long, boring constructions. Get the real noun (often a concrete thing or a person) out there and give it the verb it deserves.

PREFER THE "LOOSE" STYLE
Keep your sentences simple and conversational. Make them easy to read. How?

Recast sentences that take too long to say. If you get tangled up in a sentence, back out and start over. It probably wants to become two sentences; you need to sequence what you're saying. Much of writing is simply starting into various constructions to see if they'll say what you want them to, like trying tunnel entrances.

Keep subjects and their verbs together. Put them early in the sentences, too, and add modifying material later—either to the ends of sentences, or in sentence fragments that follow. In other words, don't layer modifiers into the subject-verb mechanism; don't mess up the driveshaft.

Adding material to the ends of your sentences (rather than the beginning or between subjects and verbs) is called *the "loose" style*, and it's the American idiomatic voice: simple, straightforward, and adding to itself as it goes. Sentences written in the "loose" style are called *cumulative sentences*; that is, they state their idea right up front in the subject and verb, then add meanings and modifications as they go. They're easy to read, and they sound like you're thinking as you go, which you are. You approximate speech with constructions like these because you just keep talking, and as you talk, you tack new ideas, like this one, onto the end of your last phrase, as they occur to you, so you can go on

forever if you feel like it. . . . See what I mean?

The sentences you want to minimize are complex ones with too much modifying material either embedded in the main clause or preceding it. (Check your grammar book under *periodic sentences* or *compound-complex sentences* for constructions to use sparingly.) For example, a sentence like this becomes difficult on the mind:

> Although you seek a bank that has the sophistication to handle large accounts yet also has the flexibility to manage smaller ones, you may think that without investing in two separate institutions you're asking too much. . . .

I still don't know what this sentence wants to tell me; it's all preamble. Periodic sentences begin not with the main clause, but with subordinate clauses and phrases, so they're coiled, delivering their full meaning only at the end. Readers have to hold everything in their minds' RAM until the payoff, and that's hard on their brains. Using some periodic sentences is fine, of course, but if you use too many—especially too many with embedded modifications—then your reader will flounder.

Let's recast that periodic sentence as loose sentences instead (and use parallelism in the last two of them):

> You want a bank sophisticated enough to handle large accounts yet flexible enough to manage small ones. But you think you'll have to invest in two separate institutions. You think you'll be asking too much of one. . . .

See how this one is easier to follow and sounds more like someone talking?

How to use loose sentences for details
You will often use copy to cite product specs, to deliver the necessary detail, the rest of the product story. You can use loose structures to do this, simply adding details to the ends of sentences. The following professional writers show how gracefully—and clearly—the loose structure handles details:

> Every so often I make an attempt to simplify my life, burning my books behind me, selling the occasional chair, discarding the accumulated miscellany. [7]
>
> —E. B. White

He [Ken Kesey] wrote like he talked, antic, broad, big-breathed, the words flowing in a slangy, spermy, belt-of-bourbon surge, intimate and muscular, the rigors of the college wrestling mat somehow shaping his way of engaging the world in prose—you got a sense of a writer grappling with this subjects, pinning the story, the paranoia in his vision offset by the relish for the stage. [8]

—Chip Brown

Each sentence is easy to follow: the first says, "I attempt to simplify my life," and the second, "He wrote like he talked," both straightforward subject-verb groupings. Then they pile up details off the end. Each sentence could have gone on almost forever, and the reader wouldn't get lost.

In copywriting this approach works well, too. You can be specific, but never let doing so overburden a sentence. Consider this example from the middle of some BMW copy:

The driver, meanwhile, sits not in a mere driver's seat, but a cockpit—behind a curved instrument panel replete with vital gauges and controls, all placed for optimum visibility and accessibility.

Sentence fragments as the copy version of the loose style

Because copy sentences tend to be shorter than other prose sentences, often you will want to hang modifications off the end of a sentence as *fragments*. You punctuate them as separate sentences, but they're really part of the main thought that preceded them. Here's an example:

So you need shoes and apparel that don't give up either. A shoe like the Air Cross Trainer Low from Nike, with the cushioning you need for running. The flexibility you need for aerobics. The stability required for court sports. And the fit and comfort your feet beg for regardless of where you tell them to go.

See how all these punctuated sentences are really fragments off the main assertion?

Fragments are almost essential to good copy

Copy is like one side of an intimate conversation, written down. Like the personal letter, it pulls the

> The lyf so short, the craft so long to lerne.
>
> —Chaucer

reader close. That's why sentence fragments (and short sentences) are so important to copy. Cutting off snippets of a sentence and writing sentences that are themselves snippets can provide the speed and openness you want. Well used, they become almost a hallmark of good copy. They focus the eye and mind. They're quick. They simplify issues and make things seem easy and convenient. Plus they sound conversational.

But don't go too far. If you chop up prose too much, it gets unclear and jumpy, too fragmented to make sense. So, like all good writers, use sentence fragments but only on purpose, when doing so helps the prose.

STUDY STYLE

This discussion of style gets back, as it should, to writing well in general. I've been telling you all along that copy is simply good prose and that you've already had a course in that. But no one ever graduates from composition class. Everyone is a lifelong student of well-made sentences. Since you're a writer now, you should cultivate a writer's habits. In addition to learning by osmosis—reading good copy and good prose—study style systematically. One book you should always keep around is your grammar handbook from freshman composition. Handbooks vary; some are short, some are long, but they're all road maps of the English language, and you can't drive long or far without consulting one.

DECIDE HOW LONG COPY SHOULD BE

In the rush to cut into your copy and keep it simple, never forget that your goal is *effective* prose, not quick prose. How long is long? How short is short? Copywriter Alastair Crompton tackles that question:

The question, "How long should an advertisement be?" is the same question as "How long is a piece of string?" There is no *rule*. An ad is too short if it ends without saying the right things to make a sale. An ad is too long if it repeats itself, gets boring, stops giving facts and information, or uses two words when one would do.[9]

Since there is no "rule" about copy length, you must decide for yourself when that string is long enough. Determine how much more information your reader wants. Look to both your client's product and your ad's concept for the amount of copy you should write. If you're making a rational argument for the product because it's complicated—a car, a $1,000 racing bike—then a lot of copy makes sense. If, however, you're appealing to emotions with a brand-image strategy, and the product is one consumers *feel* rather than understand—a diamond, a cologne, clothing—then almost any copy may be too much. You must decide for yourself how much of the story is left to tell after you've found the concept and written the headline. There are no firm rules—I have in my office a fascinating diamond ad with several hundred words in it. On the other hand, a bike or car ad may use few words, or no words, relying instead on feeling or image and counting on other mechanisms (brochures, the Web site, salespeople) to tell the rest of the story.

AVOID OVERWRITING

One reason writing well is difficult is that it never reduces to formula; every good rule can be taken to a bad extreme. You can tighten too much and sound clipped and inhuman. You can sharpen too much and sound fussy. Your search for the precise expression can lead to thesaurus-writing—trading in your natural words for artificial ones—short for long, idiomatic for Latinate, real for bookish. Never write out of a thesaurus; in fact, try never to use one at all and you'll be a better writer. Only the words you own and know will work for you; you can't substitute elegant variations and still sound real. That's why reading helps you write; you come into possession of a larger, more supple vocabulary the natural way.

Good prose must be particular enough to carry meaning but not so overwrought that it sounds like my previous ruination of E. B. White: every noun with an adjective, every verb with an adverb, the whole thing overqualified until its voice lies buried under baroque ornamentation. And copy is especially easy to overwrite: you're making a case for something, you're persuading, and it's easy to push too hard, to hype instead of communicate. Plus you're often writing description. Adjectives and adverbs pop up, as they must, and verbs wither, since you're drawing a picture rather than telling a story. The prose overgrows into a thicket, strangling both your voice and the reader's interest.

How do you know when you've overdone it? By ear. Good prose is ultimately a matter of sound. Read your work out loud, *hear* it, especially with your target audience's ear. Would they like what you're saying and the way you're saying it? Are sentence lengths varied? Are long sentences mixed with short ones? Is there a good *rhythm* among them? While sentences are generally shorter in copy than in essays—ease of reading being such a priority—you don't want sentences so short as to sound staccato. Nor do you want them all the same length; one after another, they'll drone. Is your *diction* (word choice) precise enough to serve the argument but common enough to sound real? These balances are things you can hear; they're also things that improve with practice.

How body copy is not like freshman composition

As you've seen, most of what makes an essay good also makes body copy good. Good copy is simply a variant of good writing. There are important distinctions in the variant, however. Here they are.

IT SELLS; IT DOESN'T JUST DESCRIBE

Copy is always selling something, a fact too many beginning copywriters forget. In researching the product and in employing the rules of freshman English, too many writers merely describe product specs. Description and analysis are fine purposes for many essays, but they are never the *purpose* of copy. You are making the case for a product, talking someone into wanting it or wanting more of it or trying it again after all those years ("Have you driven a Ford lately?"). Even when you're describing or analyzing something, you're doing so to make it seem more appealing, or less complicated, or so well made that it must be bought. No matter what the prose's task seems to be at the moment, you are always a salesperson (see fig. 9.4).

IT STATES THE BENEFITS,
NOT JUST THE FEATURES

If you slide into product specs and forget that you should be selling instead, you will often write about *features* instead of translating those features into *benefits*. You and I have been here before. Remember, features belong to the product, but benefits belong to the people. Your copy will be "so what?" stuff until you show the advantages to be gained

9.4. How might you sell an inessential item? By making it fun to contemplate. This amusing copy becomes its own little time travel. And just often enough it slips in a straightforward pitch for, yes, a potato clock.

from all those features. This simple headline understands benefits: "California Closets. Because whenever you need something you'll know where it is."

BRAND-IMAGE COPY HAS ITS OWN RULES

Remember, however, that brand-image, lifestyle, and attitude copy describes and sells consumer *feelings,* not hardware. Many ads don't talk about products at all. Instead they resemble short stories, character sketches, or psychological counseling. So don't lock into thinking that ads must talk hardware. Body copy really sells the *idea* of the ad in words. So if the idea is the romance of the sea or the lifestyle of the person wearing a certain brand of clothing, then write that as well as you can.

Consider, for example, the Honda ad in which the station wagon is not described at all; the owner's

lifestyle is (fig. 9.5). Instead of detailing product features, the copy narrates the changes in circumstance that the vehicle serves. (Notice the use of "you" to pull in the readers.) In following a life and its funny, endearing complications, readers not only identify with the owner but also appreciate, by implication, the capabilities of the Honda. Well-written lifestyle copy.

A final word: On rewriting

There is no writing, just rewriting.
—John Updike, novelist

I could have put this in the headline chapter, too, because you can rewrite a headline all day long. But with body copy there are even more words to get right. Rewriting is not a curse visited on bad writers. Writing *is* rewriting. I often wish it were otherwise, but it isn't. I must write lots of drafts, go through a process every time, from fumbling and stupid and incoherent prose to something less so, until sometimes I arrive at good work. Occasionally I can write a headline or short copy block that comes out okay right off. Or sometimes it has to be okay because it's going out the door, no time to fiddle. But most things take me a few drafts. They'll probably take you a few drafts too: a couple just to cover the territory, then a few more to tighten and make it make sense, then a couple more to give it some grace. But even that "sequence" isn't true. Every piece develops differently, few come easily. So learn to accept this process as natural. Rewriting is the way of writing, and eventually it becomes the fun of it, too. Honest.

Literary critic Elizabeth Hardwick captures the universality of the rewriting "lifestyle" in the following comment:

Say, it is Monday, and you write a very bad draft, but if you keep on trying, on Friday, words, phrases, appear almost unexpectedly. I don't know why you can't do it on Monday, or why I can't. I'm the same person, no smarter, I have nothing more at hand. I think it's true of a lot of writers. It's one of the things writing students don't understand. They write a first draft and are quite disappointed, or often should be disappointed. They don't understand that they have merely begun, and that they may be merely beginning even in the second or third draft.[10]

One day you get married, have kids, get a dog and buy a wagon. So you start driving to day care. You drive to the baby-sitter's place. You drive to your parents'. And, according to your grandparents, you don't drive over to their house as often as you should. Then you start taking the children to preschool. Then to kindergarten. Then to grade school. You drop the kids off at swimming lessons, ballet lessons, trombone lessons and ice skating lessons. A week later, they drop the trombone lessons. You go to the beach one summer and to the lake up in the mountains the next. And you finally decide to go see the Grand Canyon. Your dog barks at all the gas station attendants along the way. You pick the kids up from soccer practices, which soon turn into basketball practices, which soon turn into baseball practices. Then come the football games, which they don't play in, but still need a ride to. And just when you're starting to feel a little like a taxi service, one of your little darlings walks up to you, smiles sweetly, and asks for the keys to the car. You might as well enjoy the trip. The Accord Wagon ⊞HONDA

9.5. Good copy serves the ad's concept, whatever that may be. In this case, rather than detailing the features of the product, the copy details the lifestyle of its owner, demonstrating the wagon's utility in the process.

Writing checklists

The basic writing exercise is simple and unvarying: write a draft and get criticism, from your own internal editor and from colleagues and clients. Keep rewriting until it sounds right, until it works. That's the method. No tricks, no shortcuts.

During that process check for the following things:

Checklist for body copy

1. The lead: Does it pull hard enough, make a quick enough and strong enough transition out of the headline/visual?

2. The middle: Does it say something new? Advance the story? Give details? Complete the argument? Or does it just make nice noises? (You don't have to write features and benefits copy, but be sure whatever you're doing is better.)

3. The close: Does the copy end rather than just stop? Does it pull things together? Does it provide a call to action, that second "last" line?

What should readers do now that they've read your copy? Tell them.

4. Structure: Does the copy have a structure? Is the argument or story, however long or short, unified and complete? Does the first sentence follow from the headline/visual? Does the last line return to the first line and headline/visual? (You don't have to follow this pattern either, but remember that copy needs a shape and sense of resolution.)

5. Voice: Is the voice of the copy working? Does it match the headline/visual?

6. Clichés: Have you broken past clichés, both of English and of advertising?

7. Persuasiveness: Does the copy persuade or just describe? How convincing and motivating is it?

> Who casts a living line, must sweat.
> —Ben Jonson, dramatist and poet

Checklist for the English language

1. Spelling: Is everything spelled and punctuated correctly?

2. Verbs: Circle the verbs. How strong are they?

3. Alignment: Examine subjects and verbs, and align them with the agents of action and the action.

4. Transitions: Circle the transitions. Are there enough? Are they up front in the flow? Are there too many?

5. Sentences: Are they graceful? Varied? Rhythmic? Strong? Simple? How do they sound—not one by one, but all together? In short, does the copy "flow"? Have you connected thoughts and sentences so they sound like a single stream of speech, not a bunch of one-offs?

6. Tightening and sharpening: Have you tightened and sharpened the sentences? (Tightened: gotten as many words out of them as you can without drawing blood. Sharpened: replaced fuzzy, boring, general words with precise ones.)

6a. Editing: Have you edited ruthlessly? Gotten to a 1:1 ratio (the number of words you use exactly matches the ground you cover)?

7. Specificity: Are you as specific as possible? Do you invoke the senses (sight, hearing, touch, taste, smell)? Have you at least asked yourself whether you could?

8. Fun: Are you fun to read? Remember what an editor at the *Wall Street Journal*, Barney Kilgore, said: "The easiest thing in the world for any reader to do is stop reading."[11]

These are tough questions—and the reason all good copywriters read aloud (at least in their heads), solicit commentary, and then, invariably, rewrite.

10 ▪ Television

The Electronic Weedwhacker Age, when TiVo and Replay walk the earth, is here. . . . [TV ads] will have to be voluntary destinations, as all companies will suddenly be in the entertainment business—embracing the idea that they are not just carmakers or airlines.

—Jeff Goodby, co-chairman,
Goodby, Silverstein & Partners

TV advertising is often the highest-profile work done by agencies. If you're just starting your career, chances are you're most interested in creating TV spots. Print and radio are fine, but TV is where the thrills are. TV is the glamour profession.

First, however, a few sobering thoughts

1. Copywriters can't really make TV spots. They're too complicated.

2. If you're creating portfolio pieces by which to get a job, you may not need TV ads. Creative directors looking at your book often won't take the time to examine, frame by frame, your storyboards (a series of little TV frames with copy blocks beneath them). Nor will they always stop and read typed radio copy. Would you? Besides, they can determine whether you can think and sell by looking at your print ads.[1]

3. TV ads are really little films created by filmmakers. As a senior vice president at DDB Needham, Chicago, noted, "The two disciplines— feature films and commercial films— have blended together to the point now where it's just filmmaking."[2] Agencies often hire filmmakers to make their TV spots, and the list of those who've made ads gets longer every day: Robert Altman, Martin Scorsese, Federico Fellini, Francis Ford Coppola, Sam Mendes, Ang Lee, John Frankenheimer, David Lynch, Spike Lee, Tim Burton, and many others. And not only do filmmakers themselves make the spots (often only loosely based on agency storyboards), but frequently editors are hired separately to create the commercial itself from the filmmakers' footage. As you can see, all this gets a long way from you and your copy.

4. A storyboard does not bear the same relationship to a TV ad that an ad rough does to a print ad. A rough of a print ad *is* that ad, more or less. A storyboard, however, is only a map of the TV spot. It simply refers to it, the way a map of Colorado refers to the state itself. This is an important distinction. You realize it every time you look at reproductions of TV advertising in textbooks and annuals: four or five isolated stills from the video are accompanied by copy providing the voice-over and some explanatory comment. Good luck trying to re-create it. Unless you've seen the spot, you usually can't recover it, or sufficiently imagine it, from such a map. The same is true of any storyboard you'll make. You can't really express your vision, whatever it is, in such a manner.

What to do? As these limitations suggest, you'll never have the control over TV advertising that you'll have over print advertising—unless you go to film school and learn how to make movies. But you can participate in the process. You can sell by making things move, by unfolding your advertising idea, not in the space of a print ad but in the time of a TV spot.

And remember: by age 18 you'd spent 11,000 hours in school but over 15,000 hours in front of the TV.[3] By age 20 you'd seen 800,000 TV commercials, about 800 a week.[4] TV is the thing you've

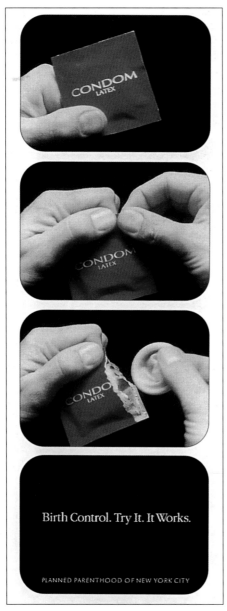

10.1. A straightforward demonstration, whose wit comes from the disarming truth of the voice-over.

studied the most. You already know so much about the language of television advertising that it's essentially a native tongue.

The first, last, and only rule: be interesting

Zipping, zapping, muting, avoiding, ignoring, and just generally hating TV commercials constitute a national pastime—unless, of course, viewers happen to love the ads; then they'll watch them over and over, which is where you come in. Make your

client's spot so inherently, compulsively, unavoidably watchable that people will sit still for it every time they see it.

Keep viewers' self-interested, pleasure-principle-seeking habits of mind uppermost in yours as you dream up your spot. Otherwise, they will dispatch you and it to Adland Abyss, lustily and with great glee (ah, the saving of fifteen seconds, thirty seconds, two minutes even!).

Make people refuse to zap your spot. I dare you.

Begin at the beginning

Start with your strategy. What are you trying to do? What's the creative brief telling you? What's your objective? TV can handle any of the kinds of strategies examined earlier: generic claim, product feature, unique selling proposition, positioning, brand image, lifestyle and attitude. Here, as everywhere, idea is king. It's not technology, it's idea, that will make or break the spot.

Think demonstration, or story, or both at once

TV's dramatic possibilities are nearly limitless, but start by considering the two techniques that TV handles so much better than print: *demonstration*, the testing of the product's selling point, and *narrative*, the telling of a story. Many, if not most, TV spots can be considered some combination of demonstration and story.

DEMONSTRATIONS

Show viewers how your product works; demonstrate its benefits. The key is to twist the format, have fun with it. You can do this in several ways.

Literal demonstration

The ad shown in figure 10.1 couldn't be simpler; the copy makes it memorable. Viewers watch a fellow take out and open a condom package, with this voice-over: "It's easier than changing a diaper."

There are no spoken words in the spot shown in figure 10.2, just rock music and people energetically building something. Viewers can see cement being mixed, wood being sawed, posts being stuck in post holes—all punctuated by title cards: "12 lb. sledgehammer, aisle 9," "8 inch anchor bolts, aisle 7," "4x4 pressure treated posts, aisle 20." The spot closes with this: "Cutsey artichoke-shaped cabinet knobs. Not in stock." . . . "Ever." "McCoy's. Go build something."

A

B

12 LB. SLEDGEHAMMER

AISLE 9

C

D

**CUTESY ARTICHOKE-SHAPED
CABINET KNOBS**

NOT IN STOCK

E

F

EVER.

G

McCOY'S
BUILDING SUPPLY CENTERS

GO BUILD SOMETHING.

www.mccoys.com

10.2. McCoy's positions itself as the real builders' store, not one of those nicey-nice, everything-for-everyone places. The rock soundtrack and energetic people make even *me* want to build something— no small feat.

Metaphorical demonstration

Dramatize the product's selling argument by comparing it to something else. What might thrill rides at the Playland amusement park be like? How about like a speedboat racing across the water and nearly flipping over into disaster. But just before the boat crashes, the picture stops and then rewinds. Viewers see the boat un-flip, land back down safely, and speed backwards across the water. Soundtrack screams at the imminent disaster are replaced by

10.3. A metaphorical demonstration. Just before the upended speedboat crashes, the film rewinds, saving the boat and its daredevil rider from catastrophe. The spot then closes with the title card. Playland argues that, just as with the speedboat video, the best amusement park rides combine excitement, physical thrills—and terror—with happy endings.

laughing and the sounds of an amusement park ride. The closing card shows the Playland logo and says, "Actual rides may vary." A terrific idea (see fig. 10.3).

Whimsical demonstration

The VW New Beetle doesn't look like other cars, but so what? How to make its shape matter? Why not compare that singular curve with all the square shapes in people's lives? The surprise is in their number and variety (see fig. 10.4). Who knew the world was this square? Viewers laugh at the squares' juxtaposition with the car's shape and the relief that curve affords. This spot dramatizes the uniqueness of the New Beetle (and therefore any consumer who owns one), not by comparing it with other cars—too boring—but by comparing it with the unexpected.

STORIES

Hook viewers with a story, and do a little selling inside it. After all, you *can* tell a story on TV, something you almost cannot do in a print ad. And you can often demonstrate within that story, wrap a demo up inside the narrative. As illustrated in figure 10.5, Yahoo's power to gather important information quickly is dramatized by a fellow who veers from being one kind of oddity (a way-too-combed-over-guy) to another (a way-too-gigantic-Afro-wearing guy). But Yahoo has made him happy, and that's what matters.

How to sell something as utilitarian as a refrigerator, how to even make it interesting? By telling, or suggesting, a story. The spot illustrated in figure 10.6 shows a husband drinking from a milk carton (something his wife obviously disapproves of), but this time she gets revenge: the refrigerator's broken and the milk has spoiled. Viewers see him spitting it out in the sink, while his wife, back turned toward him as she sits smiling at the kitchen table, says, "The fridge is broken." Then the super/announcer says, "Refrigerators on sale. Sears. Where else?" This quick, funny little spot involves viewers by tying the product to a very familiar domestic scene, one that reflects human nature with a wink and a smile. And it's the element of human truth that viewers relate to when they see this spot.

Kinka Usher, a TV ad director, emphasizes the critical importance of imbuing an ad with human truth—which he accomplishes by incorporating little stories: "I don't do ads with voiceovers. Or ads that list product points. I don't think that type of advertising is effective. I tend to want to work on branding and I want to work on original ideas. With image or brand advertising, you're more likely to be able to make a little film, with the product seamlessly woven in—so that people are having an experience based on the film and less on the product. Because you really can't get emotional about a car. No matter how much Ford may think that their car is the most emotional thing they've ever seen, the average person doesn't get emotional about it. Now

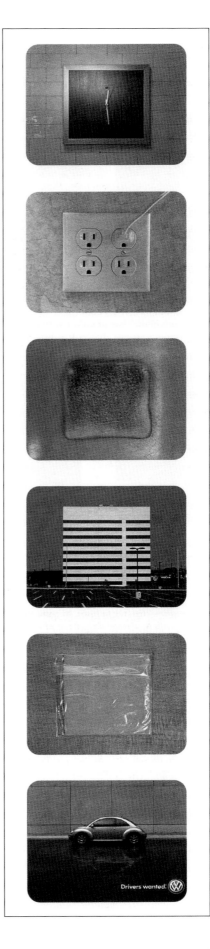

10.4. A whimsical series of comparisons that demonstrates the unique silhouette of the New Beetle.

10.5. Suggested stories, people with a life underneath the action, can be a great strength of TV spots. This man has a story to tell, that's for sure. And Yahoo obviously helped him find what he needed.

you can get emotional about the person who's driving the car. You can relate to their human nature. And that's the difference."[5]

Visual Advice

As you're developing and visually expressing your ideas, consider the following.

KEEP IT SIMPLE

In creating storyboards—especially ones for your portfolio, ones that stand a chance of capturing the attention of creative directors—make them short and simple. Twenty frames with a paragraph of copy/explanation per frame just won't do it. Reduce the concept, or rather think up a concept that can be expressed in no more than a few frames. You want it to jump out of the portfolio, leap off the page, and resonate in the viewer's mind. Look at how astoundingly simple the ad in figure 10.7 is.

MAKE IT MOVE

Start strong, close strong, don't waste anything. The same obligations of economy and speed that I've discussed with print advertising operate even more so in TV. Whatever your idea, get to it fast. Don't segue toward something interesting. Start with it.

Rely not only on consumers' sophisticated ability to unpack symbols and images in microseconds but also on their demand that you keep those images coming. If your spot doesn't move, forget it—you've probably been zapped. Part of what's exciting about TV advertising is that it moves so much: there is the illusion of great energy, all of which transfers to the product and makes it seem my client's product? Does it go around like a can opener, splash through water like a bike, squirt like a tube of toothpaste, what?"

If your client's product doesn't move, consider creating movement by changing camera angles or by finding things associated with the product that do move. The writers behind a TV spot for Ricoh copiers realized that copiers don't move but repairmen do. The ad dramatized reliability by emphasizing the omnipresence of the repairman if the viewer's firm bought the wrong brand. Viewers watched a man's feet moving back and forth through

10.6. Weave a story around your client's product. Tie it to people's lives. Let humor and human truth lend themselves to what you're selling.

10.7. A TV ad so simple that it even looks good in print.

energy-giving. Notice how much movement is a part of TV ads, even the simple ones.

IF IT DOESN'T MOVE, MAKE THINGS ASSOCIATED WITH IT MOVE

One virtue of stories and demonstrations is that, by definition, they move. Even if you're working on an idea that's neither, try to find a way to get movement into the spot. Ask yourself, "What part of my product story moves? What motion is inherent in the office, without knowing until spot's end who he was. The ad closed, "Because business should depend on a copier that works. Not a repairman. Ricoh Copiers built to work. And work. And work."

Figure 10.8 is a great example of creating movement when it seems impossible. Frost Bank is one of what are now only a handful of Texas banks actually based in Texas, and the company wanted to hang an ad on that fact. But how to make a fact move? Show a fellow lowering a Texas state flag to half mast. That's the whole spot. It's simple, funny, and surprisingly watchable—partly because it's so audible: viewers hear the flag blowing, wind whistling, birds chirping, the rope's metal buckle clanking against the pole. They watch the flag being lowered; read, first, "80% of the biggest banks in Texas are no longer from Texas"; then, "Bummer"; and, finally, "Frost Bank. We're from here." This ad vivifies the fact and does so with a dry wit, equating the loss of banks headquartered in Texas with a cause for statewide mourning.

Sometimes, of course, it's possible to be attention-getting by moving nothing. In a TV world jammed with nonstop visual extravagance, a quiet or motionless or nearly motionless spot can be arresting. Imagine an ad that shows a couple sleeping in. That's it: man and wife asleep, with summer sunlight streaming in the window; viewers hear snoring, birds twittering, clock ticking. Voice-over: "Remember what life was like before you had kids?" Camera card: "YMCA Summer Camp. Minneapolis 822-CAMP. St. Paul 292-4100."

REMEMBER YOUR MTV LESSONS

The following techniques have long since become part of TV's visual repertoire. While many of them are more the province of filmmakers than your immediate concern, you do want to make ads that fit consumers' visual expectations. Keep their expectations in mind.

Hyperkinetic imagery
Visual speed and sophistication
Ironic, wise-guy attitudes
Unexpected humor
Quick, suggestive cuts rather than slow, sensible
  segues
Narrative implications rather than whole stories
Attitudes, not explanations
Tightly cropped, partial images instead of whole
  ones

Fresh mixtures of live action, newsreel footage,
  animation, typography, film speeds, film
  quality
Unexpected audio/video relationships

Soundtrack advice

Like words in print ads, the soundtrack in TV spots is half the trick.

BE RELEVANT, BUT NOT REDUNDANT
Be sure that whatever is being said, sung, or sounded relates to what viewers are looking at. Just as in a print ad, however, don't be redundant. If people can see it, don't say it, too. Say something else. If you show a car splashing through the mud, don't say, "Built for the worst weather." Viewers can see that. Instead say how it endures what they're witnessing; talk about features or the emotional benefits to the driver.

BE SURE ON-SCREEN TYPE MATCHES THE VOICE-OVER
The only exception to the previous don't-repeat-yourself advice—and it's an important one—is that when you put type on the screen, either say nothing or have the voice-over say exactly those words. You never want to say words and show words that aren't exactly the same. People can't process separate sets of language simultaneously. Remember how irritating presentations like PowerPoint become when you're trying to read the words on the slide while the presenter insists on saying something else? Your viewers hear better and learn harder when you imprint the message visually as well as aurally.

USE MORE VISUAL THAN AUDIO
Remember the obvious: TV is visual. Don't let your storyboard talk too much and move too little. *Listen* to some TV spots. Notice that in the soundtrack there's less language—and more music and sound effects—than you supposed. (And visually, of course, there is almost always some dramatic movement.) A working rule of thumb is no more than two words per second, so a 30-second spot can manage only 60 spoken words—or fewer. Let your words breathe; give them some air. Air around your words is like white space in print advertising.

DEVELOP TENSION BETWEEN VISUAL AND AUDIO
The tension between headline and visual, so fre-

10.8. A fact—that only a few Texas banks are still based in Texas—becomes visible and audible.

quently the essence of print advertising, has its counterpart in TV advertising: the tension between what is shown and what is said. Interesting tones are created by running one sort of language on top of another sort of imagery.

Some years ago a great Sony ad showed a monkey standing in water listening to a Walkman. Part of the ad's memorability was that arresting image, but the ad elevated it by running opera music on the soundtrack. The monkey was, apparently, listening to opera and being uplifted by it—viewers could see by his expression, as he stared out to sea, that it enraptured him. Thus they got the idea that music and technology combine to help man evolve. The ad almost planted the idea, whimsically, that Sony had helped make evolution possible—as deft an example as I've ever seen of claiming the highest possible benefit for a product.

Opera music has been run over many different visuals, often ironically: sandwich-making, in one instance, thus elevating the spreading of mayonnaise into an art. Another TV spot ran a soprano's aria over the slow-motion, attempted smashings of locks—sledge hammers banged on them, cars tried to drive through locked fences, and so forth. The ad, for Masterlock, included the brand mnemonic of a rifle shot failing to crack the lock, but the soundtrack and slow-mo violence themselves created an odd, ironic tone—almost the orchestration of violence—and it was this tone, really, that raised the spot, that announced a new feeling. Viewers got absorbed in the pleasure of destruction, nicely accompanied, and the beauty of the music also suggested that everything was finally secure, thanks to Masterlock.

You don't have to think music, either. In Reebok's controversial "UBU" TV ads, old scratched recordings of epigrams from Ralph Waldo Emerson were run over weird visual imagery, creating a nicely unsettling mix. It was as though Emerson's voice itself had been resurrected, throwing viewers into the American past as the imagery launched them into a bizarre American future, an Outland of Individuality. That campaign showed just how rich a mix you can create by placing soundtrack and imagery into creative tension. So think about juxtaposition and irony. Try running something over the images that is neither redundant nor too safe. See what effects you can create.

And remember the tremendous power of audio

to alter people's response to video. In a simple TV spot, a mud-splattered Range Rover in a studio was washed off with torrents of water. A flat idea, right? But the advertisers replaced the sound of the rushing water with jungle noises—shrieking animals, rhythmic African drums, and so on—adding novelty and excitement to the spot. Now the off-road thrills of driving the vehicle were dramatized through the wild sounds viewers heard as they watched the mud being washed off. From no idea to great idea—by simply altering the soundtrack.

Two Nike TV ads do similar things with sound. One spot shows athletes warming up for competitions while viewers hear a classical orchestra warming up before a concert. In another spot the human sounds of a group of athletes running cross country are replaced by those of galloping horses. Cool synergy. Each half of the ads needs the other to complete it.

How to present TV ads

If you're not using animatics or videos, present your ideas to others by showing flat images and talking about them.

USE A STORYBOARD

The traditional way is via the storyboard. You (or your art director partner) sketch in the major moments of the spot and write in the voice-over and any other stage directions below the images. Usually the copy itself is upper and lower case, but all other explanations are in all caps. This lets the viewer see, at a glance, what is spoken and what is simply a direction.

DESCRIBE IN SCRIPT FORMAT

Rather than drawing pictures, describe them. Create two columns on a sheet of paper. In the left column, describe each key visual in a few sentences. Across from each entry, in the right column, write down whatever directions or voice-over accompanies that visual. Script format is like a storyboard sequence, except that it's all in words. This format is useful if you don't draw, and your idea can be visualized by readers surprisingly well.

PROVIDE A SCENARIO

Write up your idea without blocking it out. This is called the scenario. You simply write your TV spot in a paragraph. Explain the ad in synopsis. What do you see happening? How does the spot start? How does it end? What is the narrative, the demo, the twist? Say it out.

One piece of advice: if you can tell your story without mentioning the product, you've too loosely tied your drama to the product. Try to create a story in which the product is indispensable. The trick is not to be so blatant about product as hero that the spot becomes a sledge hammer.

Another piece of advice is to write a scenario *before* blocking out a storyboard to ascertain whether you've got an idea at all.

GENERATE A KEY FRAME

A key frame is one central visual that sums up the ad's idea and the spot itself. What is the central moment? For example, a Tropicana orange juice campaign showed people trying to stick a straw in an orange—a funny and absurd way to dramatize the brand's freshness. That was each ad's key visual: a person trying to stick a straw in an orange. Another example: a pin dropping in slow motion beside the Sprint logo. This has become a key frame as well as a visual slogan for that telecommunications company. What began as a visualization of the quality of Sprint's optic fiber network ("So quiet you can hear a pin drop") evolved into an ad-closing visual slogan.

The key frame technique is a handy way to present ideas. Rather than showing a whole storyboard, you draw just one major visual and write the paragraph explaining your idea beneath it. Key frames

are thus easier to consume, since people are looking at and reading only one thing. Provided that your copy is clear and specific, people can get a strong sense of your ad.

Even if you don't present your ideas this way, ask yourself, of every TV spot you create, "Is there a key frame? Can I reduce my idea to one central visual?" If you can't, maybe you haven't yet created a spot that's simple enough.

Best advice

While the hyperkinetic complexity that abounds on TV can make for great finished commercials, it often makes for chaotic storyboards in your book; so for ads in search of a job, simple and sweet may be best. Unless you're taking a TV course that lets you put your ideas on video, I recommend that storyboards follow the advice of TV copywriter Bruce Bildsten of Fallon, who likes simplicity and clarity: "I see a lot of commercials where there is a good idea, but it's buried in production values or too many benefits. The spot can still be beautiful and richly produced, but it's more the simplicity of the idea itself. You have to make it work so that the idea comes through."[6]

All the spots in this chapter share a simplicity of idea. Try to create a storyboard that works as economically, wittily, and powerfully, as these do. Architect Mies van der Rohe's "less is more" dictum can apply just as well to storyboards as to buildings.

11 ▪ Radio

When I sign off my television newscasts by saying,
"See you on the radio," it's my way of saying that
radio is like television, but with better pictures.
—Charles Osgood, CBS News

Osgood's insight is essential to understanding radio. He invokes the "theater of the mind" quality that you may have heard your grandparents talk about, from the days when listening to the radio, rather than watching TV or surfing the Internet, was the national media pastime. The most fundamental distinction between radio and any other medium (except reading) is its demand—an inescapable invitation, really—that you, not the medium, create the pictures in your mind. This unique-to-each-listener imagery, especially its extravagant possibilities, ought to dominate your thinking about how to advertise on the radio.

How people use radio

Some interesting facts about radio: people usually listen to it by themselves, and given the universality of car radios and portable headsets, people are frequently mobile when doing so. There are 5.6 radios per household, and people listen an average of twenty-two hours a week,[1] so everyone has them, everywhere—they're on joggers, in the malls, on the hiking trail, in the classroom, perhaps even on the ears of the person sitting next to you right now. Thus people bond with radio in a very personal way—it's a one-on-one medium—but since they're almost always doing something else while listening, they're inattentive to it. Radio is far more likely to be a background presence than the focus of awareness. These facts suggest how to use it.

Constraints of radio ads

Since people aren't listening closely, you've got to try pretty hard to catch their attention. Keep your message simple, then repeat yourself—within each spot and in the number of spots themselves—to counteract listeners' inattention. Direct-response advertising can be difficult because listeners can't cut out coupons from a radio ad or write down numbers, especially while driving. In fact, they can't remember much, which is another reason that you'll have to keep it simple and repeat yourself. If getting one point across is good advice for a print ad, it's great advice for a radio ad. One Big Idea, hammered home, sweetly. Get people to notice your spot, understand your point, remember it.

Virtues of radio ads

Since listeners' relationship with radio is personal and local, it's a terrific medium for retail advertising. People listen, often, to stations in their local area, so you can change your spot (or part of it) readily, adjusting to different targets, different offers, changing retail circumstances. Radio has immediacy and can work while listeners are mobile, so it's often close to the point of sale, perhaps even the last thing they hear before buying something; or they have the radio on *while* buying something, as at fairs and outdoor events. McDonald's, for example, uses radio heavily. Statistics indicate that 40 percent of McDonald's customers decided to eat there within two minutes of arrival (80 percent within two hours) and over 85 percent came by car, 81 percent of whom had their radios on.[2] I'd advertise on radio, too, wouldn't you?

As mass markets vanish, all markets fragment, and target marketing becomes a way of life, radio becomes ideal. Because there are so many radio stations and formats, you can reach out and touch almost any audience you target. Dream up a demographic/psychographic segment or niche, and you can literally dial that audience on the radio. You can target precisely and not go broke doing it. Also lots of people who are light users of other media are heavy users of radio. There is an invisible audience out there, almost unreachable except by radio; it thus becomes a good supplement to TV and print campaigns, extending their reach. Radio is also a great daytime medium, the morning and late afternoon being its prime times, before America turns on its TV sets for good. In fact, radio listening is greater than TV watching from 5 A.M. to 5 P.M.[3] And, of course, overnight radio has become a huge phenomenon.

How to create radio advertising

You create a radio spot by manipulating no more than three things: words, sounds, music. With them, and only them, you create entire worlds, the miniature auditory universes that are radio ads.

THINK WORDS, WORDS, WORDS

Radio is a copywriter's medium, obviously, since your words become everything. Almost. The talent cast to deliver those words adds a lot to a spot, of course, as reading the radio typescripts in this chapter will indicate—you sense how much better these spots would be if you could hear them as produced, with the great voices and their rhythms. But good radio spots are still good—funny, imaginative, persuasive, memorable—simply sitting there in type.

What words to use? The most fundamental and most common radio ad language is simply that of an announcer, someone who gets the listener's attention and then delivers a specific offer, complete with copy points, much like someone reading the headline and body copy from a print ad. Although sometimes effective, especially when read by well-known radio personalities, the genre of announcers-reading-copy often fails to prove distinctive or memorable. "Radio falls apart when people try to make it newspaper advertising on the air," says Bill West, vice president, Radio Works, Houston, by which he means that good radio should construct images in listeners' minds, not just be data read aloud.[4]

INTRODUCE CHARACTERS, SCENES, DIALOGUE

Think, therefore, in terms of characters and scenes. This can be as simple as creating an unusual persona for the announcer. Motel 6 ads, with which most people are familiar, rely on the charm of Tom Bodett's folksy persona: he embeds the motel's sell-

ing points in his whimsical monologue, and by spot's end his character and values have become the motel's. This is really testimonial advertising, in that the *who* of the message becomes part of the *what*. And it makes sense: why should people listen to Mr. or Ms. Generic Announcer when they can listen better and be sold harder by hearing an unexpected character make the announcements? A spot for the National Thoroughbred Racing Association (fig. 11.1) mimics an announcer's call of a race to make the selling argument.

The next step is to replace the announcer with a character or characters, often by establishing characters-in-dialogue, and to use announcer commentary, usually at the end, to supplement it. The key is making the people real, not shills for the product, and making the dialogue real, not hokey. Bill West and Jim Conlan of Radio Works give crucial dialogue advice:

> Break it up. One of the most common mistakes people make when writing radio dialogue is to write long copy blocks. First one person says a whole bunch of stuff, then the other person says a whole bunch of stuff. That's not a dialogue. That's dueling monologues. Effective dialogues require short lines with lots of back and forth. Since you have no visuals, the back-and-forth dynamic in a radio dialogue supplies the conversation with its action.[5]

In figure 11.2, for example, the couple's dialogue, bizarre as it is, sounds real. The man and woman are having very odd conversations, but real ones; they aren't windy position statements or recitations of product benefits from a creative brief. Robert Frost said that "the ear is the only true writer and the only true reader."[6] It's the only true listener, too. Hear how people talk, and get that down. If you let the pitch overwhelm the people, your spot is dead.

And as crazy as the conversations in figure 11.2 are, the wild premises don't hook listeners at the expense of the product benefit; rather, they dramatize it. OurHouse.com promises "Tools. Advice. Housecalls. Sanity. Everything you need to fix up your house, or have it done for you." Both conversations/stories dramatize the need for exactly that. Can you think up a scene with characters-in-dialogue that engages interest *while* dramatizing the product benefit? You can if you try.

11.1. Think in terms of character: who is relating the spot? In this case a racetrack announcer turns boredom itself into a horse race, demonstrating, without having to argue for it, just how much fun watching an actual horse race might be.

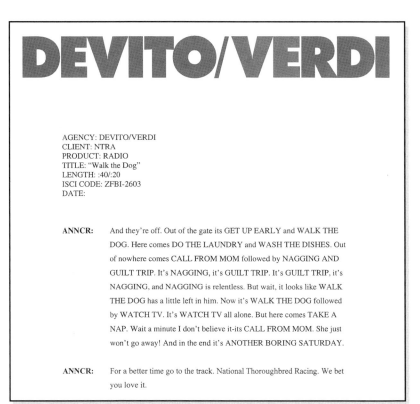

DEVITO/VERDI

AGENCY: DEVITO/VERDI
CLIENT: NTRA
PRODUCT: RADIO
TITLE: "Walk the Dog"
LENGTH: :40/:20
ISCI CODE: ZFBI-2603
DATE:

ANNCR: And they're off. Out of the gate its GET UP EARLY and WALK THE DOG. Here comes DO THE LAUNDRY and WASH THE DISHES. Out of nowhere comes CALL FROM MOM followed by NAGGING AND GUILT TRIP. It's NAGGING, it's GUILT TRIP. It's GUILT TRIP, it's NAGGING, and NAGGING is relentless. But wait, it looks like WALK THE DOG has a little left in him. Now it's WALK THE DOG followed by WATCH TV. It's WATCH TV all alone. But here comes TAKE A NAP. Wait a minute I don't believe it-its CALL FROM MOM. She just won't go away! And in the end it's ANOTHER BORING SATURDAY.

ANNCR: For a better time go to the track. National Thoroughbred Racing. We bet you love it.

OURHOUSE.COM
Brand Radio
:60 Radio "Finishing" – As Produced
©2000 Black Rocket

ROOM SOUNDS. WE HEAR A DOOR UNLOCKING. WE HEAR A WOMAN WALKING IN.

WOMAN: Hi honey.
MAN: Monkey cakes.
WOMAN: What's that smell?
MAN: I'm redoinging the floors.
WOMAN: You're redoing the floors?
MAN: Yep. With shellac. Shellaca-dack-adoo.
WOMAN: Oh come on honey. Jeez open a window. Bob, you're drooling.
MAN: I like it. Drooling.
WOMAN: Were you shellacking all day?
MAN: Heeeeeeeee.
WOMAN: Oh my god.
MAN: Hoooooo. ("HOOOO" GOES UP AND DOWN LIKE SLIDE WHISTLE.)
WOMAN: Bob, sweetie, look at me. I'm right over here.
MAN: Mommy....mmm
WOMAN: That's it. I'm calling Dr. Levine.

ANNCR: Tools. Advice. Housecalls. Sanity. Everything you need to fix up your house, or have it done for you. Ourhouse.com. We're here to help.

ANNCR2: Partnered with Ace.

OURHOUSE.COM
Brand Radio
:60 Radio "Pet" – As Produced
©2000 Black Rocket

MAN: Hey, honey?
WOMAN: I'm in here hun.
MAN: You'll never guess what I bought.
WOMAN: What?
MAN: (PAUSE) What?
WOMAN: What?
MAN: A kangaroo.
WOMAN: A what?
MAN: (AS IF TALKING TO A PUPPY) Come on, it's okay, it's okay. This is your new home. This is my wife.

ALL OF A SUDDEN WE HEAR SOUNDS OF A HOUSE BEING COMPLETELY DESTROYED: THINGS CRASHING, FALLING, BREAKING, PEOPLE GROANING, STRUGGLING AND FALLING, ETC.

WOMAN: That's my lamp! Put it on a leash! Get a leash.
MAN: No, no, down! Down!
WOMAN: What are you doing?!
MAN: Down boy. Down boy.
WOMAN: What have you done?
MAN: Bad kangaroo! Bad!-Heel!

ANNCR: Tools. Advice. Housecalls. Sanity. Everything you need to fix up your house, or have it done for you. Ourhouse.com. We're here to help.

ANNCR2: Partnered with Ace.

11.2. Characters-in-dialogue. Everyone loves to be a voyeur—
and with conversations like these, what pictures they see.

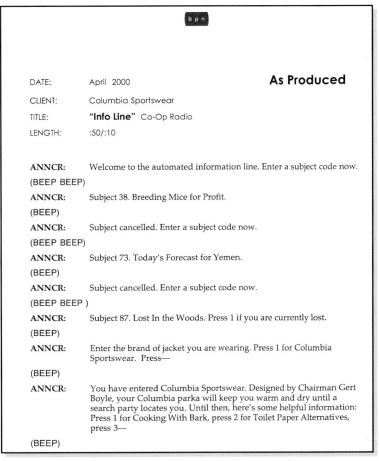

11.3. A humorous take on getting an automated voice when calling a help line.

Figure 11.3 offers another unusual dialogue, one that relies on a funny exaggeration of the automated phone responses everyone has encountered.

USE "EARS ONLY" PROSE

Remember that you're writing for the listeners' ears only. Listeners will not have the chance to go back and look at what you've said, so keep it simple and readily consumable (no more than two words per second). Use a tape recorder to play your work back to yourself. Let your ears tell you what to do, not the look of the words on the page. And don't neglect the "white space" of radio advertising—silence. By rushing to cram lots of copy points into a small space, far too many ads yell at listeners with breathless announcers. Unless you're satirizing that tradition, avoid it.

DRAMATIZE SOUND AS SIGHTS

Sound effects (SFX), an invaluable tool for radio writers, offer unlimited possibilities—libraries of sounds are available, and with minimal equipment you can, of course, create your own sound effects. Think how readily and completely sounds evoke whole places and things. They become parts standing for wholes. Rain drumming on a tin roof, the rhythmic slapping of waves—listeners are suddenly somewhere exotic, in the Caribbean or South Seas. A howl of wind, dry crunchings, one after another—listeners could be walking across the Antarctic. An echo to a droning voice—they find themselves in a large hall, listening to a speech. Dogs barking—listeners are in a kennel. Dogs barking with an echo—suddenly the dogs are in the hall, *not* listening to the speech. It's all possible. On the radio.

Not only are sounds rapid transits to almost any scene or situation, however outlandish, but they're emotional triggers, too. Hearing may well be a person's first sense—babies can hear sounds from inside the womb—and the association of feelings with sounds is almost instinctive. Think of how readily people associate feelings with sounds.

AGENCY: DeVito/Verdi
CLIENT: For Eyes Opticals
PRODUCT: Radio
TITLE: "Sushi"
LENGTH: :60
ISCI CODE: ZFBI-R154
DATE: 6.21.01

ANNCR: There are some things you shouldn't pay 40 to 60 percent less for. Like Sushi, for example.

SFX: man vomiting violently.

ANNCR: Or say, Parachutes…

SFX: Parachute rustling and a loud thud.

ANNCR: Shotguns…

SFX: Gun going off.

MAN: (screaming) Ahhhh, my face!!!

ANNCR: Pit bulls…

SFX: Dog snarling and barking.

ANNCR: Condoms…

SFX: Baby crying loudly.

ANNCR: Mail-order brides…

SFX: A pig squealing and snorting.

ANNCR: A prosthetic leg…

SFX: Sound like a tree breaking.

ANNCR: A brain surgeon…

DOCTOR: How many fingers am I holding up?

MAN: Thursday!

ANNCR: Aromatherapy.
SFX: Farting sound.

ANNCR: Denture cream.

SFX: A man sneezing hard followed by glass breaking.

ANNCR: Shower radios.

SFX: Sound of shower and radio being tuned, followed by zapping electrical sound and scream.

ANNCR: But when it comes to glasses, you should pay 40 to 60 percent off. Because at For Eyes you get the same designer eyewear you get at other stores, just for less. For Eyes. The store for people who can't see paying a lot for glasses.

11.4. What's a clever way to set up the argument for designer eyewear at discount prices? Get people to imagine all the things they'd regret buying at a bargain price. Wit may be your best friend, but sound effects are a close second.

Take, for example, that Caribbean rain. If it's a hard rain, with lightning and thunder, listeners edge toward fear. If it's soft, they feel cocooned, dreamy. As rain slows to a drizzle, they grow restless, expectant of change. Almost all sounds "mean" something, so consider using sound not only to establish place and mood in a spot but also to forge emotional linkages to products. Figure 11.4 presents a spot for an eyewear retailer that uses a variety of sounds to evoke a lot of pictures in the listener's mind.

See you on the radio

As this chapter's small sample of radio typescripts suggests, radio can be a way to create imaginative, compelling advertising. (Check out the Radio-Mercury Awards at www.radiomercuryawards.com to hear how good radio ads can be.) Nonetheless, young creatives often dismiss radio in their rush toward TV and other more glamorous advertising genres. Let's give the last word about the value of radio to someone who should know—Jeff Goodby, co-founder of Goodby, Silverstein & Partners: "The smart ones love doing [radio]. It teaches you how to think clearly. You can develop a style, learn how to cast and direct properly, and how to work with actors and actresses. Smart writers always welcome radio work."[7]

> Radio is really the most intimate medium of all, which is why you have to be so careful in how you create it. It's so intimate because the listener is actually the art director . . . all the listener has is the words and the sound effects, so in effect the listener becomes a collaborator.
>
> —Joy Golden, radio copywriter

12 ▪ Other Media and Genres

> If you can get people to stop thinking about making ads and to start thinking about making pieces of communication, then something fresh is apt to arrive.
>
> —Dan Wieden,
> co-founder, Wieden + Kennedy

As an advertiser, you will never be asked simply to create visual/verbal relationships in the abstract. Nor will you always be asked to create a magazine ad or radio or TV spot. Your work will encompass a variety of tasks—from naming things (products, promotions, exhibitions, collections of software or silverware) to writing and editing brochures, point-of-purchase displays, catalogs, packaging, transit posters, Web sites, you name it. In today's media-driven society, the following comment by Keith Reinhard, chairman, DDB Needham, captures the challenge faced by advertisers in the twenty-first century: "In simpler times, advertising people had two concerns: what to say and how to say it. Now the issue is where, when and how can advertising reach receptive prospects. . . . Today's toughest question is how to find your customers at the most strategic time—that's why media is the new creative frontier." [1]

Each medium contains its own particularities, and you can't solve all advertising problems by invoking some variant of the mythic trinity of headline, visual, body copy. Here are a few such cases: often-encountered advertising genres and media whose characteristics influence how you approach them:

Direct-response advertising
Catalogs, brochures, annual reports
Business-to-business advertising
Out-of-home advertising
Guerrilla advertising
Interactive media
International/multicultural advertising

Longer forms

I'll start with the first three because they often require more than just short, snappy language. Direct-response advertising, promotional and capabilities brochures, catalogs (printed and Web-based), annual reports, and the like—much of it business-to-business writing—all require a lot of words.

When you're working on such a project, you'll be getting together often with your client and design team. Consider the following steps:

1. Study up. Ask your client for all available informational material. Read that and everything else you can find on the client, the client's product, the competition, and so on. Become an instant expert.

2. Figure out where this thing you're creating fits into the whole communication scheme. What's its mission? What's it supposed to accomplish? Where are the target customers before they read it, and where do you want them to be after they read it? Selling is a series of steps. Which one is this?

3. Determine where, literally, this thing will live. Will salespeople hand it to prospects as a "leave behind"? Will it fit in a rack at the point of sale? Are there companion pieces that will piggyback with it in a direct mailing? What, exactly, are you making?

(Steps 2 and 3 sound too obvious to mention. But I've headed off without knowing where to and lived to regret it, so I share that basic advice with you here.)

4. Think through your creative brief. Who are you talking to? What advertising promise are you making? Why should consumers believe you?

5. Conceive the Big Idea for the piece. Don't start on the copy until you've found the Big Idea, and don't assume finding it will be easy. This is the hardest part, but the most essential. Without a Big Idea, your piece is just another hunk of Adland flotsam floating past people too busy to care.

6. Organize your copy. That Big Idea needs to unfold in parts. Create a structure for what you'll be saying. Remember how you had to organize those research papers you wrote in college? Okay, do that again, but be more interesting this time.

7. Write like an angel. Once you've got the grand scale figured out, lay down all "the little words," as William Bernbach called copy, and lay them down so irresistibly that people read every one.

DIRECT-RESPONSE ADVERTISING

> The trouble with many copywriters is that they think their job is to write copy. That is equivalent to a salesperson saying, "My job is to talk." The job is not to "talk." For a writer, the job is not to "write." For both the job is to sell.
>
> —Don Kanter, vice president,
> Stone & Adler, direct marketers

Last week I got catalogs from Pottery Barn, Lands' End, and the Art Institute of Chicago, plus a piece selling various retirement options from TIAA-CREF (are they trying to tell me something?). My phone bill had inserts encouraging me to consider new telecommunications exotica. At my last aerobics class the instructor handed out coupons for a yogurt shop; today, fluttering on my car windshield, was an invitation to get a free car sponge with a BP fillup; and last night, while watching TV, I found myself mesmerized by a "long-form" infomercial for Soloflex body-building machines. This morning amazon.com's home page welcomed me by name and suggested books it had picked out just for me. Tonight, while writing this paragraph, I got a phone call from a telemarketer offering me a free ten-day preview of the Time-Life Book Digest. I won't even count how many commercial e-mails arrived today.

As different as these scenarios seem, they're really all the same: *direct-response advertising.* "Direct" because no retailers or wholesalers stand between me and the product: I am hooked up, one to one, with the advertiser—through a phone call, a letter, or a print, TV, radio, Web, or e-mail ad. And "response" because I'm asked to use a response device—an 800 number, a reply card, a coupon, a click-through—that connects me to the advertiser and completes the transaction, whether I'm buying the product or requesting more information. This interaction, unmediated by retailers, is thus "direct response."

Even though, as a week in my life shows, direct-response advertising uses many media, let's think about the direct-mail piece. You'll probably get several versions of it today, and the chances of your writing a direct-mail piece are high, since it's the third biggest advertising medium (after TV and newspapers). Direct mail also models the rhetoric of direct-response copywriting, regardless of the medium.

Appreciate the hole you're in

It's a big one. Americans get almost four tons of "junk mail" every year and never even open 44 percent of it. You want your piece to be in the 56 percent they do open, yet most direct mail looks alike, talks alike, and has the whiff of the pretend-personal.

Your copy must do a lot: catch attention; stimulate interest and desire by stating, then proving, the benefit(s); overcome general skepticism and specific objections; make the product tangible in the face of its intangibility (there's usually no store a consumer can walk into to check out the product); and close with a strong enough call to action that an immediate, positive response becomes not only convenient but inescapable.

You've got to work within the genre yet still be original enough to transcend trash-can-seeking stereotypes. How to do that? Know the rules, then consider creatively breaking them.

1. Be attention-getting. Put some language or design or both on the envelope to get it opened. The envelope (or whatever part of your piece first confronts the target audience) functions like a print ad's headline or dominant visual as the grabber (see fig. 12.1).

2. Think of the copy as a letter to a friend. Since direct-mail advertising can often be tight-

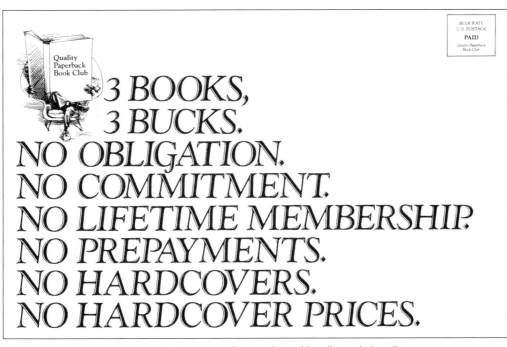

3 BOOKS, 3 BUCKS. NO OBLIGATION. NO COMMITMENT. NO LIFETIME MEMBERSHIP. NO PREPAYMENTS. NO HARDCOVERS. NO HARDCOVER PRICES.

Quality
Paperback
Book Club

BULK RATE
U.S. POSTAGE
PAID
Quality Paperback
Book Club

12.1. Notice that the copy on this envelope, like all good "headlines," piques the reader's interest *as* it expresses benefits. This isn't a blind headline or borrowed-interest headline. The book club's language, with its strong use of parallelism, is both the attention-getter *and* the complete selling promise.

ly targeted, chances are you'll have a specific audience to write to: current Porsche owners, women who have previously bought expensive lingerie, men age 35 to 50 who have dyed their hair, and so on. And as technology and database tracking grow—along with people's reliance on credit-card assisted, touch-pad, keystroked, stay-at-home shopping—such accuracy will only increase. You will know, to a greater degree than with mass-media advertising, just who you're talking to.

This is good. It's one-to-one sales; you're speaking directly to one consumer. Be as warm and informal as the situation allows, use the language of the consumer, share his or her mindset. Although the offer itself will have the greatest effect on sales, how you phrase that offer, the voice of your copy, will go a long way toward separating your piece from "junk mail."

3. Cover all aspects of the transaction. Unlike traditional national-brand advertising, direct advertising functions as a complete sales message. You're not just piquing interest, tinkering with an attitude, or laying down one more stratum in the geological structure of a brand

image. You're conducting the whole deal, from getting the target audience to open the envelope to closing the sale. As advertising professors Jerry Jewler and Bonnie Drewniany point out, "Advertising sells products. Direct marketing sells offers, using deadlines to produce swift responses."[2]

Since you're addressing someone already interested in the product, once this prospect begins to read a direct-mail letter, he or she is likely to stay with you. So write longer, with more selling facts. Sell harder and straighter. If some aspect of the persuasive sequence doesn't happen, then the sale doesn't happen. You're it or nobody is.

Bob Stone, one of the best of the direct marketers, advises following a seven-step formula in such letters, one open enough to let you steer past clichés but still sequenced well enough to cover the arc of persuasion:

1. Promise a benefit in your headline or first paragraph—your most important benefit. [You may want to start with the problem your target has, in order to set up the benefit your product

delivers, the way it solves the problem.]

2. Immediately enlarge on your most important benefit.

3. Tell the reader specifically what he or she is going to get.

4. Back up your statements with proof and endorsements [testimonials].

5. Tell the reader what he or she might lose if he or she doesn't act.

6. Rephrase your prominent benefits in your closing offer.

7. Incite action. Now.[3]

4. Use multiple pieces within the mailing.
The classic direct-mail piece contains several items: a letter; a brochure; a separate reply envelope (often with an "involvement" device, like a punch-out tab or perforated tear-slip); sometimes an accompanying gift offer for ordering immediately; and a final, shorter letter to try one last time to catch prospects if they've been unmoved by everything else. The exact contents of a direct-mail piece vary, but many direct advertisers feel that several items, in concert, carry the selling argument more effectively than does one element alone.

But rules are there to break. An award-winning direct-mail letter for the *Economist* magazine contained just that, a letter, and it came shredded. Recipients had to put it back together—how's that for an involvement device?—and when they did, they were congratulated for their curiosity and energy, their can-do spirit, exactly what the *Economist* is all about, and they were encouraged to subscribe to keep rewarding those virtues.

A direct-mail piece from jeweler Blue Nile wanted to encourage men to shop at its Web site (fig. 12.2). But instead of detailing specific items, catalog style, the little book lived up to its title and then some: in addition to the title's topics, there was advice to men on how to read a palm, how to park a boat, and why scars are cool. Once men started reading, the book pulled them through with a voice that was funny, charming, and, not least, informative. Starting with this book was a smart strategy since it's difficult to sell important, expensive things like diamonds with only a Web site and without the hands-on, eyes-on tangibilities that benefit local retailers. So Blue Nile first established itself as an entity men could identify with and value as a source of information and expertise. The booklet laid the foundation for trust that precedes any buying experience, especially one like this.

5. Analyze your own mail. Direct mail, unlike most advertising, can be so readily measured that it's the ultimate testing ground for what works. Advertisers can adjust all aspects of headline, copy, promise, and so on and then exactly determine the results of those changes. Consequently, your own mail is an experimental laboratory of the art and science of persuasion. Study it to discover what techniques do and don't work on you. What makes you throw something away unopened? What compels you to open it? How much of it do you read? What makes you keep going or stop?

CATALOGS

Catalog copy, whether print- or Web-based, may sound like dreary work in small point sizes, but in many ways it's the essence of copywriting and the litmus test for a copywriter: can you talk someone into buying something simply by what you say?

Lands' End writes catalog copy as well as anyone, and since this year's fat, December issue just thumped into my life, I've turned to a page, almost at random, and read this headline beside a picture of a man and woman in similar sweaters:

New hand-framed 4-ply Merino Cardigans that could last a couple of lifetimes.

All Lands' End headlines sell; they say, straightforwardly but energetically, what each product is and why readers should buy it.

Here's the copy:

Though these beautiful sweaters have a full hand, they are soft. After all, Merino is one of the world's finest wools. And our 100% Merino is worsted-spun (in Italy, no less) for extra softness and smoothness. Our new cardigans are double-breasted. And have fully fashioned "j" armholes, which have a comfortable modified drop to them. Men's has a shawl collar for snugging around the neck. Women's, a classic reverse (or notched) collar. Both sweaters are hand-framed by an intimate, painstaking firm located near the headwaters of the Clyde. And won't both make a very comfortable alternative to a classic blue

HOW TO CARVE A TURKEY

HOW TO BRIBE A

MAITRE D'

HOW TO BUY A DIAMOND

A book from

blue nile

12.2. An unusual way to sell diamonds, this little book gave advice to men that was both funny and serious. All of the advice was highly readable, only some of it about diamonds. By providing guidance and counsel in "guy" issues, Blue Nile encouraged men to feel that it could help them with diamonds, too.

Some for Junior.

angle to the blade. There may be guests waiting, but take your time. This is no time for a trip to the emergency room.

Begin by cutting off the leg and thigh by finding the joint on the underside of your bird. The key is to cut through the joint, not the bone. Separate the drumstick from the thigh by again slicing through the joint. Cut some big pieces of dark meat from the drumstick and thigh by slicing parallel to the bone. Now, cut the wing off by finding the joint and slicing through it.

You're ready for the breast.

A little for Grandma.

Using long, even slices, cut parallel to the rib cage. Go with the grain of the meat. Make sure you are cutting even pieces — not thick on one end and thin on the other. You're done. Have a shot of whiskey.

Note: Before you begin carving, allow the bird to cool for at least 30 minutes or up to an hour. This lets the juices settle and makes carving easier.

And some for you.

If you're left-handed, pretend the turkey is a chicken and follow the instructions above in reverse order. And if your guests are getting restless or heckling you, have a shot of whiskey after cutting the leg.

Have a nice dinner.

HOW

to buy a diamond

All women are in some way, beautiful. (This is one of the wonderful things about being a man.) Some women are supermodels, ideal and perfect. Other women are simply beautiful. The interesting thing is that no two women find beauty in the same way. Diamonds are like that.

Behold, the marvel of geometric perfection.

It takes some of us a lifetime to find the perfect woman. Finding the perfect diamond for her should be less difficult. To help in your search you need to learn the "four C's." The C's stand for a diamond's cut, color, clarity and carat weight. (To help in your search for the perfect woman, we have nothing to offer. Stay strong.)

Cut is the craftsmanship that brings a rough diamond alive and gathers light into the stone. In a round diamond there are

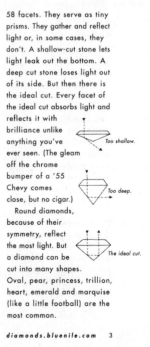

58 facets. They serve as tiny prisms. They gather and reflect light or, in some cases, they don't. A shallow-cut stone lets light leak out the bottom. A deep cut stone loses light out of its side. But then there is the ideal cut. Every facet of the ideal cut absorbs light and reflects it with brilliance unlike anything you've ever seen. (The gleam off the chrome bumper of a '55 Chevy comes close, but no cigar.)

Too shallow.

Too deep.

The ideal cut.

Round diamonds, because of their symmetry, reflect the most light. But a diamond can be cut into many shapes. Oval, pear, princess, trillion, heart, emerald and marquise (like a little football) are the most common.

blazer? Dry clean. Made in Scotland. Navy (with Plum tipping on cuffs and waistband).

Copy is specific, complete, persuasive

The Merino cardigan is not even a featured item; it's one of two items on one of 259 pages. Yet even in a catalog filled with entries, in a section stuffed with sweaters, I know the peg on which this item is hung. I know this sweater's story. In fact, every sweater—every piece of clothing—in Lands' End has a story, and the copywriters tell it: the Lands' End Expedition Parka was designed by Antarctic explorer Will Steger; the Matterhorn Parka is three layers warm; the locker bag was actually designed to fit lockers; even the cotton socks are "knit with a special blind-loop process that eliminates the bulky toe-seam found on ordinary crews." The reader leaves even the most mundane item with a stronger sense of its individuality, its material distinctions and their benefits. Vigorous research, vivid specifics, a warm voice, and sheer will-to-sell combine and triumph. No item is ever allowed to be simply a thing.

The following copy for a watch comes from Levenger's Web-site catalog ("Tools for serious readers"). It's straight as an arrow, is full of features and the benefits they provide, and describes the watch so thoroughly that if there weren't a picture, I could still see it:

> Our Unpocket Watch is designed for a belt or a bag. The dial is inverted so when you look down, you can read the time without craning your neck—and probably without your glasses, as the convex lens acts as a magnifier. This quartz clock takes a standard watch battery (included) and weighs just 3 ounces. The 1¼ inch alloy case is brushed and polished silver and hangs from a ½ inch-long black leather fob. A lobster claw clasp keeps it secure but easy to open. You may be surprised at how convenient a watch that goes more places than on a wrist can be.

Creating a clear, succinct argument for any product is harder to do than it may seem and a deeper pleasure than you may think. As Barry Tarshis puts it in *How to Write Like a Pro*:

> Clarity is so elemental a consideration in writing that to single it out as simply one aspect of the process seems almost silly, rather like offering as part of a cooking school curriculum a course on how to make food taste good.

Far from being simply a rudimentary skill you master early in your career in order to move more quickly into the more "creative" and "imaginative" aspects of writing, clarity is the very essence of the craft. It could be argued, in fact, that if you haven't conveyed your ideas or images clearly to your reader, you haven't really *written* anything, you've simply put a lot of words on paper.[4]

Each catalog creates its own persona

There are lots of ways to be persuasive. The J. Peterman Company catalog sells the romance of items instead of their utilitarian selves. It doesn't even use photographs, relying instead on mere gestural sketches of the items. In the near-absence of product, the copy voice becomes everything. Eccentric and literate, singular and self-assured, the voice is Gatsby-esque in its evocation of the romance of life. The copy wraps the product up in a feeling. Readers really want to buy the voice and its attitude, so they buy the closest thing to them, the product:

> IN THE GARDEN ROOM.
>
> Lunch at Commander's again. Table by the big oak looking out on Lafayette Cemetery No. 1. World's best Ramos gin fizz, live jazz drifting up from downstairs. The topic, unfortunately, is new business. Smile, nod, study reflection of ceiling fan rotating in my soup spoon . . . then I notice her sitting nearby. She's several degrees more than gorgeous. Something out of time. The band singer on her break? An escapee from a suffocating garden party? . . .
>
> [We're working our way toward a silk halter dress.]

With well-created catalog copy, the consumer should be able to recognize the brand on the basis of the voice alone. Make that one of your goals: to create a distinct sense of self for your client's brand—trustworthy, interesting, one people want to spend time with and, not least, buy things from. There are many compelling catalogs and voices. Find them. Learn from them.

Catalog headlines are mini-lessons in persuasion

Whenever you're advertising anything and have gotten lost in the funhouse of witty headlines and wacky ideas, drifting farther and farther from any real selling promise, pull out a catalog and see how headlines by, say, Lands' End or Sharper Image express—in a condensed but pungent way—the selling argument. They'll help pull you back from the jokes-for-jokes'-sake of your errant headlines. You'll appreciate again how well catalog writing stays inside the selling idea, dramatizing the benefit and positioning the product.

Consider, for example, the following headlines from the Sharper Image catalog, a compendium of upscale, urbanite accessories. Notice how each pinpoints product and benefit:

For an electronic, pocket-sized Spanish/English translator: "5 lbs. of Spanish on a microchip."

For a teensy, clip-on reading light: "Marriage-saving light for bookworms."

For a compact home workout machine: "Tunturi squeezes 15 great exercises into 3 ft. x 4 ft."

For a 2-in-1 travel product: "Hair dryer elopes with the travel iron."

For a car cover that automatically gathers itself up: "Self-retracting instant garage."

For a talking scale: "Your weight, well spoken."

These may seem too blunt for some advertising purposes, and they are. They may also be unsuitable examples of how to write national-brand headlines, because their assertiveness may be too harsh for the softer, more understated approaches of attitude or image advertising. But they are almost haikus in the poetics of ad copy, pure forms of the selling impulse.

ANNUAL REPORTS, PRODUCT AND CAPABILITY BROCHURES, AND THE LIKE

These are big organizational tasks. By definition, they require the presentation of lots of information; they also require that readers find them interesting enough to pick up and compelling enough to stay with. Reader interest is never a given. It must be earned, usually by a copywriter and designer working together to pull readers in with an imaginative approach. Consider figures 12.3 and 12.4, two examples of a design firm's work for a travel service.

Butterfield & Robinson (B&R) tours, whether walking or biking, are heavy on real interaction with the land and people but are also upscale, gracious experiences. Michael D. Liss, B&R's marketing and managing director, presents the challenge for the design firm:

Our trips are crafted with special attention to details. We think about how the experience will unfold for you. Where it begins and ends. Which places you should see, and in what order. Where the highs are. Those are intangibles that we are selling. That stuff is so hard to explain in print. The difficulty is that a competitor can sell the same four hotels and get you to those places. On paper, it may look exactly the same and cost a third less money, and people are likely to say, "Wait a minute! What's the difference?" Through the design [and writing] of our brochures, we can convey that B&R trips are really more special.[5]

To differentiate these trips from all others, B&R's design firm, Viva Dolan in Toronto, must make sure that everything in the brochures expresses the qualitative distinctions that define the brand—from the big-picture overviews of the B&R experience to the chapter and verse of trip, maps, and itineraries.

A further challenge is that each catalogue must be unique—which means that Viva Dolan doesn't just need one Big Idea; it needs a new Big Idea every time it redesigns the guides. Designer Frank Viva explains: "One of [B&R's] key attributes is a love for the unexpected. People who take these trips want to be surprised and delighted with a one-of-a-kind experience. They feel the same way about the marketing materials. . . . Each catalogue must outdo the last, taking a creative approach that inspires people to keep it on their coffee tables and share it with friends."[6] As the writer, Doug Dolan needs to evoke that same singular, serendipitous quality of experience in the voice he creates. To do so, he brings to the copy his experience as a writer of fiction: "It's a fiction writer's instinct to try to get in the precise physical details that set up a moment that everybody can relate to. It's not a marketing voice, but a sense of a real traveler talking."[7]

In this work you can see, first, how well Viva Dolan has understood its client and, second, how clearly and persuasively the firm has presented B&R's travel experience to potential consumers.

These spreads from the catalogues pull me in and make me want to go. You, too?

BUSINESS-TO-BUSINESS ADVERTISING

Much advertising writing is not directed to the ultimate consumer at all. It's from one organization to another: an insurance company is talking to a college about handling its faculty's medical coverage; a plastics manufacturer is trying to interest a milk producer in shipping products via its packaging; a magazine is seeking to convince advertisers to use it.

Why it's hard to write

Technically one person is not talking to another, and often enough the product also seems vague—some corporation somehow is supposed to help the gears of some other large corporation run better. Business-to-business advertising can seem too amorphous to write well—there's no simple thing or service, no ultimate consumer to put it on her hair, wear it, or drive it to the beach.

The good news

Your difficulties in writing this type of ad are mostly an illusion. Everything you've learned about how to write ads to the ultimate consumer will apply here, too. Treat the company as a person, both companies as two people, and you'll be fine. Bad business-to-business advertising wrongly assumes that there is a corporate mentality different from the human one, so it talks stiffly, gets too far into specs and jargon, and engages in corporate meta-discourse (talking about talking about something). Bad idea. Boring headlines, boring copy.

Your readers are still themselves—regular people—when studying business proposals, just more seriously so. They define self-interest in a broader sense—what's good for their company? what's good for them as its employees?—so your advertising's attitude and tone become critical. If you're too flip, hip, and in-their-face (a voice that often works well in consumer advertising, especially for products where risk or ego-involvement is low), then you might alienate them. They're at work, after all, and in some sense their jobs are on the line. They want to make the right decision, not just an interesting one. Your voice must be serious enough to be trustworthy but singular enough to be human.

Figure 12.5, for example, shows a bank talking to corporations. Sounds sleep inducing, doesn't it? But notice how the ad hooks readers with a human truth and sounds like a real person all the way through.

Do your homework

One real difficulty with business-to-business advertising often isn't the speaker-subject-audience triangle. It's the writer not wanting to do the homework required. You've got to understand the businesses involved. What does Company A make or do, exactly, and what could Company B possibly get out of it? Who, exactly, will be reading this copy? And who else is a player in this game?

If you're writing an annual report for a lumber company, what are the issues, both in the industry and in the environment? What would shareholders want to know? If you're writing a capabilities brochure for a semiconductor business or a third-party corporate reinsurer, then you've got some studying ahead, right?

Do enough research to wipe away the fog so that you can clearly see the buyer, the seller, the product, and the competition. You need to visualize the commercial situation well enough to write about it. But once you do, you'll realize that that the whole large, vague scenario resolves itself into the usual transaction: a product helps someone solve a problem, and your task, as always, is to dramatize the benefit.

Find the balance

Too often copy errs on the safe side—it's sober and serious but never speaks with enough verve and authenticity to reach its readers. That's why many people consider business writing interchangeable clap-trap. Put your own life into the corporate voice as you write it. Remember, your readers didn't leave themselves at home when they came to work. They brought along their needs and anxieties, their hopes and plans, so write to them as real people, and your copy will have the life it needs. After all, corporations never look at ads; people do.

> If you work for an institution, whatever your job, whatever your level, be yourself when you write. You will stand out as a real person among the robots.
> —William Zinsser, *On Writing Well*

Martha suspects
the monks never
used the pool

Elegant châteaux, historic villas, charming inns, renowned wilderness lodges — we find the very best accommodations along every B&R route. It might be the legendary Château de Bagnols in Burgundy, a luxurious oasis with a drawbridge and moat. The Sirenuse in Positano, with its sun-drenched terraces above the Amalfi Coast. The exclusive Auberge du Soleil, on a hill overlooking Napa's golden-lit Stag's Leap vineyards. Or the Lake Palace, a 17thC maharajah's retreat surrounded by water, with spectacular views of Udaipur and the Rajasthan hills. At B&R, we have one simple rule: if the hotels don't meet our standards, we don't bike or walk there.

Le Collegiata, our luxurious hotel near San Gimignano, is a restored 16thC monastery whose frescoed rooms have incredible views of the rolling Tuscan hills and Chianti vineyards. Like all of B&R's hotels, it's an ideal place to unwind after an active day — and maybe spend the next day walking and relaxing by the pool.

The best hotels along the way The B&R Difference **13**

12.3. A specific detail, quirky and real, can stand for many other experiences possible on such trips. This sixteenth-century restored monastery, now a hotel, is one place trippers might spend the night in Tuscany. Another spread, featuring a chef in Asolo, has this headline: "Signor Baggio can do dinner when you're in town."

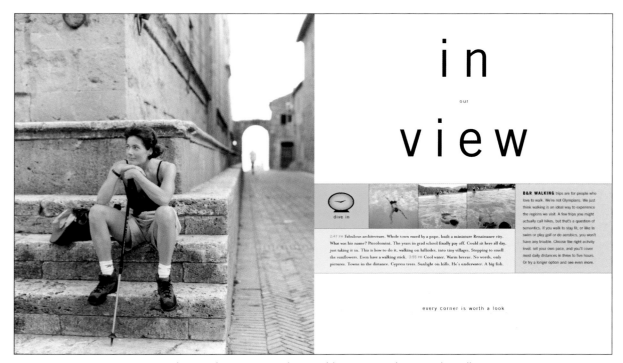

in
our
view

dive in

B&R WALKING trips are for people who love to walk. We're not Olympians. We just think walking is an ideal way to experience the regions we visit. A few trips you might actually call hikes, but that's a question of semantics. If you walk to stay fit, or like to swim or play golf or do aerobics, you won't have any trouble. Choose the right activity level, set your own pace, and you'll cover most daily distances in three to five hours. Or try a longer option and see even more.

2:47 PM Fabulous architecture. Whole town razed by a pope, built a miniature Renaissance city. What was his name? Piccolomini. The years in grad school finally pay off. Could sit here all day, just taking it in. This is how to do it, walking on hillsides, into tiny villages. Stopping to smell the sunflowers. Even have a walking stick. 3:55 PM Cool water. Warm breeze. No words, only pictures. Towns in the distance. Cypress trees. Sunlight on hills. He's underwater. A big fish.

every corner is worth a look

12.4. Another guide is organized around language in large and small point sizes, the words creating phrases that can be read in two ways. Other headlines: "I would never **GO** on a group tour," "**AT** this pace a life of **EASE** is a way of life," "**IN** no time, we get **DEEP** into the culture," and, on the farewell page, "**SO** where should we go and how **LONG** do you want to stay?"

Other Media and Genres / 129

The economy can be accused of many things. Predictability is probably not one of them.

This economic fickleness can place your company in a rather vulnerable position. As you charge boldly into the future, eyes on the horizon, even a fairly minor fluctuation in interest rates can sneak up on you and bring your company to its knees.

Or to some even humbler portion of its anatomy.

The same thing can happen, of course, if exchange rates or commodity costs decide to dance a little jig.

Clearly, something should be done to deal with this threat. At Continental Bank, we suggest financial risk management.

In brief, risk management allows your company to specify exactly how much rate variation you're willing to tolerate. If rates rise or fall beyond the limits you've specified, you're protected.

Whether the rate in question is the prime or Eurodollar, yen or deutschemark.

Beyond the obvious peace of mind it offers, financial risk management confers numerous other benefits.

It controls your cost of funds. It allows you to budget your interest expense with greater confidence. It prevents unforeseen depletion of your capital. On the whole, it permits you to do business in a much more orderly fashion.

Risk management is a relatively recent arrival on the financial scene, but it is already being heralded as the ideal mix of prudence and opportunity. It accords well with our philosophy—which is to bring our customers the most innovative, most effective financial tools we can find, develop or invent.

To learn more about how risk management can help your company, talk to a Continental banker at (312) 828-5799. There'll still be bananas in the world. But at least you won't be stepping on them. **Continental Bank** A new approach to business.

Let's say the foot is your company, the banana is a change in interest rates, and the floor is extremely hard.

12.5. Financial risks are given a human context, both visually and verbally. A trade ad with a human heart.

Out-of-home advertising

[Outdoor is the hardest to do] because it has to fit on a postage stamp. It's not a magazine page a foot in front of your face. You've got to get the logo, get the proposition, get the message and get a laugh—all while you're picking your nose at 35 miles per hour. It's hard to find ideas that stop on a dime.

—Tracy Wong, principal,
WongDoody

The major formats are outdoor boards and transit ads, but there are empty spaces to be filled everywhere: little placards on shopping carts, sponsored bulletin boards in schools and health clubs, ads everywhere people look—even when they look down (see fig. 12.6).

Out-of-home advertising usually functions as a supplemental medium (only occasionally as a campaign's central medium) and works best to help introduce new products, build brand awareness rapidly, add reach to a campaign, or serve as reminder advertising for well-known brands and products. In today's increasingly cluttered digital world, their value may be increasing. Rob Morris,

creative partner at Grounds Morris Campbell, London, explains why:

With digital TV coming along with all these channels, the question becomes, how do you attract and hold the attention of the consumer? With posters, people literally can't turn them off. Also, our cities are becoming more congested. Traffic rates in London were clocked at an average 10.9 mph last year. With people sitting in traffic, some billboards now represent just about the cheapest 30-second commercial any advertiser can hope for.[8]

Try applying the following guidelines when your assignment is out-of-home advertising:

1. Be simple, be fast. If advertising must be simple in order to be quickly comprehended, out-of-home advertising must be telegraphic. After all, people are cruising a highway at 65 mph or dashing down an airport concourse or taking steps two-at-a-time on their way to class. If a public ad is too wordy or too complicated, it's shrugged off as an incomprehensible blur.

Posters inside buses and subways, however, are an important exception; seated passengers can study them for a while, so these can be more text-heavy. (And if people are stuck in traffic, who knows how long they may stare at your message?) Generally, however, think in terms of one image and a few words. Or perhaps just a few words and the logotype.

2. Think big. One of the main strengths of outdoor boards is that they invoke respect for the monumental. Where else are you given the chance to shout at the world with gigantic words and images? This monumentalizing ability is something Marlboro has played like a tune over the years, with its great Montana skies and mountain ranges, massive horses and horsemen, buckles and boots, the huge Marlboro logo riding over it all. Don't forget that you're using a medium that can inspire awe. Adidas outdoor boards in Tokyo and Osaka, for example, featured a live soccer match (tethered players and a tethered ball). Two fellows playing soccer while hanging sideways above a building can draw a crowd, with the people staring not just at the spectacle but also at that Adidas logo.

3. Take advantage of placement. Placement of out-of-home advertising can be quite specific; you often know, in a way you rarely do in other media, just exactly where you are. You know who your audience is and what's on their minds. "158 more oils than this gas station," said an outdoor board, beside a gas station, for a Monet exhibition at the Art Institute of Chicago. A sign in front of a Dairy Queen in a residential district said simply, "Scream until Daddy stops the car." (See figures 12.7 through 12.9 for more boards that know where they are.) Regarding figure 12.8, Merkley Newman Harty's Dan Sutton explained the pro bono campaign: "If you need to get your head and spirit together, a chapel is better than a bar or phone booth."[9]

4. Consider manipulations and sequences. Outdoor boards, bus cards, subway cards, airport posters, and the like also allow, even invite, successive manipulation over time and/or space. You can say something on a board and then add to it the next week, add to that a week later, and so forth. Or you can ask a question on one board and answer it farther down the high-

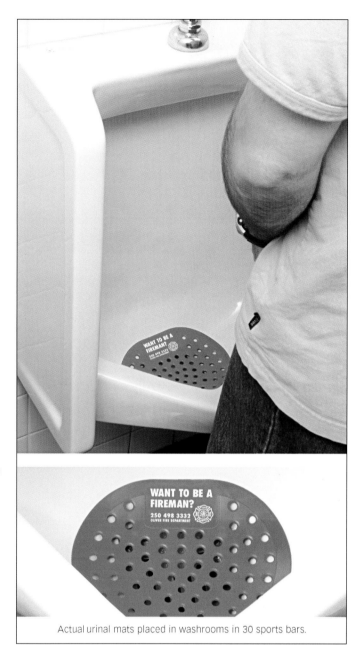

Actual urinal mats placed in washrooms in 30 sports bars.

12.6. Medium and message coincide.

way or airport walkway or subway line. Or begin something on one board and complete it on another. Or demonstrate the product's benefit by making changes in the board.

Nike boards showed an Oakland Raider quarterback throwing a pass in one board and a receiver catching it in another farther down the freeway. An outdoor board for a shopping center said, as people drove toward the center, "Wearing that again?" (in smaller type: "South Coast Plaza 17 miles ahead"). As people left the center, a second board said, "You look fabulous"

(in smaller type: "South Coast Plaza. Thanks for shopping").

Guerrilla advertising

> You have to try to sneak under the BS radar. Everyone's so media savvy these days that unless you play it perfectly, you're going to get killed.
>
> —John Pearson, art director, Wells Rich Greene BDDP

Ads that don't look like ads—that's a good definition of guerrilla advertising. Use nontraditional media, often in nontraditional ways, to bypass people's filters, get their attention, and do positive work for your client's brand. Spring up in unexpected places and ways. Ambush your target audience. Let's say they're walking through an airport and see a guy all pretzeled up, arm bent above his head, holding a piece of luggage that says, "Give me time to unwind. I didn't fly Sun Air's Exec Economy." They probably won't dismiss him as an "ad" right away; they'll notice him and smile. He's harder to ignore than an airport poster, that's for sure. This contortionist, hired by Sun Air, is guerrilla advertising.

So is a guy dressed up like a rat and "dying" of cyanide poison on the streets of Manhattan, as part of Truth's anti-smoking campaign—demonstrating that cigarette smoke, just like rat poison, contains cyanide. Yet another example is the airline Virgin Atlantic's practice of slipping trays of unbroken eggs labeled "Handled by Virgin Atlantic" onto the baggage carousels of competing airlines at airports. In each case, passersby are caught unawares by this form of advertising, hence the term "guerrilla." (Because the events often take place outside while people are on the move, guerrilla advertising is sometimes called "ambient advertising.")

But street theatre is only one of many ways you can bend advertising out of its traditional forms. Mini Cooper has done lots of unusual advertising for its little car: placing it on top of an SUV driving around town ("What are you doing for fun this

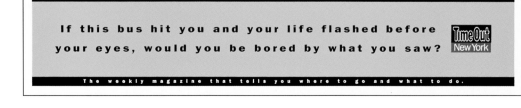

12.7. Most out-of-home ads pretend not to notice where they are; these ads take advantage of it. (The quotation-marks board is for The Weather Network.)

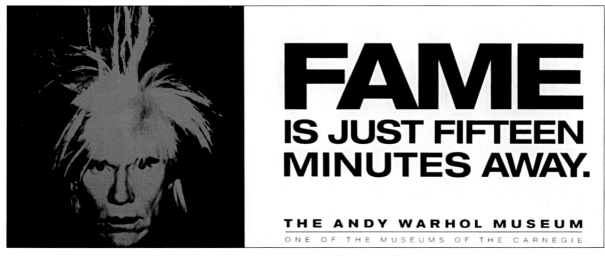

> *Does anyone really know their estimated time of departure?*
>
> THE INTERFAITH [i] AIRPORT CHAPEL
> *Located in the atrium*

12.8. A perfect union of idea and place. Another board said: "Just passing through? Aren't we all?"

> FAME
> IS JUST FIFTEEN MINUTES AWAY.
>
> THE ANDY WARHOL MUSEUM
> ONE OF THE MUSEUMS OF THE CARNEGIE

12.9. An outdoor board in Pittsburgh lets people know they're close by playing off Andy Warhol's most famous line: "In the future everyone will be world-famous for fifteen minutes."

weekend?"); attaching it to the sides of buildings ("Nothing corners like a MINI"); putting tire marks on airport floors, as though the car had been careering through obstacles; placing a Mini hobby-horse in front of stores ("Rides $16,850"); and playing tricks with changes in scale (see fig. 12.10).

Think of guerrilla advertising as partly location, partly concept: find a new place—out there and in consumers' heads. (see figs. 12.11 and 12.12.) And don't be limited by your traditional preconceptions of what constitutes an ad. Especially when it comes to guerilla advertising, the words of advertising pioneer Charles Austin Bates ring true: "More things enter into advertising than are generally supposed. In fact, everything that connects a name and a business in people's minds is advertising."[10]

12.10. Whimsy, Mini style. An ad that doesn't feel like one.

WHEN TO DO IT

Guerrilla advertising makes a lot of sense for start-ups and other small clients with teeny advertising budgets. Like guerrilla warfare, it's asymmetric, making the most of whatever you have, maximizing results while minimizing cost. But it makes sense even for big players because people so distrust and tune out advertising that if you do something that doesn't seem like advertising, something unexpected, you improve your chances of getting through, and you encourage consumers to feel good by interacting with your client's brand in this new way. Another benefit of guerrilla advertising is the attendant publicity and press coverage—the bounce or buzz—it creates. That may be even more important, since it can reach more people, than whatever the original guerrilla event or placement was. In fact, advertisers often link publicity and guerrilla advertising, the one feeding off the other. Stage the event, then try to get as much coverage as possible.

TWO VARIANTS, AMONG MANY

Viral marketing is advertising people participate in by passing it on. The ad or event has gotten into their bloodstream like a virus, and they pass it on like a virus—either because it's funny and interesting, so they want to share it with others, or they've been "paid" to do so, given a reward. Viral marketing can use any medium; the key idea is that consumers enlist themselves to spread the ad around. Burger King, for example, launched a Web site, subservientchicken.com, in which a man dressed in a chicken outfit would do whatever people asked (within reason). The idea was to take literally Burger King's have-it-your-way claim: "Get chicken just the way you like it. Type in your command here." This was good guerrilla advertising not only because it was an unusual way to get BK's differential into people's heads but also because it was an idea nutty enough to generate a lot of buzz. And the site did exactly that, scoring twenty million hits in its first ten days and quickly spawning 700 Google links to sites discussing Subservient Chicken.[11]

Jonathan Bond, president of Kirshenbaum Bond + Partners, points out the value of getting consumers to spread a message: "People don't trust advertising; they trust other people. No one ad is as credible or effective as the recommendation of a friend. But good advertising can program people to say what you want about a brand, to forge the kind

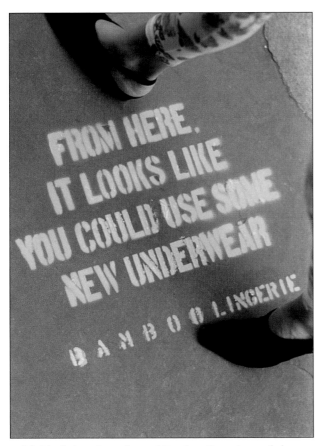

12.11. Sidewalks in front of Bamboo Lingerie retail shops were stenciled with a message both clever and unexpected.

to get it done? Stay true both to the campaign's goals and to the essence of the brand. In a clever guerrilla ad campaign, VCU Adcenter students parked an Audi TT in the driveway of potential buyers, then photographed it and hung the photograph (and a Web-site link) on the front door. Research had shown that people thought Audis were more expensive than they actually are. By fitting the car right into people's driveway and life—by making the car closer to reality than people supposed—the campaign dramatically addressed the problem.

2. Be fan friendly. You run a real risk of offending people by "wilding," that is, sticking your message in their eye and ear without asking permission. You're also intruding on the landscape—often an open, public, supposedly

of connection consumers make with Volvo and safety. That's the word-of-mouth channel, and you can't *buy* time on it. You earn it with a message that has actual news value and gets people talking."[12]

Stealth marketing occurs when people don't realize that what just happened was an ad. A classic example is trendy people in a bar talking up a brand of beer or liquor and encouraging others to drink it, too (but the trendies are actually "plants" paid to spread the word). There are a lot of "plants" in Guerrillaville. Questions like "Who's real?" and "Who's fooling whom?" may be interesting philosophical puzzles, but they often make for advertising that hurts, rather than helps, the brand. People want to trust word of mouth and often resent being fooled this way.

Advice

1. Be relevant. You're not just staging a stunt, you're communicating a brand truth. Stay on strategy. What does your client's brand need to do or say, and can guerrilla advertising be a way

12.12. A South African gun-control group placed vending machines containing apparently real handguns on university campuses and in shopping malls. (Putting money in the machines was a way to donate to the cause.) People are so used to seeing innocuous products in vending machines that this substitution shocks them—and dramatizes the argument.

advertising-free zone. Such an intrusion can irritate people mightily. Therefore be funny, be temporary, don't mess with people unduly. See things from their point of view, not just yours. As advertising writer and editor Warren Berger asks, "How would you feel if this particular sidewalk ad were stamped on the walk in front of your own house—would you still find it amusing? What if it showed up in the halls of your kid's school?"[13]

For example, a guerrilla campaign against SUVs in the San Francisco Bay Area surreptitiously tagged SUV bumpers with this sticker: "I'm changing the climate! Ask me how!" It's funny if someone is against SUVs, but it's not funny to the SUVs' owners. The campaign definitely raises awareness but probably inflames opinions rather than changes minds.[14]

3. Take advantage of your surroundings. Use them, interact with them. Make your idea fit this place and this medium. For example, in twenty low-income, high-rise apartment buildings in Beijing, Ikea transformed the interiors of the elevators to show residents what could be done, cheaply, with small spaces, implying that residents might change their apartments for the better on a budget, too. In Berlin, Ikea redid the lighting, walls, and color palette in a train station to show what a difference a few good choices could make. "We use nontraditional media so that we can be a big presence. It's a strategic decision to go where the competition isn't," says Bill Agee, external marketing communications manager for Ikea.[15]

A golf pro who gave lessons placed balls with his name, phone number, and the line "We need to talk" in golf course sand traps, bunkers, rough, and out-of-bounds areas—exactly where bad golfers would find them. Everyone who picked up his ball probably needed to have some lessons. (See figure 12.13 for another unusual example of fitting an idea with its placement.)

4. Be disarming. There may be greater creative pressure on you in the guerrilla arena than elsewhere, since nothing is as irritating or fails as loudly as a big gesture gone wrong. So make your guerrilla advertising friendly and fun. People will resent a same-as-usual sales pitch. Make them smile, don't overstay your welcome, hope for good press, and move on.

Multicultural and international advertising

> It took millions of years for man's instincts to develop. It will take millions more for them to even vary. It is fashionable to talk about changing man. A communicator must be concerned with unchanging man, with his obsessive drive to survive, to be admired, to succeed, to love, to take care of his own.
>
> —William Bernbach,
> founding partner, Doyle Dane Bernach

> I'm of the opinion that there is no such thing as a global advertising campaign. To try and market one product in different cities and cultures is just about impossible.
>
> —Steffan Postaer,
> creative director, Leo Burnett

Part of why advertising is so difficult is that both men are right. People are and aren't the same. The trick is knowing how so and how not.

HOW TO DEAL WITH PEOPLE'S DIFFERENCES
If you want to cross international borders with the greatest of ease, follow the two universal guidelines discussed in this section.

First, don't use words. Use pictures. (If you're a copywriter, life just got easier.) Ideas in one language won't always cross over into another. For instance, "curiously strong," the key phrase for Altoids mints, doesn't translate well, if at all, into other languages, thus limiting the campaign to speakers of English. Similarly, a Saab campaign whose headlines pivoted on "versus" (for example, "Saab vs. Oxygen Bars" or "Saab vs. Parenthood") didn't work in Japan because Japanese has no ready equivalent for "vs."[16] To give you an idea of how big a problem language can be, I'll just mention that Singapore alone has four national languages, and if you're aiming a campaign at all of Asia, you'll encounter hundreds of languages.[17]

Even if the language will translate, assumptions may not. Avis's celebrated 1960s car rental campaign, whose theme line was "We're no. 2. We try harder," wouldn't have worked in Asia. Ian Batey, former CEO of Time, Inc., and author of *Asian Branding*, explains why: "Self-deprecation is not an Asian trait. Asians want to save face, not lose it. If you surround your brand with negative irony, they will walk away in droves."[18] This is good to know,

12.13. Direct-response vehicle and alternative medium: the stick. The Sydney Dog Home takes care of abandoned, abused, lost, and hurt dogs; nurses them back to health; and puts them up for adoption. But the home needed money to stay open and had nothing to spend on a campaign. So M&C Saatchi came up with the idea of throwing sticks with messages tied to them into public parks. When people fetched the tagged sticks out of curiosity, they would read the copy, which explained the Sydney Dog Home's mission and encouraged donations, while the headline humorously urged adoption as well.

especially since so much American advertising—from DDB's original campaigns for Avis and VW to work created last week—delights in making fun of itself.

But ads that don't trip on translation and idiom difficulties, ads that present the human condition rather than a cultural condition, ads that are entirely or primarily visual, such ads have their visa papers ready (see figs. 12.14 and 12.15).

Second, when you do use words, be prepared to translate ideas, too. The witty "Got milk?" campaign, for example, wasn't going to work, straight up, for the Spanish-speaking Hispanic market, and research showed why.[19] For one thing, "Got milk?" translated into something like "Are you lactating?" For another, milk is central to a loving Hispanic mother's duties in caring for her family. To joke about its absence, the milk deprivation strategy, calls her competence into question. Also, peanut butter and jelly sandwiches and chocolate chip cookies, central to the campaign, didn't resonate. Finally, milk in Hispanic homes is used more to cook with than to drink. For all these reasons the campaign had to undergo significant alteration—the joke and tone had to be jettisoned—to work. The theme line that replaced "Got milk?" in Spanish-language advertising to Hispanics, translated, was "And you, have you given them enough milk today?" The selling argument is still there, but it's had surgery.

HOW TO TAKE ADVANTAGE OF PEOPLE'S SIMILARITIES

It can be easy to overemphasize the differences across cultures and countries and make one of two mistakes: (1) appeal too narrowly to a regional difference or cultural predilection, or (2) bland yourself out by pulling your punches, thinking you'd better not speak specifically or engage in humor or take one single chance. These problems are twin horns of the same dilemma: be too general and go blah; be too specific and narrowcast yourself into insignificance. Or, worse, watch your selling idea backfire as your audience feels patronized, as though they couldn't handle a mainstream argument.

José Mollá, co-founder of la comunidad, Miami, makes a good suggestion: "To me, the best thing to do is have one strategy—and then to do the fine-tuning at the executional level, so that you can deepen the connection with each culture. Often, there is a small twist you can add to the concept that will make it resonate more with the Hispanic market. But the multicultural aspect of a campaign shouldn't come from just the media buy, or the casting—it should come from the content of the message. And the way to do that is to connect with human truths."[20]

Citibank's advertising has encouraged people to be responsible with their money. How to take that idea into the Spanish-speaking Hispanic market? To advertise Access Account, a starter checking

12.14. An example of an ad that will cross any border known to man. It's not just funny to one culture, it's funny to humans. Words would only get in the way.

12.15. Although this ad has been used only in the U.S., it's ready to travel. With no headline to create language problems and a visual message that's universally understandable—both as a metaphor (the beer that stands out in a crowd) and as a symbol (the brand-differentiating Corona parrot)—this ad could go anywhere.

account that facilitates money transfers, Citibank created ads spotlighting problems Hispanics encounter every day, often small things like ordering coffee or speaking with a pharmacist. Contrasting those experiences was the tagline: "There are better reasons why you chose to live in the United States. Citibank Access Account. Access to what you came here for." In other words, access to eco-

nomic advancement: making money and improving their families' lives (Hispanics send home millions of U.S. dollars to their families in Latin America).[21]

The ads, created by Mollá's agency, put into play his advice to start with a central strategy, then adapt it to connect with a particular culture. Outdoor boards in south Florida said in Spanish, "The red should come from too much sun, not too much spending." In this case the Citibank selling argument—we'll help you use your money wisely—is translated into terms that work for the audience and location. Other outdoor boards, translated, said, "We speak to you in the language you dream in."

In brief, all multicultural and international advertising will benefit from these five guidelines:

1. Appeal to human truths, universal truths.
2. Don't base the ads on culture- or language-bound idiom.
3. Be visual whenever possible. Images trump words.
4. Establish a brand identity or selling argument, then tweak that theme to fit the audience.
5. Don't shoot lower than you should. Respect your audience's intelligence.

And remember, too, that people of all countries increasingly are consuming American popular culture, advertising, and imagery (Elvis and Marilyn will never die). The Americanization of the world is binding people together with shared cultural themes and capitalist assumptions. Advertising from international corporations like Audi, Honda, Sony, Coca-Cola, and many others has a universal sensibility, so much so that you can't tell where the advertising originated. Ads created in the U.K., Europe, or the Pacific Rim rather than in the U.S. have often become a distinction without a difference.

In short, if you're creating advertising for international audiences, be aware of the issues discussed in this section, but don't let them undo your instincts. Start with basic human truths, and you'll be fine.

Interactive media

> The trend of media is not only to fragment the audience, but to shrink it. In living memory, we've gone from the collective experience of watching movies with hundreds of others, to watching sitcoms with our family, to surfing the Web in solitude. Never mind the hit counters. We are an audience of one.
> —Crawford Kilian, teacher and writer

As a copywriter in the arena of interactive media, you're likely to spend a lot of time either writing ads that go on the Web or writing the sites that make up the Web. The first is advertising; the second is copywriting, though often not quite advertising.

INTERACTIVE ADVERTISING

People usually think of advertising as an interruption, a message that jumps into the middle of things unbidden, but J. Walker Smith, managing partner at Yankelovich Partners, says, "People are increasingly turning away from being talked at by marketers. And it's changing who has the power in the relationship."[22] He calls advertising in interactive media (especially the Web) "marketing by invitation," where consumers take charge, and he points out that consumers really are choosing to interrupt themselves. They'll do so only if they think it's in their self-interest.

Internet advertising, unlike advertising in so many other media, lets consumers do something about it, right away. In fact, it wants them to. The point of any ad there is to get consumers to click through, to respond. Internet advertisers literally have an audience of one person (thousands, perhaps millions, of "one persons") sitting there looking at that ad, with a finger poised over a keyboard. You want to make that finger move.

What does it take? Usually an offer. If your ad is just a print ad with pixels, consumers may not be motivated to do anything about it—so why not just put it in a magazine or newspaper? If you're using the Internet, take advantage of the medium. It's the quintessential opportunity for one-to-one marketing.

Make your ad a resource

Ads on Web sites have great potential because they can target the audience specifically and work immediately. If people are visiting a cooking Web site, you can place kitchenware, diet, and cooking-related offers all around them. If they're visiting a site to get information about how to fix their car, you can place car parts ads or travel ads or camping gear ads next to the site's content. Whatever people are searching for, reading about, browsing through, or entertaining themselves with, its advertising equivalents can also be at their fingertips. Make your ad helpful and interesting enough that it becomes a resource, too.

> The internet is the greatest direct marketing medium ever invented.
> —Seth Godwin, *Permission Marketing*

As Keith Byrne advised in *Creativity* magazine, "Whenever possible [on the click-through idea] give the opportunity to relate directly to users' lives."[23] For example, Web ads for Parentsoup.com invite people to enter their child's name and find out its etymology or enter the child's age and find out what his or her college education will cost. Ads for CondeNet's Epicurious.com Web site invite people to type in their favorite ingredients, and the company will send them to recipe suggestions at its site.

This is direct marketing made instantaneous. It follows that all the principles of direct marketing operate here: be quick, be clear, be intriguing, offer something of value, make it matter that consumers click through, now (see fig. 12.16).

Develop a relationship with consumers

I mentioned that Web ads usually involve offers. But offers can be of all kinds, not just "2 for the price of 1," "first issue free" kinds of things. Offers can be of information or knowledge or relationship. Encourage consumers to develop a relationship with your client's brand (partly so you can build databases for future marketing). You might offer to send people newsletters or special offers in exchange for information about themselves. Get them to visit the brand's site often by giving them something of value, someone or something they can trust.

So, for example, a Web ad links consumers to Claritin's site (Claritin makes allergy products), and once there they see the button bar: "For me," "For kids," "Allergy authority," "Pollen planners," and "Free & clear." Each button controls a pull-down menu, and consumers realize that besides being a commercial site, this is a repository of material about allergies, from myths, resources, and signs of allergies in children to allergies at school, asthma information, and opportunities to develop a personal allergy profile. Consumers can even sign up for an e-mail to be delivered to them every Thursday forecasting that weekend's weather and pollen count.

If consumers or their families have allergies, Claritin wants to be their allergy consultant and health partner. That kind of payoff—relationships with consumers that lead to long-term brand loyalty—is much more valuable than a simple coupon offer that goes no further. It's the kind of payoff that Web advertising can deliver much more easily than advertising in other media can. As a copywriter, you may be charged not just with writing ads that drive consumers to the site but also with helping create the on-site value that keeps them coming back.

Realize that media may change, but psychology doesn't

The forms Web advertising can take, and therefore the things you can do, are evolving rapidly—from banners, buttons, and pop-up ads to rich-media ads, Web movies, and beyond. But remember that no matter what the technical possibilities, it's still advertising. And what works, works in any medium. Catch people's attention, don't underestimate or abuse them, let them involve themselves, address real motives, make it easy to take the next step. If you're interesting and make a credible, meaningful offer (and an offer can be of entertainment, knowledge, or experience), people will follow. And don't let your design colleagues fall in love with gratuitous graphic pyrotechnics. Visual noise is still noisy. Make whatever happens in your ad happen for a reason.

WEBSITES

As I mentioned previously, sometimes you may be writing the sites themselves. When this is the case, take some advice from Raymond Pirouz in *Click Here*.[24] Notice that it's the traditional creative brief, but with a Web sensibility:

1. Decide on your site's central purpose.
2. Define your target audience.
3. Design an overall brand identity for your site.
4. Make getting around the site—its navigation—easy, consistent, and sensible.
5. Plan a strategy to pull people into and through the site.
6. Deliver the site's content in small units of meaning. Nest pages within pages, rather than hitting people with the whole thing in a long scrolling screen. Use hotlinks to help people move around inside the information.
7. Devise ways to get people to return, regularly, to your site.

> [T]he ultimate participation in an ad is that you can buy from it.
> —Lester Wunderman, advertiser and marketer

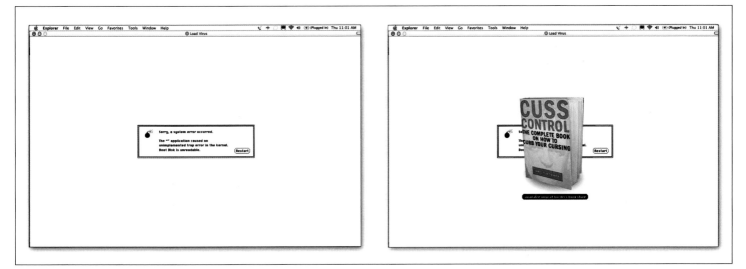

12.16. If you got this "bomb box" on your screen ("Sorry, a system error occurred. The " " application caused an unimplemented trap error in the kernal. Boot Disk is unreadable. Restart"), you might utter some of the language the book addresses (*Cuss Control: The Complete Book on How to Curb Your Cursing*) and click on the box below it, "available now at borders bookstore." No matter what the medium, the principles of good advertising operate: create awareness of a problem, announce a solution, and make getting it easy.

How to find sites worth studying? You run into plenty of them on your own, of course, but advertising and design magazines can help steer you. *Communication Arts*, for example, publishes its jurors' choices for best sites every year in the Interactive Annual (the Sept./Oct. issue). *CA*'s Web site (www. commarts.com) profiles a site every week in its "Design Interact" section.

Well-designed sites are usually also well written, so you can find the best Web writing to learn from by letting design lead you to it. The following sections address the most significant things to consider when writing Web content.

Organize first

Before you write the words, define what you think a successful visit to the site would be. In other words, what should people be able to do at your client's site, get out of it, and so on? Make that list of users and uses, then design the site and its language to fit that list. Remember, the key idea is participation, interaction. The Web isn't a passive medium, so design for it. Figure out how someone can participate in the page or site.

Just as you can write copy by asking what would persuade *you* to buy the product (using yourself as a test consumer), so too can you design the language and sequence of a Web site by asking what *you* would want at each point along the way. What questions would you have? What would you like to be able to do? If you ever outlined a research essay before writing it or while writing it, organizing a site is like organizing that paper. What are the main sections? What are the subsections? What's the sequence?

More than sentences, you're creating overall structure—you're creating forest, not just trees. This is really big writing, but in small units. The buttons running across the top or bottom of the home page, for example, the ones that tell people what the other pages are, may look like just one- or two-word bits, but they are essential organizational units that are neither inherent nor preordained. They're things you think up.

Understand how Web writing is different

The big difference between Web prose and other prose is this: on the Web, every moment is potentially self-contained. You can't count on prior knowledge by the reader. Nor can you count on one part of your writing being read before any other part, thus creating the context and prelude for it. You don't control the order of reading anymore. You've handed that over to the user, who can jump around all over the place, hotlinking between your site and others, between different pages of your site, from one paragraph to another, stopping in mid-sentence to go back to an earlier screen, and so forth.

Once you give people options, then you turn over to them the sequence and structure of the message system. Editor and writer Paul Roberts understands the freedom that Web texts afford: "Each multimedia text—and, theoretically, each word in each text—can serve as an electronic portal to an infinite number of other digital locations. With a series of clicks, you can hop from one object of fascination to any number of others, branching this way and that along various semantic trails, creating your very own, custom-built, nonlinear narrative from a vast reservoir of recombinant texts."[25] How can you use this lack of preordained order to your advantage? Do the following:

1. Think in terms of little bubbles of prose or successive layers of prose.
2. Use subheads that let people leap around if you're into anything long. Don't make the subheads clever if they're not also clear. People want to move around expediently on the Web, and cuteness that confuses won't keep them there long.
3. Don't make pages text-heavy. Use bullets. Start with the Big Idea first: make pages informative, top down, like newspaper articles in the inverted pyramiding of content (key ideas and facts up top, background and qualifications down below). Put deeper information in clearly marked links.
4. Create response mechanisms.
5. Write straightforward sentences, and write tight.

Master the art of the caption

Since everything you write has to be self-contained and self-explanatory, Paul Roberts also suggests that you study captions. *National Geographic* and other magazines have well-written captions for their photographs and illustrations: full explanations shrunk to super-small size but tasty and nutritionally complete nonetheless. Sit down and read a magazine with good captions before writing the bite-sized prose so often required on the Web.

One happy note in the midst of all these stern commandments: screen resolutions constantly improve, and people's habits are malleable. They'll grow more willing and able to read text on a screen. As a writer, you should leap for joy at reading this statement. Minimal, telegraphic prose is not the inevitable fate for writers in the twenty-first century. On the other hand, as the Web approximates TV more and more, perhaps people will re-adopt that model's mindset and once again become less willing to read. Stay tuned for further details.

Redefine yourself

When you write for the Web, you're often not quite writing. You're arranging material in multimedia presentations, creating ideas that take visual form, writing for video and motion graphics, and helping order the hierarchy of information on the site. Sometimes you're putting sentences together, but not with as many words and not all in the "linear flow"—the coherent, sequential style—of print-based writing.

So what do you call yourself? A friend of mine, a creative director at a marketing firm, used to be a writer but now calls himself, with a degree of smiling irony, an "information architect." He's building structures only some of whose materials are words. You will be, too.

PART THREE

THE TOOLBOX

Things come toward you when you walk.
— William Stafford, poet

What follow are techniques to help you come up with ideas. Think of these techniques as tools. People accept the need for tools in other areas—no one thinks about working on wood without hammers and saws, or gardening without spade and shears, or playing baseball without bat, ball, and glove—but they'll try to think without anything at all. The techniques in the following chapters are tools for thinking creatively about advertising. They lie like objects on a workbench. Pick up the ones that seem right for the task. Let them give shape to your ideas.

13 ▪ How to Be Creative

Inspiration is highly overrated. If you sit around and wait for the clouds to part, it's not liable to ever happen. More often than not, work is salvation.

— Chuck Close, painter

Creative skills, like any others, improve with practice, and creativity follows, however idiosyncratically, a method. You get better at being creative by exercising these inventive skills, and you improve your invention by going at it step by step. How to do so?

Create a routine

I need a fence before I'm motivated to climb out. So clarity and order are important. Establish a discipline up front, and then I feel free to explore.

— Harry Jacobs, chairman,
The Martin Agency

Whenever you are solving any advertising problem, don't neglect practical matters. Establish working routines that follow your mental instincts. For example, I start early work on a clipboard, making lists of phrases, words, and strategy-like statements, all done as a gathering process. I'm pulling words together that seem to belong to the problem. Soon I take this list-making into the computer; but for early efforts, there's still nothing as comforting to me as a sharp pencil and a clipboard full of paper. Art directors often think best with markers and a sketchpad in front of them. Find your own comfort zone and enter it. John Vitro, from the ad agency VitroRobertson, talks about his process:

As I'm coming up with ideas, I'm usually scribbling on a little pad. Somebody once told me, "It's not a good idea unless it's a good idea on a plain white piece of paper." [My partner and I] get together once or twice a day and pass paper back and forth between us. Usually, at this stage, we're trying to come up with an idea in the form of a line—often a headline—that gets to the heart of what we're trying to say.[1]

Let the assignment set some boundaries

Small rooms discipline the mind; large rooms distract it.

— Leonardo da Vinci

The specifics of your advertising problem will help center your thinking. Are you writing copy for a corporate capabilities brochure? If so, you'll be thinking about what categories to present the discussion in, how to organize the piece, and what will unify it, page to page (an issue you'll develop with the designer sharing the project). Maybe instead you're writing a series of newspaper ads for a local dry cleaner, so you realize that these will have to be quick and simple, probably price or service oriented. Perhaps you're writing a self-promotion piece for a photographer. The use of photos as samples is usually a given in such self-promotions, but what would you say about them? A more original advertising strategy might be to mail out only copy, no photos, in order to get attention (see fig. 13.1). Or perhaps you're creating print ads for a packaged good for your portfolio, in which case the only limits are those of your own devising.

In short, *how* you think through an advertising problem comes from the nature of the project. It will lead you in certain directions—and give you ideas. The cool thing about working on something is that you don't have to be a genius. Just start trying to solve the problem, and ideas will arrive. Teacher and ceramics designer Eva Zeisel explains it this way:

> I came to the conclusion that what we call limits—yes, industrial design is very limiting—was just the opposite; it was very unlimiting. I set my students this project. I said, "Please sit down and do the most beautiful thing you can imagine. You must have been thinking a lot about it." And they were sitting around totally frustrated, without the slightest idea of how to fulfill their dream. Then I gave them limitations—"Make something this high, with this function"—and suddenly they were all sitting there working like beavers.[2]

Start with basic thinking techniques

> I always write a thing first and think about it afterwards, which is not a bad procedure, because the easiest way to have consecutive thoughts is to start putting them down.
> —E. B. White, essayist

If you've taken a creative writing or thinking course, you've probably used free association, brainstorming, and list making. They are ways to provide structure to the notion of having ideas. They're the first techniques, really, the first how-to's.

Free association is the process of letting one idea suggest another, one word imply the next, one image beget two. (*Brainstorming* is this process performed by a group, in which the members become one speaking, collective mind.) Free association of either sort should be fast and loose—a rapid-fire, automatic-thinking kind of thing. No one can really prescribe anyone else's free association because the connections in people's brains are so individualized. But I can offer suggestions.

Give yourself a working topic, a focus for the free association. (Let's assume that you've already done research on the product and the target audience, so you have a store of information.) Write down rapidly whatever comes to mind *as* it comes to mind. Don't stop. Peter Elbow, a nationally influential teacher of writing, calls such a thing *freewriting*, and suggests that you write for ten minutes without stopping.[3] The only way to do a freewriting "wrong" is to go slowly and edit your thoughts as you have

[1]

I'm a commercial photographer.

This is a self-promotion piece.

So where's my photograph?

Where's the image or two or three that say, "Hire him"? Well, I haven't made yours yet, and besides, it can take a while. I've been 3 days on a shirt for Abercrombie & Fitch. A little white-on-white shot — keep the edges, control the grays — but it can take time to make it breathe a little, feel like someone just slipped out of it, the right someone.

On the other hand, I recently shot 45 catalog set-ups in a day and a half and felt good about every one of them.

Call me. I'm sure we can agree on how fast you'd like me to work for you. — John

13.1. In this direct-mail campaign for John Strange & Associates, commercial photographers, Crit Warren and I created a series of poster-sized "letters" from John to prospective clients. I wrote them in a straightforward voice to represent John's, and Crit designed them to be striking but also suggestive of handwriting. This is the first of thirteen such letters, each explaining why John wasn't sending out photos.

them, deciding which are worth saying and which not, what's grammatical and what's not, and so on. Such interference defeats the purpose of scanning your brain and letting it, at speed, show you connections. If you slow down, your associations become less free, more arranged. You can't surprise yourself if you peek around every corner first.

One way to freewrite / free associate is to imagine that the product itself is a friend, and you're explaining the relationship to the reader. Imagine that you're the target market, and try to say what you get out of using the product. Write it like a letter to someone about the relationship; confess: "The thing I really like about Wheaties is their athletic associations and their goofy orange box. I feel more masculine when I eat them. They're American, they're traditional, they taste good, no frills, not a complicated food. Somehow they center me for the day. They also go great with strawberries and blueberries in the summer since they're flakes and they . . . " (This can work as a strategy creator, too, since you can investigate such confessionals for *strategic* ideas.)

Lists are a favorite of mine; maybe you use them, too. They're like the first outlines, helping me get my head on straight, start seeing the issues and possibilities. Make different kinds of lists: lists of benefits delivered, problems solved, items associated with your client's product, objections to the product, strengths of the product, and so on. If I can list it, I can see it, and often I can get something started.

The value of lists is that they give you things to think with; they help give expression to your selling ideas. A common error with early work is to rush past items, closing each up and going on, rather than letting them linger open. When you've made lists, you can suspend yourself in each word or phrase, let yourself nurture it for a while. What does it suggest? What images do you see? How might it lead to an idea?

Suspend judgment

> Be fearless around bad ideas. There is no such thing as a bad idea when concepting. Often the worst ideas are your tour guide to the best ones. It wouldn't be a cliché if it weren't so damned true. My ratio of bad to good is probably 50 to 1. I fill pages with bad. I build a monument to good on a trash heap of crap.
>
> —David Baldwin,
> executive creative director,
> McKinney & Silver

Get those half-ideas, bad ideas, and nonsense ideas out of your system and onto the page. All of them either imply transformations or let other, related ideas slip out that would have stayed hidden otherwise. The next time you're brainstorming in a group or simply working inside your own mind, notice how pervasive is your self-critical editor, the "Oh-never-mind-it-was-a-stupid-idea" self who kills thoughts before they even hit the floor. Suspend judgments. Be a critic later, not now. As Edward de Bono says in *Lateral Thinking*, a very good book about creativity:

> The purpose of thinking is not to be right but to be effective. Being effective does eventually involve being right but there is a very important difference between the two. Being right means being right all the time. Being effective means being right only at the end. . . . The need to be right all the time is the biggest bar there is to new ideas. It is better to have enough ideas for some of them to be wrong than to be always right by having no ideas at all.[4]

Use both lateral and vertical thinking

> I think brainstorming and coming up with concepts is like a muscle, and the more you work it, the better. We push our people to try to think of a lot of different ideas . . . so they don't feel that if something gets killed, they can't start again. You don't want people to think, Okay, this is it, this is the idea—and stop there.
>
> —Tracy Wong, principal, WongDoody

Creating ads is an alternating process of expansion and contraction. That is, you must be abundant and uncritical—generating a variety of approaches, a number of different starts and little thumbnails and half-ideas (de Bono calls this *lateral thinking*)—but then you must take the few that seem strong, the hot spots, and worry them into shape. You must exercise analytical skills—see what's wrong with a headline and fix it, prune extraneous images to their essentials, take that half-idea and really think it through, and so on (de Bono calls this logical, analytical process *vertical thinking*).

Accustom yourself to shifting between these two kinds of thought. Each needs the other: you must find ideas outside the boundaries of the obvious, but then you must make them work. As you think up your ideas and then sweat them through, notice how you alternate modes—dreaming and judging, inventing and refining, thinking loose and thinking tight, being generous and being cold-blooded.

Throughout exploratory thinking, you will continually wander as well as leap away from your strategy. This is inevitable. The trick is to keep your strategy/objective in your mind like a porch light while you wander around in the dark. When you feel too out-there-in-nowhere, come back to that light: *what, exactly, are you trying to communicate and to whom?* Always use the strategy as your centering device. Come back to it after exploring in the dark for that Big Idea.

Hang tough

> A good ad is a tricky, slippery, evasive beast that doesn't like to be caught, won't stand still, won't come out when called. A good ad is a greased pig when it comes time to put your hands on one. Masters of disguise, good ads sneak out of you in bars, the shower, dreams, even in advertising meetings, and run away to lost pages in your workbook or torn up sheets in office wastebaskets.
>
> —Mark Fenske,
> advertising creative director

Creativity doesn't arrive; it's earned. Don't get frustrated because a great idea simply will not come when called. Its elusiveness does not mean that you're "uncreative"; it simply means that good ideas require work and that problem solving resists shortcuts. Cultivate open-mindedness and relaxation when facing the "I-don't-have-an-idea-yet" state. Too many people feel anxious over this uncertainty and rush to end it with the relief of an idea, any idea. Learn to suspend yourself in a problem without being panicked by the sense of weightlessness that comes with no-idea-yet. It's not an easy skill to acquire, but as you solve advertising problems, going from nothing to something, you'll get accustomed to both the free-fall and the saving parachute of a good idea.

Bill Westbrook, then creative head at Earle Palmer Brown, commented on the difficulties, even at a major shop, of finding a good idea:

> There's basically a time line when the writer and art director sit down to do an ad. The first things they think of are all the puns and clichés and the really stupid answers that their psyche knows from somewhere else. Then they go through a period where they think they're hacks, they don't have a clue and they think they're worthless: "How did I get into this business?" And then they come out of that into getting very smart and focused on what they have to do. And they get a good idea. [If you rush yourself,] your answers can't

be as smart or as sophisticated as they should be because you haven't had time to be stupid yet. You still have to go through that time line to get the really good work.[5]

Find more than one solution

> You cannot dig a hole in a different place by digging the same hole deeper.
> —Edward de Bono, *Lateral Thinking*

Most people get a pretty good dose of analytical (vertical) thinking in their educations. They are taught to take things apart, label constituent parts, a-n-a-l-y-z-e (literally, "loosen throughout"). But one of the skills you'll need most in advertising is the opposite habit of mind: lateral thinking. Given an advertising problem, how many *different* solutions can you find—and how quickly? Are you able to see a problem from multiple points of view? How dissimilar are your ideas from each other? Can you leap around, or is each idea just a logical half-step away from the last?

Sometimes the best solution isn't arrived at logically. How, for example, might you sell a magic store? You could do something sensible like focus on the things in it or maybe on famous magicians of the past, but what about seeing magic from the other end—the person on whom it is practiced? Take a look at figure 13.2. Copywriter Mike Roe, who created these transit posters with art director partner Jason Wood, explains their development: "I usually try to create advertising that builds on a human truth. Something that most of us believe in. However, when we tried to find a logical connection on why adults should practice magic, we couldn't find any. Okay, we found some connections, but they were horribly boring. So, we threw out all the logical reasons and just had fun. And boom! We had a campaign of non-believers who were now pleading for their life back. The moral of the story is stay loose and stay open. You never know."[6]

Consider multiple points of view

One way to get stuck when creating ads is by continuing to consider only one person's point of view—usually the consumer's, the target audience for your client's product. But every scenario has lots of players, so take a little time and list them. If you're selling shoes, don't just limit yourself to the wearer. Consider, for example, feet themselves. A copywriter for Rockport created a clever campaign

13.2. A magic store is sold, not by considering magicians, magic tools, or the history of magic, but by thinking about the person on whom magic is practiced. What if it worked?

underneath the theme "Your feet have feelings, too." All the ads whimsically made consumers consider those poor guys below their ankles, and if you read enough of those ads, you almost began to feel that someone was living down there who deserved better treatment—not only a clever campaign but an effective one for shoes like Rockports. Other possible players? The surface you walk or run on: "Soften the sidewalks" was a campaign theme for another shoe company. How about the dog who jogs with you? Ever see that great Nike TV spot narrated from the visual and verbal point of view of the dog accompanying his owner on a jog? If you haven't, here's the copy, written by Mark Fenske. The dog is talking:

> I used to like it when she ran. She really didn't go much faster than now when she's walking, but she'd tire out quicker. And then we'd go home and she'd fall asleep in front of the TV. I

used to like that. I'd go sit on the chairs I'm not supposed to and she couldn't do nothing about it. Now, we go 3 miles a day, 10 miles on weekends. You know dogs were meant to sit in the sun and sleep. They ought to engrave that on the president of Nike's forehead.

Every advertising situation has more *points of view* than you are currently considering. Find them. Can you make an ad from a less-than-obvious participant, from an unusual point of view? Yes, you can (see figs. 13.3 and 13.4).

Restate the problem

One way copywriters get hung up is by resaying the problem without re-imagining it. They keep pounding on that same nail, that same strategic thought or problem-to-be-solved, and getting nowhere. Force yourself to say the problem another way; make yourself restate it in other terms. Often this

Some eat better than others.

If you're looking for a suit that's a bit more substantial, come into Britches of Georgetowne. Our suits are made with the finest of fabrics, exceptional workmanship and of course, meticulous tailoring. We're certain you'll find one that demonstrates your impeccable taste.

BRITCHES of Georgetowne

13.3. The argument isn't unusual—that this place sells great clothes—but the presentation is. Seeing clothes from the moth's point of view makes them all the more desirable.

HEY, CAN I JUST GET UNDER THERE FOR A SECOND?

Zoop is a nutrient-rich, manure-based compost produced from well-fed zoo animals. Use it as a fertilizer or soil conditioner and watch your garden grow.

13.4. Ad writers may think readily enough of the consumer who buys Zoop, the animals who make it, the flowers that benefit from it, but have writers ever thought of the guy who collects it? They have now. And this point of view puts the product's unique difference even more vividly in mind, don't you agree?

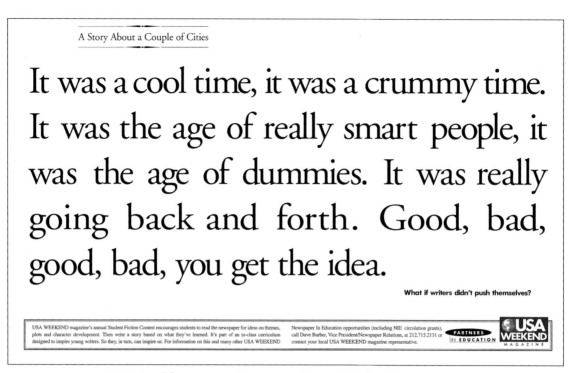

13.5. A call for entries to the magazine's annual Student Fiction Contest has fun butchering Dickens's classic opening of *A Tale of Two Cities.* But you can't have fun with Dickens unless you've read him.

will free you from the hole you're in. Goodby's famous "Got milk?" campaign happened only when its creators stopped thinking about milk as something unto itself and started thinking of it as half of a duo: it was always milk *and* something.

Paula Scher, a partner in Pentagram Design, spurs invention this way: "In my work, I always try to adopt the perspective of a first-time user. If I'm designing a package, a book, or a magazine, I approach it as if I've never heard of it before. If it's signage or an identity project, I approach it as if I were a foreigner and didn't speak the language."[7] When Scher was branding a hotel in New York City, among the signage she changed was the door tag that always says, "Do not disturb" (which is strictly hotel language). She changed it to "Go away," which is everyday people's language (at least in no-nonsense New York). This small but important gesture is an example of Scher seeing the situation freshly, noticing that the corporate voice had usurped our own.

Let the client solve the problem

This sounds flippant, but I mean it: listen closely when talking with your clients. They know their business better than you do, and often when they're

talking, a phrase or idea will slip out that, if you can hear it, will be what you should say. Or it will help you see what you should say. Ad writers try so hard to be clever that they often fail to hear the simple truth when it's spoken. Paula Scher comments again:

Creativity requires a certain optimistic naïveté. You have to develop simple solutions to complex problems and ask, "Why not?" My best ideas are usually sparked by some innocent observation or comment the client made in the initial meeting. I've found that if I don't get an idea immediately thereafter it's because I have too much information or I've done similar projects too many times before—and I have become jaded.[8]

Read, stay curious, try to know at least a little about a lot

Every really good creative person in advertising whom I have ever known has always had two noticeable characteristics. First, there was no subject under the sun in which he could not easily get interested—from, say, Egyptian burial customs to Modern Art.

Every facet of life had fascination for him. Second, he was an extensive browser in all sorts of fields of information. For it is with the advertising man as with the cow: no browsing, no milk.

—James Webb Young,
A Technique for Producing Ideas

It's hard to be creative without raw material. The more you've got, the better. Keep filling up with ideas and images from history, art, movies, music, travel, psychology, literature, fashion, photography, children's books, walks in the park, flea markets—you name it. The more strings you've got, the easier it is to pull on one. And the more things you know, the better your chances of getting two old things to combine in some new way—a common definition of creativity (see fig. 13.5).

And when you're tempted to settle for having created a so-so ad, one that could be better if you dug deeper, think about the following comment from Jay Chiat, co-founder of Chiat/Day. Perhaps you'd even like to put it up where you work as challenge and inspiration: "A lot is said in this business about excellence and order, but not enough about mediocrity and chaos. Too many ads don't intrigue, don't work. They are worse than forgotten—they are never even noticed. Forgettable is unforgivable."[9]

14 ▪ How to Write a Headline

Headlines are everything in my book. They serve as a direct window into how a copywriter thinks about a marketing problem. They tell me everything about their personality. If they have a sense of humor. If they're stealing lines from *CA* or *The One Show*, or worse yet, the Columbus ADDYs. If you can write good headlines, you'll always have a job in this business.

—Mark Hillman, principal, Method, Columbus, OH

It usually takes a hundred headlines to come up with one great one.

—Sally Hogshead, copywriter, co-founder, Robaire & Hogshead

Remember rule number one in writing a great headline: stay on strategy. Nothing works if you're saying the wrong thing. Once you know what to say, the problem becomes *how* to say it. Which is where rule number two comes in: pull up a chair and plan to stay a while. Sally's right: it'll take a lot of saying it wrong to say it right.

You're looking to generate energy among the words: create collisions, make sparks, get some drama going. You may think such energy is a mysterious affair, but there actually are ways to be clever, techniques writers have used for centuries to make language interesting all by itself—ways to write a line that, if it won't exactly hum down the corridors of time, will at least bounce around inside your readers' skulls for a day or two.

When you're sitting there writing those hundred headlines, you're running techniques through your head like beads on the rosary, whether you know it or not. You're turning phrases around, searching for synonyms, trying to say something paradoxically or in a hipper tone of voice, trying—one way or another—to get words to bump into each other and release some energy.

When you've written a bunch of headlines but haven't yet found magic, try the techniques in this chapter. I'm grateful for knowing them. You will be,

too. The more tricks you know, the more beads you've got.

Wrap it in a smile

He didn't like his facts bare and stark; he wanted them accompanied by comedy—you unwrapped the laugh and there was the fact, or maybe vice versa.

—James Thurber, explaining *New Yorker* editor Harold Ross's approach to the magazine's personality

Thurber's sense of how to write a *New Yorker* piece can work for ads just as easily as magazine articles. I'll show you what I mean. A coffeehouse in my neighborhood has a policy it wants me to know about, one I read as I walk through its door: "No pets allowed in the store, unless you bring a walrus, then who are we to say no?" It tells me something I can't do and gets me to smile about it, in the process communicating the vibe of the place: friendly. "No pets" would have just growled at me.

So wrap your idea in a smile, and watch it work better. Figure 14.1 is a great example of a headline putting a light human touch on a product benefit.

If you're selling a product fact or feature, make a little joke about it. As an example of a selling fact

THREE REASONS TO OWN A GOOD PAIR OF WINTER BOOTS.

1) THE. 2) DONNER. 3) PARTY.

Anyone who remained awake during history class would remember the Donner party. Those unfortunate emigrants *Chairman Gert Boyle* who, upon being stranded for the winter in the Sierra Nevada mountains, decided that friends weren't just good for talking to, they also made good eatin'. Pity they didn't have a few pairs of Silcov boots. With waterproof breathable Omni-Tech, a serious sole and Thermolite insulation for comfort down to −45°F, there's no better boot for long walks in the cold. So next time you attempt to cross a few states you may want to bring some along. That way if you happen to find yourself in a similar situation you'll be able to rethink your dinner plans. After all, the only thing that should taste like chicken, is chicken.

Columbia Sportswear Company.

14.1. "Keeps you warm in cold weather" wouldn't have been nearly as good, would it?

wrapped in a smile, consider the headline for a VOX vodka ad:

Most people can't tell the difference the fifth distillation makes. Let them drink their dirty little vodka.

See figure 14.2 for yet another example of a feature being sold with a smile.

Reward your reader

You don't have to write jokes to write good headlines. But you should reward your reader for his or her time. Lee Clow, chief creative officer, TBWA\ Chiat\Day, explains the value of doing so: "The essential rule is to always understand that your job is to create a bridge between the brand or the company you're talking about and the people you're trying to talk to. And that bridge better be rewarding. It better be likable, engaging, entertaining, charming, interesting, funny, fun. . . . You've got to create a bridge that, one, doesn't allow them to ignore it and, two, makes them feel good for the 30 or 60 seconds they've spent with that company or brand."[1]

The sections that follow discuss other techniques that can help you create that bridge, deliver that effective surprise. Let's see just what the possibilities are.

Parallelism

One of the workhorses of headlines (as well as slogans and body copy) is parallelism. The best way to define it is to show it.[2] Here are two sentences:

George liked Jean and often walked beside her on the way to school.

Jean was also accompanied sometimes to school by Ronald, who also liked her, but who often could be seen walking behind her.

A joke is the shortest distance between two people.
—Victor Borge, pianist and comedian

TWO ZIPPERS
UNZIPPED
MAKES YOU
COOL AND
COMFORTABLE.

THREE
MAKES YOU
A PERVERT.

Zippers have finally redeemed themselves. As evidence we present the Trekker Convertible Pant: Zip-on zip-off legs allow you to readily adapt to changing temperatures. In a matter of seconds you can convert pants to shorts or shorts to pants. Thus saving you the embarrassment of tromping about in your boxers. In addition to this adaptability, a number of features help make it the ultimate multipurpose pant. Nylon Dura Trek™ canvas offers protection, durability and style. An Omni-Dry™ wicking finish keeps you from steaming up inside. A purposeful cut with a gusseted inseam allows easy movement. And let's not forget the additional zipper up front to serve the usual purpose. Whatever that may be. *For the dealer nearest you call 1-800-MA BOYL. www.columbia.com* **◆Columbia** Sportswear Company.

14.2. The product feature sinks in better because it's going in with a smile.

Made shorter:

George liked Jean and often walked beside her on the way to school.

Jean was also accompanied by Ronald, who walked behind her.

Made *parallel:*

George liked Jean and walked beside her to school.

Ronald liked Jean and walked behind her to school.

Now you can actually *see* the meaning, can't you? Now you know who will win the girl, and who will worship from a distance. *Parallelism* is the notion that sentence elements identical in thought should be made identical in grammatical form, that form and function should coincide.

Parallelism involves repetition—often of words, but more important, of structure; and as you'll see, you can choose to repeat long structures or short ones. The point is to say similar things similarly. To do this, you'll need to realize which of your ideas are equivalent in meaning, and then express them in equivalent structures: a word for a word, a phrase for a phrase, a clause for a clause. Parallelism is to language what twins dressed alike are to childhood. Find your twins (or triplets or quads) and then put them in the same clothes.

For example, one of the most famous phrases in history is Julius Caesar's "I came, I saw, I conquered" (*Veni, vidi, vici*), and parallelism is what makes it so memorable. Had Caesar said, "I came, things were seen by me, and victory ensued," I wouldn't be quoting him now. (Nor would New York Jets football fans have used his phrase on signs celebrating quarterback Vinny Testeverde's great year in 1998: "Vinny, Vidi, Vici.")

Parallelism throws a sharp light on your ideas, clarifying your distinctions. It also makes an otherwise ordinary idea *sound* better, if only because it now has new clothes. It looks dressed up, cleaned up, sharp:

For the price of something small and ugly, you can drive something small and beautiful. (Fiat)

If an air freight company can't fly on the ground, it doesn't matter how fast it flies in the air. (Emery Air Freight)

How to keep food you can't finish from

becoming food you can't identify. (Sterilite food containers)

In persuading people they would win big at Mystic Lake Casino, this headline uses parallelism to joke about how money can change people:

Walk in a Democrat. Walk out a Republican.

Rockport justifies the price of its hiking boots:

We could make them less expensive. God could make rain less wet.

Notice that in addition to being parallel, the last two examples are *balanced:* the second parallel clause is about as long as the first one. The virtue of this technique is that it allows you to raise an issue on the one hand and complete it nicely on the other. You appear both reasonable and complete—what more need be said? Balance parallel structures when you want to add resonance and authority to the expression.

Parallelism is so powerful that even its absence is audible. Consider figure 14.3, an ad for United Hospital that encourages parents to talk to their teenagers and conveys the need to do so right in the headline. The poignance comes from readers' desire to hear that missing ending; its absence pulls them into the ad.

GO IN ONE WAY, COME OUT THE OTHER

Try reversing the elements of succeeding parallel constructions—go in one way and come out the other. Greek rhetoricians had a word for this figure of speech (*antimetabole*), but you can forget the name. Just remember the trick.

A famous example is JFK's "Ask not what your country can do for you, ask what you can do for your country." People hear how it goes out in one order and comes back in another—reversed, a mirror image—and they like it for having done so. Mae West, the sexy 1930s movie star, used the same structure to comic effect: "It's not the men in my life, it's the life in my men." This sort of cleverness lingers in the brain pan. Try it. If you hit on one that works, the structure will resonate with your readers, too.

We don't design ideas to fit machines. We design machines to fit ideas. (Oakley footwear)

14.3. Parallelism creates such strong expectations that readers can hear it even when it's not there, and that's the power of this headline.

Should your back fit the chair, or should the chair fit your back? (Steelcase/Coach office chair)

You shouldn't have to sacrifice everything you own to own a car that has everything. (Honda Civic EX Sedan)

Consider an example from a TV spot:

Voice-over: The only time he removes his car from the road is when he removes the road from his car.
Visual: A dusty BMW is washed, then immediately driven back out onto the road.

Parallelism can be visual, too. People like seeing things lined up as much as hearing them lined up ("two-fer" ads, discussed in chapter 17, are a kind of visual parallelism). Often you can "break" the last of a series of visual items for comic effect. Or complete parallelism with an image:

Headline: You can tell from the outside which Scotch they serve on the inside.
Visual: A mansion with its gates open (Johnnie Walker Black Label)

The double headline for an American Tourister luggage ad:

We've made some hard decisions. (photo of hard-shell suitcase)
We've made some soft decisions. (photo of soft suitcase)

But with parallelism you often do lose the verbal-visual synergy discussed earlier—that tension between headline and visual so many good ads employ. Instead you place tension within the language itself, relying on a kind of verbal-verbal synergy embedded in the paired parallel phrases:

Life is too short to get there too fast. (Cunard Lines)
If it weren't so tough out there, we wouldn't make it so tough in here. (Pace University—A Real Education for the Real World)

HOW TO THINK ABOUT PARALLELISM

Start by having something to say. You can't just stick mumbo-jumbo into parallel structures and expect an advertising miracle. As always, you need to create a real distinction, benefit, or promise.

How? Go to your list of benefits for the client's product and start looking for "two-fers," language that separates out into "this versus that," or "this plus that," or "this but not that," "either this or that," "not only this but also that," and so on. You're trying to take the benefits and deliver them in a one-two punch. And you're usually looking for some kind of opposition, a contrast to throw into relief.

Look at all the so-so headlines you've written. Can any of them be made parallel? Often it's not what you're saying that's wrong, it's how you're saying it. Throw ideas into parallel structures and see if they get better:

No: What's best about Holiday Inn is how there's never a bad surprise.
Yes: The best surprise is no surprise. (Holiday Inn)

No: A young person shouldn't get pregnant unless she's prepared to be a mother.
Yes: Because she's old enough to have a baby, doesn't mean she's old enough to be a mother. (visual of 14-year-old pregnant girl)
Tagline: Planned Parenthood. Abortion is something personal. Not political.

No: We developed our soft luggage to handle the difficulties of travel.
Yes: We didn't forget the hard side of travel when we developed our soft luggage.
Tagline: Beautiful on the outside. American Tourister on the inside.

Note that parallelism frequently relies on punning repetition, where the meaning of a repeated word or phrase changes:

Don't squander your disposable income on a disposable car. (BMW)
Stop handguns before they stop you. (Handgun Control)

See figure 14.4 for another example of punning repetition.

Parallelism is appropriate in a remarkably wide variety of contexts (and isn't even limited to two-ness, though that's a good place to start). But it's not infinitely appropriate, as this disparity indicates:

Vermont. A lot goes on when the skis come off.
A world of wonder. A world of value. (Mexico)

The Vermont line is vivid and memorable, the Mexico line flat and forgettable. The moral? If you don't have much to say, parallelism won't say much for you. A cliché is still a cliché, however gracefully concealed.

Parallelism is handy, if not indispensable. Besides shaping headlines, it can add clarity and punch to otherwise meandering or mushy sentences in copy. For more examples and discussion, turn to any grammar handbook and you'll find plenty of both.

Introduce misdirection: the kicker

> The basic two-step in humor is (1) to state some commonly acceptable problem, frequently with a cliché, and (2) in the last word or two change the expected ending to a surprise.
>
> —Melvin Helitzer,
> *Comedy Writing Secrets*

A lot of great headlines are essentially jokes: they have a surprising twist at the end, a stinger in their tail. This last word, phrase, or sentence—the punchline or *kicker*—surprises by subverting expectations. You get a sequence or line of thought going and then pull the rug out from under it. This is an ancient and honorable comedy trick often used by writers. It's a kind of verbal bait-and-switch technique that involves misdirection. People are led down one path, only to be surprised by a sudden switch in point of view or by an unexpected drop-off point. Here it is from a comedian (Woody Allen):

> It's not that I'm afraid to die, I just don't want to be there when it happens.[3]

From a journalist (Hunter Thompson):

> The music business is a cruel and shallow money trench, a long plastic hallway where thieves and pimps run free, and good men die like dogs. There's also a negative side.[4]

From ad guys:

> The wind is screaming in your ears. Or are those pedestrians? (Roces in-line skates)

> It's like Mom used to make. Just before she was arrested. (Cider Jack Hard Cider)

> $4 haircuts. Because you're worth it. (Moler Barber College)

> You know all those smug, wing-tipped, perfectly coiffed, $2000 suit–wearing, perfect-smile guys you see flying charter? Be one. (Corporate Express)

See figure 14.5 for examples of misdirection. And consider the following headline, which accompanied a visual of a woman working out with weights in a health club:

> Because power comes from within. Because strength gives me freedom. Because a cute

14.4. The surprising switch in the meaning of "freeze" creates the joke that powers the headline.

> guy just joined the gym and I don't think he's gay. (Marika)

The headline begins with a litany of accepted truths (clichés, used intentionally) of women's empowerment language as applied to so many products; then the last of the three is the kicker, the comic surprise that saves and makes the ad.

Although it doesn't have to, misdirection often uses parallelism to deliver the setup and punch line, to establish the pattern that the last item breaks—to the reader's surprise (see fig. 14.6). The Marika line above uses parallelism to encase the joke, and so do these:

> Headroom. Legroom. Bathroom. (Winnebago)

> Some devote their lives to charity. Others, to science. For us, it's cocktail weenies. (Hillshire Farms)

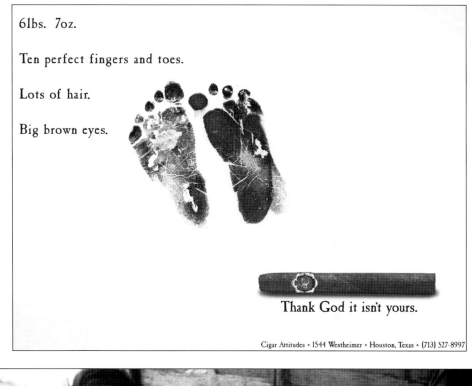

61bs. 7oz.

Ten perfect fingers and toes.

Lots of hair.

Big brown eyes.

Thank God it isn't yours.

14.5. In the Checkered Past Records ad, the kicker makes readers laugh and positions the company. In the Cigar Attitudes ad, the opening language, baby footprints, and congratulatory cigar argue for one interpretation; the kicker provides another.

The following headline for fishing reels surprises with its last item. The argument is a cliché ("good but cheap"), yet it's expressed freshly enough to stick:

> Overthought. Overdesigned. Overbuilt. Underpriced.

Kickers don't have to be funny. They can be quiet and serious. Just punch your readers at the end, as does this headline for Aveda's all-natural, no-preservative line of skin-care products:

> The ingredients in our products aren't purchased, procured or acquired. They're borrowed. From the earth.

The following cover headline, the most famous in *Rolling Stone's* history, accompanied a photo of the Doors' Jim Morrison:

> He's hot. He's sexy. He's dead.

A poster for the Violence Against Women Coalition has this headline:

> By age six, many little boys have already learned to tie their shoes, ride a bike and abuse their wives.

Periodic sentences (sometimes known as suspended sentences) can be used to deliver a kicker. A *periodic sentence* withholds an important part of its meaning until the end, piling up phrases and clauses while delaying the readers' ability to understand the whole thought. It makes them wait, and they will, as you build toward completing your meaning, as you build toward your climax. You can slide the kicker in right at the end, as does this ad's headline for L.A. Gear Jeanswear:

> Before he loves you for ever and ever 'til death do you part and brags to his friends about how smart you are and becomes the father of your children, he has to call back.

Kickers also work well for brochures. Set the kicker up on the front panel, pay it off inside. Greeting cards do this for a living.

You can use visuals to help create kickers. Write a headline that demands one visual, then surprise with another. Or show something that demands one headline, then give another (see fig. 14.7).

You might think the difficulty with kickers is that you have to be funny, and not everyone is. But part of being funny, or at least clever, is knowing *how* to do that, the forms that witticisms take. Just as you can ask yourself to express a thought in parallel form, you can ask yourself to try the repeat-and-vary principle of comic deflation. Set up expectations and break them. Besides, where is the ad as funny as Chris Rock or Jon Stewart? You need only to rise above common thought commonly expressed. You don't need to be a professional comedian. Just get your readers going one way, then surprise them—drop them off somewhere else.

Emphasize repetition

People like to hear things repeated, as any good songwriter or speechwriter knows. Sometimes simply *repeating a word or phrase* works all by itself. Repetition is what keys Gertrude Stein's memorable quip about why she left Oakland: "There is no there there." In the examples below, I write a blah version of a headline, then follow it with the real headline, so you can see how a repeated word or phrase gives it energy. Read my bad, fake headline and then the good, real one. Hear the difference?

Bad headline for Stanley Sharpshooter staple guns:

> You'll notice that our handle is easier to squeeze than the ones on other brands.

Good one:

> You'll notice a difference the first time you squeeze the handle. Starting with the fact that you can actually squeeze the handle.

Bad headline for PMS Escape:

> From now on, he won't seem so irritating.

Good one:

> From now on, if he's irritating you, it's because he's irritating.

Here are other headlines whose "pop" relies on repetition:

> No telephones. No computers. No boss. There sure as hell better not be no fish. [Photo of fishermen at water's edge] (Stoddard's, America's oldest fishing store)

> A day without coffee is like a day without coffee. (Caribou Coffee)

14.6. The parallel items couldn't be more brief; nice surprise at the end.

Why your all terrain shoes should come from a place with all terrains. (Dexter shoes, made in Maine)

Many repetitions of word or phrase rely on punning (even the ones above rely on slightly different meanings in the second use of the word, so they're puns, though quiet ones). You're changing the meaning of the word:

Women run companies. Women run households. Women run nations. Women run. [Visual of woman jogging] (Insport apparel for women)

The recipe for a great dish starts, surprisingly, with a great dish. (CorningWare)

A Lava soap print campaign showed dirty hands becoming clean hands, with this theme line: "Leave work at work." Again, Lava is punning on "work," meaning the grime the first time and the job the second. I like it. See figure 14.8 for another example of word repetition.

During World War II many Brits were angry at the special treatment and status of the Yanks who came to England. They said the Yanks were "overpaid, oversexed, and over here." It was said that the problem with the Brits was they were "underpaid, undersexed, and under Eisenhower." Both state-ments surprise by switching the meaning of the last word in the sequence.

Use opposition

> In a sense the whole point of language is to give separate units that can be moved around and put together in different ways.
> —Edward de Bono, *Lateral Thinking*

Copywriters sit down, after filling up on product information, and play around with words, trying to get them to interact, trying to spark something, create collisions. As a writer you are constantly moving words around to get them to release their power.

Look at language you find interesting and notice how often oppositions are doing the work. The following title of a chapter about grammar in a how-to-write book actually sounds interesting because of opposition: False Rules and What Is True about Them. The title of a book about memoir, *Inventing the Truth*, catches the reader's attention with an apparent conflict between making things up and remembering them. The following sentence from David Denby's *New Yorker* review of the movie *The Italian Job* gets its strength from opposition: "Yet even though everything in this summer spectacle moves—heavy safes and trucks fall through the air —not much really happens."[5] The slogan for Perdue chicken hooks the reader with opposition: "It takes

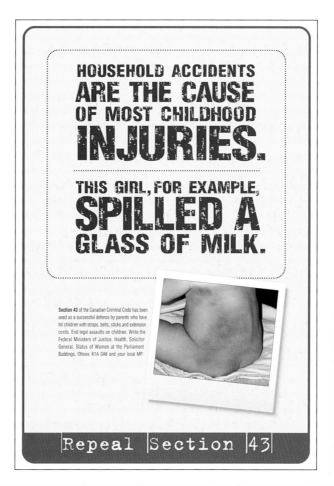

14.7. One of these ads is funny and the other deeply disturbing, but both use the interplay between headline and visual to generate misdirection. The kicker in the Repeal Section 43 ad, the visual, is set up by the headline. The kicker in the VW ad, the headline ("Hey, there's a black one"), is set up by the visual.

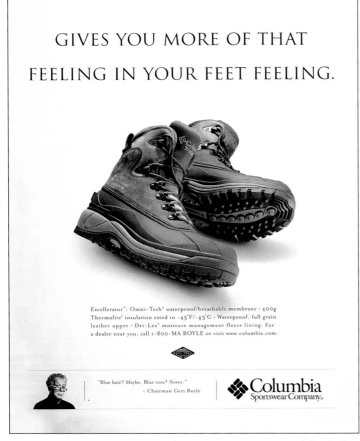

GIVES YOU MORE OF THAT
FEELING IN YOUR FEET FEELING.

Excellerator™: Omni-Tech® waterproof/breathable membrane · 400g
Thermolite® insulation rated to -45°F/-43°C · Waterproof, full grain
leather upper · Dri-Lex® moisture management fleece lining. For
a dealer near you, call 1-800-MA BOYLE or visit www.columbia.com.

"Blue hair? Maybe. Blue toes? Never."
- Chairman Gert Boyle

Columbia
Sportswear Company®

14.8. It's amazing what repetition can accomplish. Without it, you've got this piece of nothing: "Gives you more feeling in your feet."

a tough man to make a tender chicken." So, too, does this line from comedian/actor Dan Aykroyd about his friend John Belushi, whose self-destructive excesses eventually killed him: "He was a good man, but a bad boy."

GET WORDS TO COLLIDE

Play around with all sorts of collisions between words: head-on, at an angle, tail-light to front bumper—you name it. Make some noise.

Circuit City (an electronics retailer) could have sold big-screen TVs with this lame headline:

The bigger the TV, the better.

But it had the wit to write this instead:

There are no TVs too big. Only rooms too small.

A trade ad for Cigna corporate insurance showing an employee's face in pain could have said:

Is ensuring against employee disability a problem for your corporation?

But the copywriter did better:

Why should his backache be your biggest headache?

This headline uses opposition to create surprise:

Before it leaves the factory, it gets the once over. Twice. (Honda Accord)

See figure 14.9 for another example of opposition.

An ad for a healthcare system encourages awareness of genetic health risks with succinct opposition:

You may not choose the same path as your father. But your body might.

Another headline puts numbers in opposition:

In a world that can't wait 24 hours for a package, there's a place that still waits 18 years for a whisky. (Glenlivet)

SAY WHAT CANNOT BE

A related kind of opposition is *paradox*. Have you discovered something in your product's story that just doesn't seem possible, something that hooked you with its incongruity or unlikelihood and might hook your target audience, too?

Beat your wife and your son will most likely go to prison. (Milwaukee Women's Center)

That's a powerful headline because it expresses, as a paradox, the truth that children often learn violence at their father's knee.

The following headline, also for the Milwaukee Women's Center, is an example of paradox using the kicker format. The ending surprises because of preceding misdirection:

He threatened her. He beat her. He raped her. But first he married her.

Can you express your selling argument *as* a paradox? Lots of times you don't find a paradox as much as you create one:

Most tennis balls are lucky to last 3 sets. This one has lasted 14 years. [Photo of a tennis ball] (Wilson was advertising its continuing sponsorship of the U.S. Open.)

Is it possible to specialize in things that haven't happened yet? (Credit Suisse First Boston, financial services)

You can't see nematodes, but you can make them disappear. (Counter, an agricultural pesticide)

Heroin can end your life. Even while you're still in it. (Partnership for a Drug-Free America)

See figure 14.10 for two more examples of paradox created by copywriters.

GET PAST THE OBVIOUS

Is it possible to be too predictable and Adland-y with oppositions? Sure. Headlines like "Big savings on small appliances" or "Tomorrow's solutions today" or "Get more, pay less!" are junk. But this headline for a Toyota SUV isn't: "The true measure of a sport utility vehicle is not where it can go. But rather, where it has been." Neither is this headline for BMW: "Foot goes down. Pulse goes up."

Highlight omission

> I always listen for what I can leave out.
>
> —Miles Davis

Ad writers are familiar with visual cropping: show just part of the image—the hand rather than the whole arm, the eyes rather than the whole face, a slice of the product or scene rather than all of it. The ad gains power through its immediacy and simplicity. And, most important, it gets people involved. They have to do some work themselves: they have to complete the image.

You can do the same thing with headlines: cut them down, shave them off, start them in the middle, stop them before the end—one way or another, crop their completeness. Keep in mind the timeless comment by the eighteenth-century French writer Voltaire: "The secret of being a bore is to tell everything."[6]

ANSWER QUESTIONS THAT HAVEN'T BEEN ASKED

Recently I saw a person working out at a health club and wearing a college T-shirt that said on the front "Duke Crew" and on the back "I can't. I have crew." That line is something crew members say all

LIFE IS MEASURED IN YEARS.
BUT WHEN YOU LIVE WITH CANCER,
IT'S DIVIDED INTO MOMENTS.

Altru
THE NEW ALTRU CANCER CENTER

14.9. Opposition provides the poignance and power of this headline.

the time because they're dedicated to the team and its arduous training. It's a tough-but-we-love-it bonding statement. It's also the answer to a question people haven't asked. They have to back up and supply the question themselves ("Want to go shopping? To a club? To a movie?"), and in doing so they feel the team's commitment and drive. A cool T-shirt. Omitting the questions, the way this T-shirt does, can pull people more quickly into an ad; they're involved before they know it.

One ad in a Winston cigarette print campaign presents a hip young gal looking right at the reader

FORTY-TWO PERCENT OF ALL MURDERED WOMEN
ARE KILLED BY THE SAME MAN.

Each day women are beaten to death by their husbands or boyfriends. Just as frightening,
each day neighbors just like us make excuses for not getting involved. For information about how
you can help stop domestic violence, call 1-800-END-ABUSE.

THERE'S **NO** EXCUSE
for Domestic Violence.

Family Violence
Prevention Fund

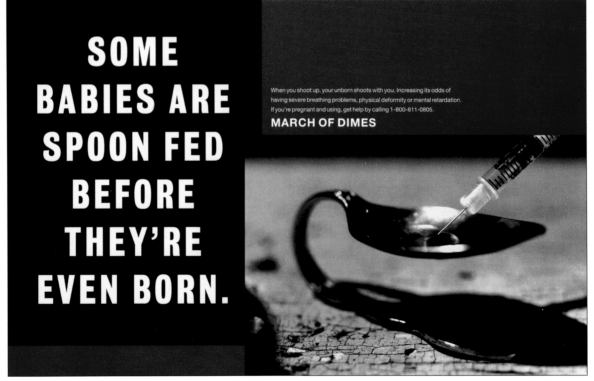

SOME BABIES ARE SPOON FED BEFORE THEY'RE EVEN BORN.

When you shoot up, your unborn shoots with you. Increasing its odds of
having severe breathing problems, physical deformity or mental retardation.
If you're pregnant and using, get help by calling 1-800-811-0805.

MARCH OF DIMES

14.10. Paradox drives both headlines.

and saying, "Yeah, I have a tattoo. And no, you can't see it." (Winston's slogan: "Leave the bull behind.") Again, readers are pulled in more quickly by finding her answer—to a question they haven't asked—already in their face.

An outdoor board for Crystal Springs bottled water shows a picture of the Loch Ness monster with this headline: "Because you wouldn't believe what's in other waters." By assuming readers have already asked "Why drink bottled water?" or "Why drink Crystal Springs bottled water?," the headline jump-starts their involvement. (It's also a good joke, surprising them by switching the meaning of "waters.") Figure 14.11 is another example of an ad kick-starting itself by answering an unanswered question.

IMITATE SPEECH RATHER THAN WRITING

People talk in truncated, fragmented, often urgent ways. So make your ads sound the way people talk. For example, an ad announcing a Marilyn Monroe U.S. postage stamp could have had this headline beside the stamp's image of the gorgeous star: "She's so beautiful that you almost want to lick the front of the stamp rather than the back." But the copywriter had the good sense to jump in more quickly: "The back. You're supposed to lick the back." Another good example is the title of a profile in *Texas Monthly* of actor Bill Paxton, on the verge of making it big: "Bill, due." Here the omissions reinforce the pun.

MAKE THE CONSUMER DO SOME OF THE WORK

Don't discuss the product; discuss what happens after the consumer uses it or what precedes or necessitates it (see fig. 14.12).

START IN THE MIDDLE

If the product's story often elicits objections or comments, answer that unspoken thought in your headline. Leap ahead a little bit. Don't start at the beginning of the conversation; intersect it deeper in. A clever campaign to get young people to vote showed moments in their lives when they'd made other choices easily enough—one ad showed an empty pizza box, with the olives in a little pile. The headline on all the ads: "See, you do have an opinion." Notice how the headline jumped ahead, as though a conversation had already been started.

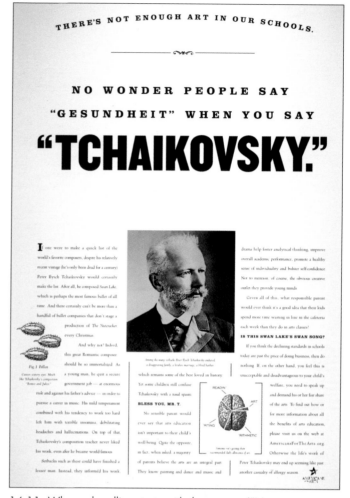

14.11. When a headline starts with the answer ("No wonder people . . . "), as this one does, readers involve themselves in the ad to find out the question.

Be specific: Find the corner of 4th and Pulaski

> I've never been much for the vague, planetary, philosophic school of songwriting. I'm from the start-with-the-detail school.
> —Warren Zevon, rock musician

Elsewhere I've argued that if you've got an interesting fact about your client's product, you should use it. Nothing cuts through the crap and clutter of advertising better than a real, true fact about the product. Nothing is more persuasive. But even if you're being general, try making up facts to express that general point. Replace generality with specifics.

Let's say that you're encouraging people to license their pet. You could show a picture of a bewildered cat against a white background and say, "License your pet because it might get lost and not

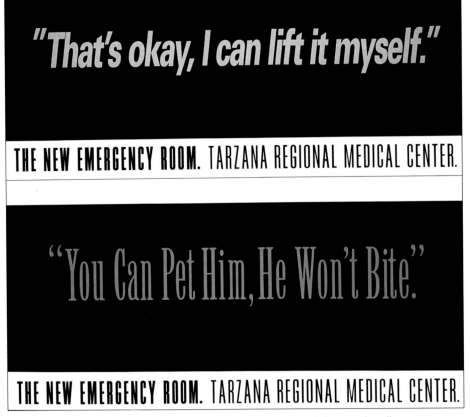

"That's okay, I can lift it myself."

THE NEW EMERGENCY ROOM. TARZANA REGIONAL MEDICAL CENTER.

"You Can Pet Him, He Won't Bite."

THE NEW EMERGENCY ROOM. TARZANA REGIONAL MEDICAL CENTER.

14.12. Since the best pictures are often in our head, let your headline create them. I'd rather imagine the calamities surrounding these headlines than read them or see them, wouldn't you?

be able to find its way home." But imagine describing that scenario specifically (see fig. 14.13). Even though your readers were probably never lost in quite that spot, the specifics perform their miracle: they stand in for, even help readers *see*, their own lost places. Plus the headline pulls their pet more closely to them, relating its problem to one of theirs when they were young.

In figure 14.13 the copy flows directly from the headline, continuing the specific recollection of being lost as a child (notice the sweet, tight tie-in of the first line):

Or was it the vast expanse of the Small
Electrics department? After that experience,
they pinned a name and address on you.
Remember? . . . For your free pet licensing
kit, call the Wisconsin Humane Society . . .

Look at figure 14.4, another ad from the campaign. Its headline uses the kicker: it gets a sequence going and then alters it, to the readers' surprise. What's

important in both figures, though, is that the headlines are specific. That's what makes them memorable.

Almost any advertising problem can be solved with specifics if you think into it enough. Would you find this headline memorable: "Are you spending more on your kid's shoes than on her helmet?"? Of course not. But you might remember the one shown in figure 14.15.

The following example is one more instance of being specific even if you're making it up. In a Dewar's scotch whisky ad, a beautiful young woman looks right at the reader, beside this headline:

Trust us, she does not want to hear the story
about you and your friend Danny doing
watermelon shooters in Daytona.

The general argument is, "Grow up. Get the attention of adult women. Drink Dewar's." But the specifics of the headline conjure up two immature kids. Generalities would conjure up nothing.

Dare to pun

Common advice about writing headlines is never to use puns. A *pun*, of course, is a figure of speech in which a word means more than one thing; people hear and respond to the double meaning. If someone said, "I'm dying for a cigarette," people might say, "Yes, you are," responding to the unfortunate double meaning in "dying." John Deere's slogan, "Nothing runs like a Deere," is a double pun. People hear the two meanings of both "run" and "Deere"— "run" like an animal and "run" like a machine; "deer" as in animal and "Deere" as in brand of machine. Kind of complicated for a simple phrase, but it works.

The criticism against puns in headlines is that, first, they're dopey (puns are often called the lowest form of wit); second, they celebrate themselves more than sell the product; and, third, they're lazy. Puns are among the first things copywriters think up when trying to solve an advertising problem, the argument goes, so they should be bypassed for something earned with more sweat. Puns replace further thought; they're something catchy that will do in the absence of a better idea.

Ironically, the people who tell copywriters to lay off puns are often the same people who judge advertising for competitions, and if you open up an annual of the year's best ads, you'll find that puns abound. The judges are smart people who know a good ad when they see one. It's just that they're moving down those tables fast as judges, the same way most people are moving across ads fast as consumers. Puns work fast; they quickly do a lot of what ads must do (capture attention, lodge in the brain, communicate some fairly simple product virtue).

Puns aren't bad. *Bad* puns are bad ("A science fiction offer that's out of this world!" or "Do your cookies crumble? Ours don't."). I think what the critics really mean is: don't use *bad* puns; use good ones. Don't make readers groan; make them smile. And connect your pun to the selling argument.

How to pun

1. Use one word, but surprise readers with its double meaning. Let it straddle two meanings or contexts or uses. Consider the following headline from Jewelry Depot: "A diamond is formed by thousands of tons of pressure. And if you've ever bought one, you know what that feels like." The surprise comes in

14.13. The miracle of specifics: they put the reader right there.

14.14. Would "She can sit. She can speak. What she can't do is find her way home" be as good?

using "tons of pressure" with two different meanings, one literal, one metaphorical.

Two recent Volvo slogans, "Drive safely" and "For life," both make the brand's safety argument with puns. "Drive safely" means "drive carefully" and also "drive a car that will help you avoid injury." "For life" implies both long-term loyalty and the avoidance of injury or death. Another example is Tabu Lingerie's "It's better than nothing." The double meaning? It's better than not buying anything; it's more exciting than simple nudity. See figures 14.16–14.18

14.15. Inventing numbers gives this argument punch. Putting them into opposition helps, too.

for other good examples of headlines that know how to pun.

Double meanings often work most powerfully when you jump categories. In other words, get way off the usual meaning of the word. The ad shown in figure 14.19 puns on the advertising buzz-word "honest." People are always being told about an "honest" this, an "honest" that: an honest scale, an honest beer. Hey, okay, an honest beer. What would "a brutally honest beer" say? You'd be surprised.

A paper campaign punned on the paper's printing-capability claim that "Everything turns out better on Domtar paper" by rewriting famous novels and plays so they did indeed "turn out better" (see fig. 14.20). Funny and memorable.

2. Repeat a word, but change its meaning.

We raise questions that raise eyebrows. (*Harper's* magazine)

The shortest distance between two points isn't the point. (New Balance running shoes)

A novel concept in a New York hotel room: room. (The Waldorf Towers)

3. Substitute a word that sounds like the expected word. Major League Baseball's Col-

orado Rockies use the slogan "Baseball with an Altitude," in which readers hear both "attitude" and its clever substitution. Bridgewaters restaurant, which caters large events, announces, "Eat. Drink. Be married." See figure 14.21, as well as the two headlines below, for more good examples of effective word substituting.

Didn't sleep last flight? (British Airways)

Think someone under the table. (*Economist* magazine)

4. Pun later off a word used earlier; that is, pun off a meaning inside an earlier word.

The new Chrysler New Yorker has a huge trunk. But it doesn't come with a lot of Detroit baggage. ["Baggage" is a pun made possible by the preceding "trunk."]

You can't run away from your problems. But you can wade. [Both the extension of a cliché and a pun.] (Stoddard's fishing store)

Want to rekindle an old flame? Try a blowtorch. [Visual of red lingerie in white space] (Tabu Lingerie)

5. Let the picture be half of the pun. Pun off the visual. Figures 14.22 and 14.23 illustrate

Fish are cold blooded. You can be too.

The Sigma 2200 reel: anodized aluminum, machine tooled brass and stainless steel. Take no prisoners. *Shakespeare* SINCE 1897

14.16. The switch in the meaning of "cold blood-ed"—for fish a metabolic state, for people a killer instinct—is the surprise that makes the ad.

Hundreds of chairs. And occasional tables.

Fleetham
FURNISHINGS & DESIGN
Hennepin Avenue at Lake Street

14.17. Possibly my favorite headline, ever. I laugh every time I see it. A wonderful pun on the double meaning of "occasional."

OF ALL THE REASONS TO BUY A VOLVO, YOU'VE PROBABLY GIVEN BIRTH TO A FEW YOURSELF.

14.18. One meaning of "given birth" is probably sitting in the back seat right now.

The cartilage in your nose never stops growing.

A BRUTALLY HONEST BEER.

14.19. "Honest" has been given another meaning, a literal one. Other "brutally honest" headlines in the campaign: "Nearly 80% of your brain is water" and "General Douglas MacArthur's mother dressed him in skirts."

the double-whammy that a good ad can achieve when the visual is an essential part of the pun.

As a writer, you're trying to generate energy. That's why (good) puns are good. They're energetic by definition: you've said two or more things in one spot; the language has an extra jolt right there. The poet Ezra Pound said, "Great literature is simply language charged with meaning to the utmost possible degree,"[7] and although one pun is a long way from great literature, it does charge the language with (double) meaning, making it richer and denser, giving it more stopping power. Shakespeare loved a good pun. So did Joyce. So should you.

Twist or extend a cliché

> If you can't say something good about someone, sit here by me.
>
> —Alice Roosevelt

Clichés, which are overused ideas and expressions, are bad and should be avoided like the . . . well, you know the next word, don't you? And that's the problem. Everyone knows the next word in a cliché, so your chance for "effective surprise" is zero, unless the next word isn't what people expect. Then you may have something. So clichés *can* work in advertising, drawing people in with their familiarity but surprising them with your witty alterations of the

How to Write a Headline / 169

and Juliet walked into the tomb to find Romeo, lying cold and still on the stone. "What's here?" she asked, knowing all too well the answer. Carefully, she bent and kissed her lover, then picked up his dagger and prepared to plunge it into her own heart. And at that moment Romeo awoke, looked at Juliet and said, "Oh this darn narcolepsy. I fell asleep again, didn't I?" And Juliet put down the dagger and they ran out to discover that their families had reconciled and were playing volleyball and lawn darts together and had bought the happy couple a brand new utility vehicle.

The End

EVERYTHING TURNS OUT BETTER ON DOMTAR PAPER

14.20. *Romeo and Juliet* turns out a lot better than you remember.

TASTE ONE TO KNOW ONE.

Chipotle

GOURMET BURRITOS & TACOS.

14.21. Makes me smile. Makes sense, too.

expected language. Take that cliché and change it, extending the line or replacing something in there with something else, something surprising but appropriate, just as Alice Roosevelt, gossip-loving Washington socialite, did by altering her cliché's expected ending (". . . then don't say anything at all"). Drop your readers in a new place, rather than the old one. Surprise them.

Harvest clichés that might work with your client's product. Where to find them? There are books of clichés and Web sites that list them. Find ones particular to your client's product, brand, category, or commercial circumstance. Or think more broadly. What part of your scenario or your audience's mindset could you use? What clichés best express the benefit?

How to tweak a cliché

1. Take the cliché literally. Often clichés contain a dead metaphor, "dead" because people no longer hear it. Surprise your audience by taking the metaphor seriously. Bring it back to life. Help your audience hear it again:

> Opportunity is knocking. Or is that just your knees? (Investor's Business Daily) [*Slogan:* Don't read it. Use it.]

> Opportunity no longer knocks. These days, it darts past the door before you can even react. (SAS e-Intelligence, a data access service)

See figures 14.24 and 14.25 for more examples of clichés whose literal meaning works to maximum effect in an unexpected context.

2. Substitute a new word or phrase for something in the cliché. Follow Alice Roosevelt's example: change the ending, change a word or phrase, change something. Get your audience's attention again:

> The big engine that could. Introducing the SLK 320. (Mercedes-Benz)

> See how the other two-thirds lives. (Seattle Aquarium)

See figure 14.26 for another example of substitution.

Write slogans and theme lines

Learn to write great theme lines. Nothing makes a creative person more marketable than the ability to write the "phrase that pays."

—Phil Dusenberry, chairman,
BBDO, North America

Lots of products use *slogans* (sometimes called *tag lines* or *theme lines*). These usually run alongside the logotypes (as well as in voice-overs and on supers in TV spots) and state the essence of the campaign, brand, or company—memorably, advertisers hope. Slogans stand by themselves as language, as a selling argument. They're purely verbal in this way, not requiring a visual. Certainly people remember the good ones, and they do help place the brand, quickly identifying its value in consumers' lives.

Slogans are portable pieces of persuasion, little chunks of language people carry around in their heads (Nike's "Just do it," Apple's "Think different"). They're durable—often meant to last for years, if not decades. Motel 6's "We'll leave the light on for you" has identified the chain since 1986. "Nothing runs like a Deere," the slogan for John Deere, a farm and lawn equipment company, has run since the mid-1970s. "I ♥ New York" and "Virginia is for lovers" have been ubiquitous state tourism slogans for over twenty-five years.

Many ad writers recommend distilling a product's selling idea into a slogan or theme line whenever you advertise anything to focus your thinking, whether you end up using the line or not. Writing slogans also teaches you, in a compressed form, many copywriting lessons that longer exercises can obscure. As a copywriter, you'll often be asked to give short but interesting names to all sorts of things: presentations, exhibitions, events, and so on. Copywriters are in many ways phrasemakers. For all these reasons, writing slogans is good practice.

It's worth noting, however, that a number of important advertising people think slogans aren't worth the trouble. They argue that it's impossible to say anything in a few words, and that too many slogans sound too much alike—interchangeable claptrap. And since marketing circumstances change more and more rapidly, trying to write a line that

14.22. Write a pun based on the visual.

14.23. The can opener is a double pun: Warhol is famous for painting soup cans, and the museum is "opening."

YOU CAN'T SQUEEZE BLOOD FROM A TURNIP. HEY, YOU'RE NOT A TURNIP, ARE YOU?

1.877.BE.A.HERO   THE BLOOD CENTER

DONATE BLOOD

14.24. Everyone has heard this saying, but who has ever gone further with it?

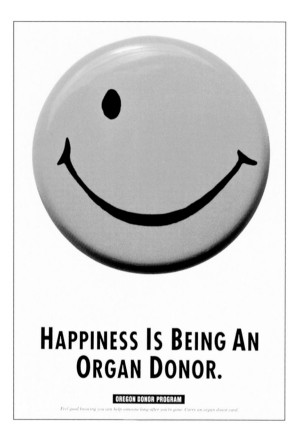

HAPPINESS IS BEING AN ORGAN DONOR.

OREGON DONOR PROGRAM

Feel good knowing you can help someone long after you're gone. Carry an organ donor card.

14.25. Clichés can be visual, too. This worn-out image is being taken literally, and that has made it powerful again.

will last for decades is a fool's errand. These are valid arguments. But I like slogans—good ones, that is. If you have a chance to do some work for your client's product, why not take it?

MAKE THEM SMART, NOT JUST PRETTY

Slogans are often clever—rhyming, punning, or in some way using wit to create a rhetorical flair that makes them memorable. Slogans are the art of the well-made phrase. But their real job is to be an ad in miniature: make the case for the product, position it relative to its competition, justify it. In short, more than being clever, slogans need to be smart.

For example, one of the great slogans was Campbell's "Soup is good food." But at first it didn't seem so great—it wasn't witty, it was all monosyllables, and its promise seemed banal. What it really was, however,

was durable and right on a smart selling strategy. The monosyllables helped emphasize soup's simplicity—its basicness—and the message positioned soup (in case people might think otherwise) as real food itself, not just an accessory to a meal. Smart. But not glittery. The Campbell's slogan illustrates the difficulty in distinguishing a good line from a merely glittery one. So be thorough and thoughtful when creating and critiquing slogans. Hold them up to the light. Turn them this way, then that.

The Campbell's line redefined soup in a positive way, and the strategy is fundamental. Often consumers need to be shown that products aren't just regular, boring, ordinary things, but are instead much more. Use slogans to elevate products in consumers' minds, make them see these products in the best possible terms. Bally's health spa slogan,

"You don't just shape your body, you shape your life," is a classic example of this principle.

It's no surprise that good slogans incorporate many of the techniques good headlines do. In fact, if you're writing a bunch of headlines, chances are you've written some slogans, too. Headlines and slogans aren't always interchangeable—slogans need to be short, must stand alone, and should be memorable and durable—but they do share techniques.

One way to get the knack of writing slogans is to run a number of them through your head. You'll see how similar their purpose often is and how variously it can be expressed. Do this enough, and you'll notice patterns.

How to think up slogans

1. Elevate the product. It's not just one more damned thing. Look for the highest possible benefit. Climb that ladder:
- Federal Express: "It's Not Just a Package. It's Your Business." See how FedEx raises the stakes? This slogan typifies the fundamental strategy, not only of slogans, but of advertising itself: claim the highest possible meaning for the product, assert its importance to life well lived.
- Maxwell House Instant Coffee has called itself "Instant Sophistication," perhaps as overt a statement of selling strategy as you'll ever see.
- "BMW. The Ultimate Driving Machine." You can't climb higher than this.
- People aren't wasting their time watching the TV game show *Jeopardy*. They're having "The most fun you can have with your brain."

2. Differentiate it from the competition.
- New Balance: "Shoes that fit better perform better." New Balance sells itself as the only athletic shoe that comes in widths. Its slogan *is* its position. Tight parallelism, too.
- "Beef—Real Food for Real People." An attempt to downplay the health negatives of beef by insulting the bean-sprout eaters and flattering the beef eaters.
- MasterCard: "It's more than a credit card. It's smart money."
- Altoids: "The curiously strong mints." Made me curious. You too?

3. Don't sell features; sell benefits.
- Little Debbie snacks: "Unwrap a Smile."

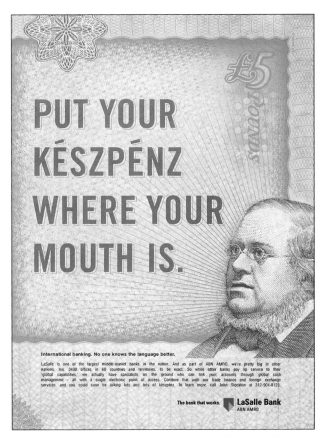

14.26. The bank announces its international services by taking money clichés and tweaking them into other currencies. Cheeky. This ad doesn't talk like banks talk, and that can be good. Another headline in the campaign: "Show me the xianjin."

- VW: "Drivers wanted." It's not just for getting around, it's for *driving*.
- Braun shaver theme line: "We thought about shaving so you could think about something else."
- Black & Decker: "How Things Get Done."
- Marshalls, a discount retailer of brand-name clothing: "What will you find this time?" Marshalls realizes that bargain shoppers are really on a treasure hunt.
- For another slogan that looks beyond mere things to what they might become, see figure 14.27.

4. Lean it up against something else.
- Downtown Cincinnati is on the Ohio River. How can businesses across the bridge cash in? Here's how: "Northern Kentucky: The Southern Side of Cincinnati."
- A poster advertising Harold Pinter's little-known play *The Birthday Party* clarifies

GO BUILD SOMETHING.™

14.27. Slogans that promise (in this case, demand) a benefit help people see the big picture.

GOODWILL

Good clothes. Good prices. Good cause.℠

14.28. Truth in parallel form.

things: "Part Hitchcock, part 'I Love Lucy,' part film noir, part vaudeville."

• The National Pork Board, realizing that people weren't eating pork, allied itself with ever-popular chicken: "Pork: the other white meat."

5. Find the human truth. Say what people are thinking.

• Harvey Hardware: "Sometimes it is the tools." Usually the *homeowner* is the problem with home repairs. But not always.

• Rogaine: "Stronger than heredity." For men worried about losing their hair, that *is* the hope, isn't it?

• Contemporary American Theatre Company's slogan makes fun of most people's reluctance: "Live theatre. It won't kill you."

6. Try parallelism.

• Round-Up weed killer: "No mercy. No pity. No weeds." Misdirection: the last item surprises and makes the point.

• NicoDerm CQ stop-smoking aid: "The power to calm. The power to comfort. The power to help you quit."

• Moen (well-designed faucets, sinks, etc.): "Buy it for looks. Buy it for life."

• Continental Airlines: "Work Hard. Fly Right."

• Radio Shack: "You've got questions. We've got answers." This line stakes out a position in a crowded field—Radio Shack as demystifier of technology, a place with not just hardware but help.

• *Survivor* TV show: "Outwit. Outplay. Outlast."

• Las Vegas: "What happens here, stays here." Would "What happens here won't be

brought up later " work? The succinct power of parallelism and repetition wins out.

• Figure 14.28 shows how parallelism is often lying there waiting to be invoked; here it helps you take advantage of a brand's name.

7. Try opposition.

• The new Thom McAn: "Your feet won't believe your eyes."

• Audio Books: "It's a great way to read. Just listen." Not only true, but it makes reading sound easier. Good benefit.

• Crunch fitness clothing: "Outerwear for your inner self."

• MasterCard: "There are some things money can't buy. For everything else, there's Master-Card."

• Air France: "Making the sky the best place on earth."

8. Try parallelism *and* opposition.

• Sony PlayStation: "Live in your world. Play in ours."

• MassMutual Financial Group (investment and insurance): "You can't predict. You can prepare."

• Yamaha watercraft: "Solid thinking for a liquid world."

• Bigg's superstores: "Where men who hate to shop love to shop."

• Nynex yellow pages: "If it's out there it's in here."

• Figure 14.29 demonstrates how parallelism can throw a spotlight on the problem-solution scenario.

9. Tweak, twist, or add to a cliché.

• Slogan for Outdoor Products USA on a student's backpack: "Life is a journey. We'll help you pack."

LIVING BRINGS IT IN. WE TAKE IT OUT.^{SM}

14.29. If you want to stress an opposition, nothing does it better than parallelism.

• Caribou Coffee: "Life is short. Stay awake for it." Caribou Coffee invigorates the cliché by adding a joke.

• Fatbrain.com (books and software for Webheads): "Because great minds think a lot." Here the line twisted is "Great minds think alike."

• The *Village Voice*: "Not America's Favorite Paper." Reversing the Adland cliché that this, that, or the other thing is "America's favorite."

• See figure 14.30 for the reinvigoration of another cliché.

10. Use metaphor.

• The American Floral Marketing Association updated the original FTD slogan "Say it with flowers" by extending the metaphor: "Increase your vocabulary. Say it with flowers."

• MET-Rx (high-performance food supplements) has used "Food has evolved" and "Engineered nutrition." Both metaphors (one organic, one technical) elevate the product by making it more than, better than, food. Bringing in language from other contexts can change the way consumers see your client's product.

• Bell helmets: "Courage for your head."

11. Invoke the Rule of Threes. I can't explain why, but a whole lot of things come in threes—from the Holy Trinity to Larry, Curly, and Moe—and are better for it:

• Mack trucks: "Heart. Steel. Promise."

• Starbucks, introducing pre-packaged coffee: "At grocery. At home. At last."

• Sony PlayStation PS one: "wherever. whenever. forever."

• PlanetOutdoors.com: "Get on. Gear up. Get out."

• C-SPAN's *Booknotes* series: "One Author. One Book. One Hour."

12. Play tricks with type and punctuation.

• Baker's Bourbon: "Best. Sipped. Just. Like. This."

• Wrangler: "Real. Comfortable. Jeans."

• Friends In Deed (the name of a helping community for victims of AIDS and other serious illnesses)

13. Stop making sense. Be evocative instead. Tell it slant. I admire this slogan for Walking Man, a brand of urban clothing: "Challenge. Neatness. Fury." Quirky and original, it suggests more than it states, expressing the principles of

14.30. A slogan whose witty reversal of a cliché encourages people to smile about sad music.

the clothes (or, more important, the clothes wearer). This line's a long way from something crummy like "Quality clothing that works as hard as you do." It invokes the Rule of Threes, too.

14. Mix oil and water. Combine unexpected *kinds* of words. David Letterman calls his production company "Worldwide Pants," two words you'd never heard together before. A Columbus rock band, Movieola (the name itself an unexpected combination), calls its music company "No Heroics Music" after a member saw the category "no heroics" (that is, use no extraordinary measures to save a life) in a nursing home file. The band's lyrics use the phrase "durable dream," another unexpected pairing. Copywriters need to pay attention to the potential energy such wordplay offers. It's often what they're hired to deliver.

But ad writers are so accustomed to making sense that unusual combinations can be hard to create. When you can't get fresh phrases, try "cut ups," the term for cutting your prose apart and sticking it back together in odd combinations. Or splice your words with words from other places—magazines, Web pages, flyers, street signs, pop music titles, slang, posters in windows, your mail, a supermarket's bulletin board, police talk, diaries, famous novels, anything—to create new combinations. As novelist William S. Burroughs, himself a cut-and-paste man, said, "You cannot *will* spontaneity. But you can introduce the spontaneous factor with a pair of scissors."[8]

15. Don't shun puns. I recommend being smart before being glittery, and many writers recommend avoiding puns altogether. But a quiet, well-chosen pun still works for me:

• Kelly Springfield invites people to see the literal and psychological benefits of good tires: "Get every mile you can out of life."
• Tecnica in-line skates: "Advanced thinking on your feet." The pun, of course, is the two senses of "thinking on your feet."
• American Express Gold Card: "Worth Its Wait." A high-quality pun that not only asserts the achievement of getting the card, but also deftly invites the reader to complete the meaning: "(worth its weight) . . . in gold."
• Mitsubishi: "Technically, Anything Is Possi-

ble." Adverb as pun, and a good one, too, considering the wide range of Mitsubishi hi-tech products, from TVs to cars.
• Travelocity.com: "Go, virtually, anywhere." Another punning adverb.
• "What's holding you back?" Slogan for various organizations encouraging people to buckle up before driving.
• "When you've got Epson, you've got a lot of company." The pun invites people to think of Epson as widely used and powerful—"a lot of company" in both senses of the term.

16. Oh, okay, rhyme.
• Ocean Spray: "Crave the wave" (copy line in TV spots: "Tartly refreshing. Refreshingly tart.")
• Oil of Olay: "Love the skin you're in."
• Mars candy: "Pleasure you can't measure."
• Half Price Books: "Waste Not. Read A Lot."
• "To help stay well, Purell." (hand cleaner/sanitizer)

17. Use euphony. Make your slogan memorable by maximizing the way the words sound together:
• "Intel inside"
• "OnStar On Board"
• "Power to the pedal" (Shimano)
• "The softer side of Sears"
• "The incredible edible egg" (American Egg Board)
• The slogan for *Mother Jones* magazine uses alliteration (the repetition of initial sounds): "Truth-telling, tree-hugging and titan toppling for 22 years." All the t's create fun, but readers realize *Mother Jones* is serious about its journalism, too. The line helps lighten what readers might otherwise assume is the too-heaviness of investigative reporting.
• Saturn's slogan "A different kind of company. A different kind of car" relied partly on consonance, repeating "d" and hard "c" (or "k") sounds throughout. They added impact and authority to the lines. Take them out—"A different sort of company. A unique kind of auto"—and even though the line still uses parallelism and still says the same thing, it's lost a lot of punch. When copywriters write, whether headlines, slogans, or copy, they should always listen to how the words sound together.

18. Forget clever, be clear.
- Iomega data storage: "Because it's your stuff."
- refdesk.com: "The single best source for facts on the Net."
- The Home Depot: "You can do it. We can help."
- Alibris: "Books you thought you'd never find."
- "Got milk?" As Goodby, Silverstein & Partners say, "How many other campaigns have been able to compress headline, tagline, product name, and brand positioning into two words?"9

19. Don't just claim it, prove it. Slogans that merely assert something often make people doubt the claim. (The surest way to show you're not cool is to claim you are.) Nike didn't say, "We're the best." It *proved* its core position as sports authority and tough-love coach by speaking in that voice: "Just do it." So don't claim something. Body it forth. Talk in its voice. Say what that person would say:
- Bruegger's Bagels: "Totally completely obsessed with freshness." Sure, there's a claim here, but with its over-the-top repetition and breathless lack of commas, the voice proves the claim. These people *sound* obsessed.
- Blue Cosmos Design wanted to express this idea: BCD's designers are smart professionals, but also fun people to work with. Instead of saying it, copywriters tried to prove it: "Serious strategic design. Say *that* fast 3 times."
- See figure 14.31 for another example of a slogan embodying a claim rather than just asserting it.

20. Release the figure from the stone. When slogans are too long, they fall out of the reader's head—or never get in there. So cut yours down; circle hot spots and see if they work all by themselves. Frequently two or three words in a seven- or eight-word slogan are the heart of the matter. Look for the quick, punchy, tight version of your thought.
- Slogans often slim down over the years. Ace Hardware's original slogan was, "Ace is the place with the helpful hardware man." Now it's "The helpful place." Wordiness,

rhyme, and sexism are gone.
- Sometimes a slogan can incorporate the logo, not just stand beside it; for example, "The best jazz is sung with Verve."
- Adidas: "Feet You Wear." A line so compressed and oxymoronic that it becomes almost a poetic image. Anything longer would be weaker.

21. Above all, solve the problem. Slogans solve advertising problems. Say what is most needed:
- "Amway. We're Your Neighbors." Since Amway isn't well understood, this slogan goes to work on that problem, reducing any stigma and making Amway seem as inevitable as the people next door. This slogan may do as much as any three words can.
- Many people have heard of this university but can't quite place it. They can now: "Seton Hall. The Catholic University in New Jersey."

22. Modify as needed. Be prepared to change your slogan. Durable doesn't mean permanent:
- "Do you Yahoo?" worked when search engines were new. But increased competition and expanded capabilities made the question no longer relevant. Yahoo needed to promise more, so it did: "Life engine."
- Federal Express's original slogan was, "When it absolutely, positively has to be there overnight." But as business has changed, so has the slogan. "The World On Time" succinctly expands FedEx's mission beyond mere overnight delivery, claiming the high ground of the product category—and doing it all without even using a verb.
- Saturn's "A Different Kind of Company. A Different Kind of Car" used parallelism to make the case that an American automaker had restructured itself enough to build an internationally competitive car. Written in 1990, the slogan lasted until 2002, when it was shortened to "It's different in a Saturn." In 2004 Saturn decided to quit being coy and say what it meant, changing its slogan to "People first," a line it had used internally for years.

KEEP THREE THINGS IN MIND WHEN CREATING SLOGANS

First, the difference between a not-so-great slogan and a great one can be just a word or two, so exam-

14.31. Power Trip sells motorcycle gear. How to say "we're tough" without saying it.

ine carefully what you've written. You're trying to do a lot in a few words; any change will have a big effect. See what a different word or word order does.

Second, it's hard at a glance to tell what a good slogan is. I'd have nixed Campbell's "Soup is good food" and held out for something more glitzy. But it proved an extraordinary slogan, wearing well over the years and selling a lot of soup. So turn slogans around and look at them from all angles. See what you've got.

Third, as Dan Wieden of Wieden + Kennedy points out, it can take a while for a slogan to become good, to grow into the culture: "By itself, especially in the early days, [a slogan] feels shallow, but as time goes by and as more ads are put inside of that basket, the more weight and imagery it carries. When we first presented 'Just Do It,' there was a resounding silence, and we just went on. That's just the way a really strong theme line works."[10]

BEYOND SLOGANS

Lots of times you'll be asked not to write a slogan, exactly, but to do something similar: name a conference, campaign, exhibition, event, sale, sales promotion—anything that needs a handle. If that's the case, then be vigorous and specific. Give people a peg to hang this thing on. For example, when a Minneapolis typographer and copywriter were speaking to the ad club I belong to about that city's

advertising, the club could have called the presentation "How Concept and Typography Make Great Advertising," but since type-dominant layouts were what Minneapolis advertising was all about then, the club called it simply "Big Words." More enigmatic and interesting, don't you think? If you've got the room and the inclination, you can have it both ways—at least with the titles of some things—via the colon. Start with the punchy title, then explain it after the colon: "Big Words: How Concept and Type Make Great Advertising." (For another example of a theme line, see figure 14.32.)

Learn to name things

Whatever you're asked to name—a product line, a brand, a company—you want the name to express the gist of the thing and do so memorably, to sink a hook into it. Accomplishing this task is harder than it looks. Sensible can often be too sensible, and unusual can simply be odd. English has only so many words, and a lot of them are already taken. Naming gets tougher when you add marketplace crunch—20,000 new products every year, accelerating global competition, the hyperspeed of digital and Internet innovation. More people are creating and selling more things more often in more media than ever before. And most of these things need a name. Keep lawyers and naming consultancies handy for the big stuff.

But let's put off the lawyers and consultants for now. As simply a language issue, how do you name something?

As always, do your homework. Research your client's product, audience, and competition. Ask and answer these questions:

1. What are you trying to accomplish? What problem are you trying to solve?

2. What do you want to emphasize about the product? What's its key idea? What should its name describe?

3. How does your client's brand distinguish itself from the competition? What's its position? What positions are competitors claiming? What names are they using?

4. Who are you aiming this name at? How should those people be addressed? What are they expecting? How might you surprise them?

5. Do you have any constraints? Are you adding a name to a group of names already in place? Are you extending a brand? Constraints reduce your wiggle room, but they also provide direction.

After you've established answers to those questions, you're ready to tackle the naming game. Read on.

How to choose a good name

1. Take words right out of the dictionary. These can be good because people already know what they mean and can apply them to your client's brand. You're looking for something appropriate, but unusual. For example, a startup ad agency called itself Anomaly because the principals thought their approach to business was just that. Zip is a good name for Iomega's digital storage disks. It's a verb, and it's quick, with just the right meanings. A fast zipper for my stuff? Cool.

Metaphors can be a good way to go: Sprint, Mustang, Ocean Spray. Vivid and specific, they *show* what the product does. Find the essence of your thing-to-be-named, then express that metaphorically. National Public Radio's interview show *Fresh Air*, with Terry Gross, uses a metaphor and a pun. "Air" is a metaphor for radio and a pun, as "[a breath of] fresh air," on new ideas. Bank One's "Maximum Strength

Checking" uses pain relief language for a checking account.

2. Create completely made-up words. You can make these out of whole cloth (Oreo, Kodak, OXO) or partly so (the portmanteau words I talk about below). The downside of completely made-up words is that it costs a lot of money to teach them to your audience (they're not in consumers' heads already), but once you get them in there, people won't mistake you for someone else. Connotations, as always, count plenty.

3. Invent portmanteau words. Two words, or parts of them, fused to create a new word, are easier to grasp since they contain identifiable parts. Portmanteaus come in all flavors. Sometimes they're a true fusion of part of this word with part of that one to create a word people have never seen before. Other times they're two words, more or less unaltered, simply pushed together to create a "new" one (PlayStation, WordPerfect, ChemLawn, PowerPoint, Fire-Wire).

How to create portmanteaus? Cut and paste prefixes, suffixes, and word roots. Stick half of this word onto half of that word; stick all of that word onto the front or back end or middle of another, get some Latin and Greek into the mix. Lewis Carroll coined the term "portmanteau" because such combined words reminded him of the way different things could be crammed into a suitcase, or portmanteau, and they're widely used. Such words can be good: KinderCare, DieHard, Volunteen (for teenage volunteer programs), Synchilla (Patagonia's synthetic chinchilla), the recipe Web site Epicurious.com ("epicure" and "curious"). But such words can be stinky when they're too obvious or too dumb. I called an early version of this book *AdThink*, and reviewers rightly rejected it as too glib, too mechanical, an invitation to make ads by the numbers. Connotations again.

Why create portmanteaus? Because you get three words for the price of two: the two original words plus the energy of the new, invented word. Netscape is a brand name that's also a new thought, compounded of "Internet," "landscape," and maybe "network." Allegra, an allergy relief medicine that doesn't cause drowsiness, is also a new thought. Consumers can hear "allergy" in there, and also "allegro"

14.32. The theme line and central visual of a capital campaign for the Ontario College of Art & Design shows how word and image, when they're working well, interrelate; each relies for part of its power on the other.

(fast tempo), implying that the pills work fast and won't knock people out. Good name. Consumers don't consciously hear the portmanteau, but they subconsciously do, don't you think? The word sounds fast, and it sounds new (see fig. 14.33).

4. Use acronyms and letter clusters.
Acronyms you can pronounce (AIM, NOW, Sunoco); letter clusters you can't (IBM, BP, ESPN, VW). Combine the initial letters or parts of words (Sun Oil Company became Sunoco) into a new "word." English lexicographer H. W.

Fowler called all these truncated coinages "curtailed words," and they include, if you think about it, words people use every day: ad(vertisement), (in)flu(enza), photo(graph), sit(uation) com(edy), cab(riolet), and a host of others. Everyone loves shorthand, reducing something windy to something quick.

Can you be too quick? Some people think that when Kentucky Fried Chicken reduced its name to KFC, the company lost a lot. Now people couldn't tell whether they should eat there, let KFC insure them, or hope the company got to the bargaining tables with NATO and OPEC. That confusion may be why the Colonel's face still accompanies the logotype. You gain speed with acronyms, but you lose clarity. Also, the initials should have some kind of cohesion—either say something when pronounced, as do acronyms (FUBU, NASCAR), or sound good together as letter clusters (NPR glides smoothly off the lips; ABC, NBC, BBC, and CBS all have nice consonant- and vowel-sound sequences).

5. Find words that are place names. The unique specificity of a place transfers to the thing named: Columbia, North Face, and Patagonia sportswear; Southwest and Northwest airlines. Where was this thing you're trying to name invented, or where is it from? Look around. Grab a name from its geography.

6. Find words unique to the corporation— maybe the founder's name (perhaps the most common naming technique) or names inside the company. Wendy's, for example, is named after one of founder Dave Thomas's daughters. Kinko was the college nickname of that company's founder. So get up to speed on the company and its story. Maybe the owner's dog or cat or summer retreat has a quirky name. Maybe her father's middle name was unusual. Maybe not. But check to see what's inside the company's storage box. Lift the lid.

7. Make puns. People see plenty of them, that's for sure: Primal Knead (a bakery), Blood Vessel (a bloodmobile), VanGo (an art outreach program using vans). I think every copywriter has to decide for himself or herself when a pun works and when it's too corny or won't wear well.

8. Jump out of category. Look at what everyone else is doing, then do the opposite, or at least slant away from the trends. The surest way to get lost in the mix is to sound just like the competition. If it's an e-business you're naming, don't start with "e-"; everyone does that. Start with something else. Danny Altman, co-founder of the naming company A Hundred Monkeys (from the old joke that if you put 100 monkeys in a room with 100 typewriters, eventually you'll get Shakespeare) says, "If you went to a company trying to name their airline and gave them a choice between Trans-AtlanticAir and Virgin, they'd take Trans-AtlanticAir, because it sounds like something people would take seriously. The problem is, with that name they become one of the trees in the forest."[11]

9. Ask yourself what the heart of something is, and then express this in terms a little off dead-center. Get people interested. What's a good name for an educational cable network for kids? How about Noggin? A word that says kids, a word everyone has fond associations with, and a word they remember from the phrase "That's using your noggin." When Volkswagen and Apple devised a promotion in which anyone who bought a VW New Beetle received an iPod, the question was what to call the promotion, how to theme the ads? "Pods Unite!" was the clever call-to-arms for two products sharing pod-dom.

10. Bring in language from elsewhere: from pop culture, street signs, literature, poetry, TV, music—you name it. For example, A Hundred Monkeys renamed Career Central (a career placement service) Cruel World. As Altman explains, "If you're first in a field, it works to have a name that is somewhat descriptive. But once you're facing lots of competition, a descriptive name is no longer very useful. You end up with Career Central, Career Link, Careers-R-Us. The whole point of a name is to stand out. Look at what others in your field are doing, then do the opposite."[12] The Monkeys have named an advertising agency Left Field, a unified platform for IT management Jamcracker, a personal medical database 98point6, a venture capital fund Ironweed, and mail-order windowsill gardens Farm-in-a-Box.

But the words you find "over there" have to resonate. Not just anything will do. Make some kind of intellectual or emotional sense. However odd the word, it should strike something in the target audience and "work," as do the ones

above. With the ad agency name Left Field, for example, people hear "out of left field" and know that original ideas come from there.

11. Say the obvious. With everyone being oh-so-clever, the obvious is often ignored. A board game for dogs is called, obviously enough, "Hey, my dog can do that." A shampoo was named "Gee, your hair smells terrific." NPR calls its CD collections of favorite stories "Driveway Moments" because those were the ones that kept people sitting in their cars to hear, even after arriving at their destination. I can go to the grocery store and buy Lean Cuisine and Healthy Choice. These names are zigging when everyone else is zagging, one way to get noticed. They're

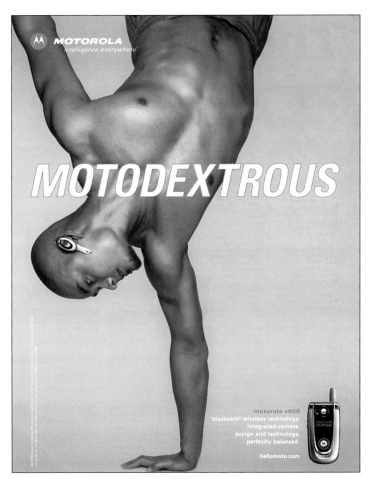

14.33. "Motorola" is itself a portmanteau word—"motor" + "ola" (sound)—so named because one of the company's earliest inventions was the car radio. This campaign for Motorola's cell phones takes that "moto" root and combines it with different beginnings and endings to express phone options. Other headlines: "Primamoto," "Gossipmoto," and "Motorazr."

also examples of "raising the obvious to the conscious," something always to consider. After I got *AdThink* out of my system, I named this book by simply saying what was in it: *Advertising: Concept and Copy*. Clever? Nope. Clear? Let's hope so.

12. Vet the name. Sooner or later you do get to the lawyers and the painful questions. Is the name in use already? Has someone trademarked it? Since globalism requires universality, will the name translate? Does it work in other cultures? Chances are you'll also want the corporate or, perhaps, product name to function as an Internet domain name, so it has to be a name that's free and clear.

Vetting the name involves performing trademark screening, doing linguistic analysis, determining cultural fit—all that. You don't want to enter the marketing texts alongside this blunder: Chevy tried to sell its Nova in Mexico, among other Spanish-speaking countries, without realizing that *No va* in Spanish means "It doesn't go." Ouch. When VW was creating advertising for the Spanish-speaking Hispanic market, it discovered that its slogan, "Drivers wanted," if translated straight-up into Spanish, implied that VW needed chauffeurs. After considering 100 variations, VW finally chose *"Agarra calle,"* slang for "Let's hit the road." Close enough.

WHICH NAME SHOULD YOU CHOOSE?

Made-up words, all connotation and no denotation, are omnipresent, especially for corporate and brand names (Acura, Accenture, Verizon, and so on). Many of these are portmanteaus in that it's easy to hear part of one word being added to part of another to make something that could be a word, if it weren't. Some people find such creations empty, interchangeable, and way over-used; others think they sound like the future. You decide. Companies specializing in naming and branding make a lot of money coming up with these things. I tend to like funky, real words more than made-up, vague ones, but I just celebrated Allegra above, so go figure. Hey, Go Figure, an accounting firm. Get it? Oh, nevermind.

15 ▪ The Power of Fact

I would want to tell my students of a point strongly pressed, if memory serves, by [George Bernard] Shaw. He once said that as he grew older, he became less and less interested in theory, more and more interested in information. The temptation in writing is just reversed. Nothing is so hard to come by as a new and interesting fact. Nothing so easy on the feet as a generalization.

—John Kenneth Galbraith, economist

Facts beat generalities every time

In this book I argue that you cannot know too much about your client's product, and that digging out facts is an important part of your research. Not only can facts inform an advertisement, they can control it. Find a strong enough one and let it be the headline, let it run the concept. If people distrust generalities (and they do) and if they distrust advertising (and they do), then present facts with which they cannot argue.

Recently I saw an outdoor board in Columbus that relied on fact for its effect. It said simply: "Roaches carry six known diseases," under which was the Orkin logo. Amazing—and, I assume, true.

Here's another example of the power of fact in an advertising world riddled with the overly general and the overenthusiastic. I was driving behind a large, slow, diesel-powered city bus, not exactly a pleasant experience. Since traffic was congested, I had plenty of time to read the signs on its rear end, one of which was: "Fully loaded, this bus replaces 40 automobiles." Suddenly I felt better about its presence. Another of its signs read: "This bus in service since 1982." As it was then more than a decade later, I wondered why tell me this? Then I realized it was to let me know, with a dramatic fact, just how careful the bus company had been with taxpayers' money. I felt better yet.

Both dramatic facts cut right into my consciousness in ways generalities like "City buses are working for you" or "Buses—the economical way to travel" simply would not. Those phrases don't have enough rhetorical flair, of course; but even if a copywriter had made them rhyme or pun, I doubt that they could be as memorable or convincing as those two specific facts.

Read this headline: "Imagine. More than 26 bones, 56 ligaments, 38 muscles, and several yards of tendons packed into the space of one foot. Yours." If people took their feet for granted before reading that Birkenstock brochure headline, they'd surely be less likely to do so afterwards. E. B. White has spoken of "the eloquence of facts," and facts really do have power to persuade—a power all the more potent in an Adland full of puffery, hoo-hah, and propaganda (see fig. 15.1). "News" is the term some advertisers use for facts. If telling people the news about your client's product helps you dig for facts, then tell the news. Apple does that every time it invents something.

Let's assume, then, that you've found potentially interesting facts about your client's product. But how will you express them? A large part of their power comes from *how* you think about and write them. The following sections offer advice on the best ways to take some good facts and say them well.

> The more particular, the more specific you are, the more universal you are.
>
> —Nancy Hale, novelist

In some families,
being the man of the house isn't easy.
Especially when you're
pregnant.

SHEDD AQUARIUM | Rediscover Shedd. See jumping whales, singing dolphins and a father who understands what it's like to give birth. Don't miss the potbelly seahorse and other extraordinary animals.

SHEDD AQUARIUM | Rediscover Shedd. Stroll through the Pacific Northwest or come face-to-face with an emerald tree boa from the Amazon who, luckily, doesn't see us as part of the menu. Open every day this summer, from 9 a.m. - 6 p.m. Visit www.sheddaquarium.org.

Three-dimensional
infrared imaging
allows her to hunt in total darkness.

Fortunately, **we close at 6 p.m.**

15.1. The challenge was to get people interested in the lesser-known fish and reptiles at the Shedd —not big stars like beluga whales and dolphins, but the little guys. Facts have a way of doing that, don't they?

Its razor-sharp teeth can bite
through a **two-by-four.**
Do we really need to explain
why he's behind four inches
of glass?

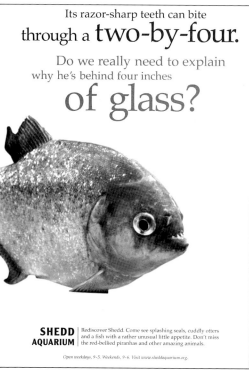

SHEDD AQUARIUM | Rediscover Shedd. Come see splashing seals, cuddly otters and a fish with a rather unusual little appetite. Don't miss the red-bellied piranhas and other amazing animals.

Open weekdays, 9-5. Weekends, 9-6. Visit www.sheddaquarium.org.

15.2. A funny way of putting it, but no exaggeration: Seattle's Pike Place Market really does cover nine historic acres.

Give your facts a human voice

It's usually not enough to just "say" the fact. Get in the habit of presenting it wrapped in your funny, warm, wry, or ironic voice. Spin it. "Voice" the fact. Sometimes advertisers say, "Wrap the fact in a smile." (See chapter 14 for more on this.)

An outdoor board for Boston's Franklin Park Zoo wanted to let people know it had birds, too, lots of them. Here's how they informed the public, with facts and a smile:

7 acres. 300 birds. Wear a hat.

See figure 15.2 for another example of a fact that relates to the human condition and speaks in a human voice.

Give your facts as sharp an edge as possible

Don't be "fact lite." State the fact specifically enough so that if feels like one. For example, it may be a "fact" that women are often paid less than men for equal work. But that statement is vague, almost uninteresting. Look at figure 15.3. The "fact" has now been made precise, and its specificity gets readers' attention.

Likewise, it may be a "fact" that England's Canterbury Cathedral is historically important, so it should be preserved. But say that specifically enough to get people's attention, as the following restoration fund headline does (also note the well-used parallelism):

St. Augustine founded it. Becket died for it. Chaucer wrote about it. Cromwell shot at it. Hitler bombed it. Time is destroying it. Will you save it?

Consider unusual quantifications

Can you quantify or measure your client's product in a new and unusual way? DDB's classic VW campaign did this repeatedly. One ad showed the Beetle with this headline: "$1.02 a pound." Another showed two VWs with this headline: "There are a

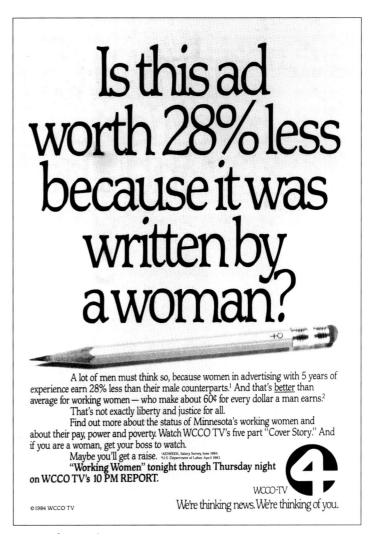

15.3. A fact made precise.

4 minutes a day. 28 minutes a week. 2 hours a month. 1,344 hours in a lifetime. Make the best of it.

Most people see shaving as something that you do for a few minutes a day. But at Braun, we see shaving as something you do for a lifetime. Which is why we've designed our shaver's thin profile to fit the contours of your face as comfortably as your hand. And why the rubber knobs on our grip actually quiet motor noise, as well as provide a firm hold. Our rechargeable shavers charge in an hour instead of the usual twenty-four; and perform equally well with or without a cord. Even our foil is ultra-thin and platinum coated to help provide a closer, smoother shave. This comprehensive approach to shaving has made Braun the best-selling foil shaver in the rest of the world. Now it's finally available in America. And not a moment too soon.

BRAUN

Designed to perform better.

15.4. An unusual quantification.

lot of good cars you can get for $3400. This is two of them." The cologne Bleu Marine for Men placed one drop from the bottle on the page, under the headline "There are only 624 drops to a bottle. Plan each one carefully." Any such unusual measurement of your client's product catches the reader with its unexpectedness (see fig. 15.4).

Lean your facts up against something

One problem with facts is that too often they're inert, just a big number, a small number, or some statistic that alone means nothing. Facts often mean more when they're placed in human contexts, especially ironic ones (see fig. 15.5). If you just say that "Henry Weinhard beer has been brewed in Oregon since 1856," people are likely to say, "Yeah, so?" The fact alone seems unimpressive, a number without a meaning. But if you say, "Oregon had a beer before it had a capitol," as an ad for Henry Weinhard once did, suddenly the fact becomes interesting, doesn't it? Likewise, you could say of Old Grand Dad whiskey, "First introduced in 1796," but

a copywriter did better: "Introduced fifty years before ice cubes."

Look for a contrast you can exploit

A lot of factual ideas strike the mind when they are presented in opposition: this fact versus that one. The tension of facts-in-opposition powers the headline. For example, what if you discovered that New Balance athletic shoes were partly created by scientists at MIT? You could just say, "The shoe that MIT created," or you could write a headline that gives the fact some contrast:

Over the years, MIT professors have been responsible for 150 computers, 47 rockets, 6 satellites and one shoe.

Following is a headline for an ad promoting prunes (beside a photograph of a prune):

There are five types of fiber your body uses. Here are four of them.

This following copy line from a World Wildlife Fund ad similarly juxtaposes facts so that readers better understand the issue:

In the age before man, the earth lost one species every thousand years. Today, we lose one every twenty minutes.

See figures 15.6 and 15.7 for two more examples of effective exploitation of facts.

Remember that facts about your client's product imply facts about the competition's

For every fact you discover about your client's product, there is a corresponding fact about the competition (see fig. 15.8). Your ad might be more impressive if it used facts about the competition in place of facts about your client's product.

Make your facts visual

Sometimes copywriters lock into thinking that facts must be statistics—quantifiable, verbal. We think the only way to express facts is through headlines. But many facts are visual—or can be visually energized (see fig. 15.9).

Demonstrate your facts

Don't claim them, prove them (see fig. 15.10). Nothing's stronger than a demonstration.

15.5. Lean a fact up against something.

15.6. How to sell an expensive salon shampoo? Invite readers to contemplate this contradiction.

15.7. A clever contrast between numbers drives readers into the ad and delivers the selling point.

They don't write songs about Volvos.

15.8. Who could argue with this?

15.9. The small-print headline, "More than 3 million readers every week," is complemented by the visual, suggesting one issue being read that many times. Funny and simple, this visual idea gives the fact stopping power.

Bernice is not a honey baked ham. Must sing? No can do. Watch the fish swim. They are Ethel Merman.

See. People will read anything on a subway poster.

TRANS AD

Your product *goes* here.

15.10. How do you demonstrate the power of transit advertising? This ad just did.

16 ▪ Testimonials
The Power of Personality

Personalities appeal, while soulless corporations do not. Make a man famous and you make his creation famous.
—Claude Hopkins, *My Life in Advertising*

One of the most durable of advertising techniques is the *testimonial*: someone speaks *for* the product. Testimonials may seem dopey and obvious—"Hi, I'm Joe Famous. I use Blotto, and you should, too"—but they don't have to be.

Testimonials are a very old technique, related to word of mouth (the first cave man said to the second caveman, "Here, use this pointy thing, not that pointy thing," and the testimonial was born). When people want to buy something, they often ask a friend with knowledge of the brand what he or she thinks of it as a way of testing its worth. With testimonials, people's interest or belief in the spokesperson rubs off on the product.

No matter what you're selling, someone can testify for it. And since people find other people more fascinating than they do anything else, why not use them?

Keep two things in mind:

1. Finding a likely candidate is only half of the job. Once you drag someone on stage, use your wits. Tie that character to the product, cleverly. Your concept and headline will make or break the testimonial more than will your choice of spokesperson.

2. Decide whether you'll press the truth button or the whimsy button. You can ask your audience to believe that this is a real person who really uses the product, or you can just have fun with the character or person without requesting our belief. Either approach can

work, though I prefer real people with a real connection to the product. There's more substance in that argument, more pull power. It's not just a joke, even though joking testimonials can be mighty good. So before you take the joke route, don't fail to look through your research for people who can help you sell the product. They're not just arresting; they're the truth.

Figure 16.1 is an example of how to use real people (rather than celebrities with no connection to the brand) in testimonials and make them interesting in the process. This approach is funny, requires just a little work from the viewer (those make for the best ads), and proves that real people with real connections to the product work terrifically well—provided the creative people give them just the right twist, which is where you come in.

Who might you pull onstage?

1. Extreme user. Find the heavy user or the over-the-top user and let that person demonstrate, often with hyperbole, how great the product is.

2. Expert. Find someone who stands outside the brand and has the expertise to evaluate it. If you're selling food, find a chef. If you're selling cars, find a mechanic. If you're selling a prison, find some criminals (see fig. 16.2).

3. President/CEO, founding mother or father, employee. Give the brand a human face. Take the monolith out of it. Find someone to person-

189

MIKE KOPP
political reporter

KXMB
NEWS 12®
"Your Local News Source"

CBS Station Of The Year

ify the corporation, one that people might otherwise think too big, too corrupt, too remote, or too something (see fig. 16.3).

4. Celebrities. There are a million of them. The key is to give your treatment of that famous person some snap (see fig. 16.4). The campaign for Bell BMX helmets used celebrity endorsers (famous BMX pros) but treated them unusually. Writer Dave Schiff, of Crispin Porter + Bogusky, explains: "BMX is probably the harshest, most cynical target audience on earth. Concepts are mocked, high production values are dismissed and authenticity—athlete-driven advertisements—is the only accepted form of communication."[1] So he and his colleagues used images of BMX pro athletes, but placed the helmets on top of demon masks. The ads were painted on urban surfaces by Miami sign painters using Haiitian voodoo-style graphics, then photographed for the print ads. The mask and copy become a kind of incantation, a prayer to ward off evil spirits—fear and self-doubt—while doing bike tricks.

The copy reads, "May the helmet which surrounds the head of Steve McCann also surround the head of me. May it protect me from unseen forces that make the sure foot stumble and the strong mind weak. Oh helmet of Steve McCann, help me to ride like Steve McCann, and bring doom to those who oppose me." Schiff got the broken English this way: "In order to get the tone right, we used one of those free online translators and wrote all the copy in Spanish, then converted it to English."[2]

5. Not the person, but something associated with the person. You may want to bypass the celebrity altogether and just use something associated with that person, as a Spiegel catalog campaign did, showing the silk gown Bianca Jagger bought or the shoes Priscilla Presley bought from the catalog. There was an extra poignance to this use of a metonym (a part standing for the whole) in place of the celebrity.

6. The wrong person. The quintessential example may have been Fallon McElligott's 1980s

16.1. Do your homework, learn about companies, and recognize that within any brand's story are people who can help sell it.

print campaign for a Minneapolis hair salon that featured famous people with bad haircuts (see fig. 16.5). The centerpiece of that campaign was an image of Albert Einstein with his famously messed-up hair and the headline: "A bad haircut can make anyone look dumb." What a smart idea. Similarly, Del Monte introduced shelf-stable, microwave vegetables by using horrified kids as spokespeople. Their unified fear: if vegetables are this easy to prepare, now we'll have them *all* the time. Yikes!

Often consumers are persuaded to buy things because of a negative endorsement. If a teenager's parents don't like a product, that could be all the reason necessary for wanting it. Spend some time thinking about who can't use or doesn't use or doesn't like your client's product. Can you twist that negative into a positive? Could the product be sold by someone unlikely? Very likely.

7. Ironic testimonials. You may want to go further and *devalue the seller*, make jokes on the idea of credible spokespeople. Given our cynical attitude toward advertising and endorsements, such ironic testimonials gain absurdist power. Some years ago the car company Isuzu played off the cliché of the dishonest car salesman by inventing one, the smarmy Joe Isuzu, whose hilariously overstated promises the spots ridiculed. E. & J. Gallo Winery created two hayseeds, one garrulous, the other silent, Bartles and Jaymes, who apparently sold the wine they made from their front porch. We were invited to laugh at their cardboard nostalgia—two guys too dumb to know they needed an ad agency. More recently Altoids has used geeky spokespeople in their ads, oddballs who humorously embody various benefits of the brand's position, mints and gum that are "curiously strong." Burger King has sent its namesake, the King (in this case a fellow in costume, wearing a great big, plastic Burger King head), around as a visitor to backyards and even bedrooms—his loom-

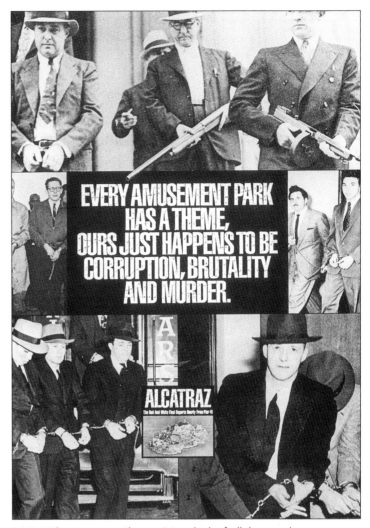

16.2. Why go to see Alcatraz? Just think of all the people who've already been there.

16.3. I wasn't interested in DuPont—until I read this ad (headline: "With a single idea she can stop trains"). It's amazing what Stephanie Kwolek, Kevlar®, and DuPont can do, isn't it? Delve into your client's product. Tell the stories. Show the heroes.

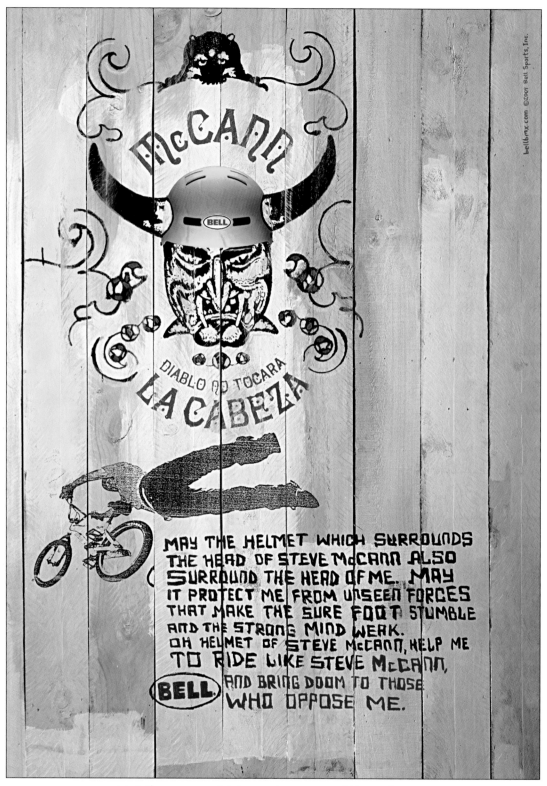

16.4. If you use a celebrity, get the most out of him: make sure the ad resonates with your audience. This ad starts with Steve McCann, but it doesn't stop there.

ing, silent, smiling face becoming both hilarious and disturbing. Many ads play ironic jokes on their own clichés, sharing a wink with us at the testimonial genre. So think about subverting, subordinating, or in some way altering the usual position of the spokesperson as authority speaking for the product. (See also chapter 21, Postmodern Advertising.)

8. Historical figures, unreal people. The person in the testimonial needn't be alive or even real. Characters from history, legend, literature, movies, and cartoons can be used for their attention-getting quality as well as their unusual "relationship" to the product (see fig. 16.6).

Apple's "Think different" campaign, for example, used a variety of famous innovators, most of whom had no relationship with computers, Apple or otherwise. Amelia Earhart,

16.5. By its witty use of the "wrong person," this campaign avoids ad clichés overused for hair salons (fashion-ad approaches, beauty shots of hair), thus creating a distinctive image for its client. Partly *because* this is so unlike a hair salon ad, people figure that this place knows its business.

16.6. Famous and infamous figures can gain attention while delivering the selling idea.

Pablo Picasso, Muhammad Ali, Mahatma Gandhi, and all the rest served as symbols of creative thinkers, risk takers, people who dared to be great. That was their "relationship" to Apple, and, tangential though it was, it worked. Apple became the computer expression of the rebel in everyone, a way for people to celebrate and encourage their own potential.

Thus you needn't limit yourself to living people, nor do you need to be reasonable. I've seen images of Laurel and Hardy used to sell windshield wipers, Franz Kafka to sell beer, James Dean for tennis shoes. Even an image of Adolf Hitler can been used to sell things (see fig. 16.7). Rummage through history or Hollywood, myth or literature. See who turns up.

9. Just plain folks. Given all the celebrity testimonials, can "normal people" with an obvious relationship to the product be effective? Absolutely. Figure 16.8 is another example of perhaps the best sort of testimonial: a real person who was really helped by the product, in this case a hospital. A great headline introduces a little girl whose congenital deafness has been overcome by surgery at Mt. Sinai. Terrific work. For me at least, the truth trumps everything else.

BOB LAMBERT · RETOUCHING · 835-2166

16.7. Viewers' "what's-wrong-with-this-picture?" feeling drives the concept, while its subject proves that almost anyone can provide a testimonial.

Two year old Patricia Puia sat on her mother's lap, unable to hear the gentle voice that tried to comfort her. Deaf from birth, her life in Romania was lived in silence. But a month after undergoing cochlear implant surgery at Mount Sinai, the silence was filled with the sounds of a world Patricia never knew existed. "I feel like I've just given birth to this child for the second time," her mother said tearfully. "But this time she hears." 1-800-MD-SINAI · www. mountsinai.org **Another day, another breakthrough.**

MOUNT SINAI

WE TURNED
A CHILD WHO
COULDN'T HEAR INTO
A TYPICAL 2 YEAR
OLD WHO DOESN'T
LISTEN.

16.8. Straightforward testimonials can certainly be effective. Even though this testimonial is the most obvious one possible—someone helped by the hospital—the little girl's story is told so well that it's inspiring.

17 • "Two-Fers"
Comparisons, Before and After, and Other Dualities

I once was lost, but now am found,
Was blind, but now I see.
—John Newton, from "Amazing Grace"

A fundamental way to get attention, organize information, and be persuasive is to use paired imagery, what one might call *two-fers*: comparison-and-contrast, before-and-after, and other side-by-side setups. Such ads float through people's memory like old reruns. On the left she is fat; on the right she is skinny. Once he was bald; now he has hair. This shirt had chocolate stains, but now it's lily white. On and on, ad nauseam.

Although my examples are clichés, two-fers don't have to be. Lots of great ads exploit this structure because it's fast, simple, clear, and often startling. Usually you consider this format only when comparing your client's brand with brand X or in a before-and-after scenario—and two-fers work well to express such intentions (see figs. 17.1 and 17.2). Don't restrict yourself to those categories, nor must you be so literal minded in using this format.

Stay on strategy

Try to express your strategy, whatever it is, as a two-fer. Does your client's product have an old image but now a new reality? An old use but now a new one, too? Is the product good not only for one kind of person but for another as well? Are there two versions of it people should know about? Two benefits? Can you show the product one way and then add to that in the other image? Can you take two benefits and fuse them into one image? Consider the following possibilities:

1. Show two different versions, benefits, purposes, or kinds of consumer of a single product (see figs. 17.3 and 17.4).

2. Compare the product with something dissimilar, something that looks the same or works the same, to dramatize the benefit. Often the more unusual and unexpected the comparison, the better (see figs. 17.5 and 17.6).

3. Try using two-fers for any strategy that addresses consumer ignorance (see fig. 17.7), corrects a misperception (see fig. 17.8), or talks about problems and solutions.

As so often applies in advertising, it's less what you show and more how you think and talk about what you show that makes the difference (see figs. 17.9 and 17.10).

Create sequential ads

Budget willing, you can create *sequential ads*: a series of two or more ads that occupy, usually, the same space on succeeding pages in a newspaper or magazine. Readers see an incomplete message and then turn the page(s) for the rest. These ads gain cumulative power: if readers page past the first ad, the repetition, with variation, of succeeding installments eventually registers. It's one way to beat clutter: repeat yourself until people notice.

You can use outdoor boards in sequence, setting something up in the first board and then paying it off farther down the highway with the second board. Or have a single board evolve by adding information to an incomplete message over time. By definition, Internet banner ads are two-fers and sequential ads: images and language succeed one another, or they invite users to click on the ad to reveal the next part of the message.

17.1. The before-and-after ad is a hardy perennial, but there's nothing old about it here, is there? Other before-and-after comparisons that dramatized this chiropractor's get-the-kinks-out services were the St. Louis Arch vs. the Washington Monument, a camel vs. a horse, and a French horn vs. a clarinet.

Before. *After.*

Happy Holidays from all of us at Dahl Chiropractic.

Whose birthday is it, anyway?

The Episcopal Church believes the important news at Christmas is not who comes down the chimney, but who came down from heaven. We invite you to come and join us as we celebrate the birth of Jesus Christ.
The Episcopal Church

17.2. In yet another hardy perennial, a comparison with the competition doesn't have to be boring. The Episcopal Church's aggressive tone gets right to the point.

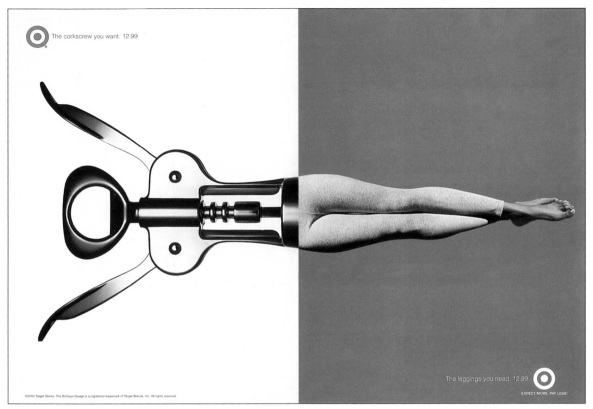

17.3. Why not compare a brand with itself—even if only in terms of shape? Target shows its range of products by fusing "what you need" with "what you want."

17.4. This ad in a beautiful campaign for San Francisco makes a surprising connection between two apparently dissimilar things, though the visual parallelism links them, as does the conceptual one: they're both iconic aspects of life in SF.

17.5. Other ads in this campaign paired the inverted body of a Les Paul guitar with a nuclear mushroom cloud and the pointed shape of a Gibson SG body with a devil's trident.

17.6. Unexpected metaphorical comparison. Another ad compared a yellow and black Mini with the business end of a bumble bee.

17.7. Can a "two-fer" be a "three-fer"? Why not? The copy line reads, "No race, creed or religion should endure the ridicule faced by Native Americans today. Please help us put an end to this mockery and racism . . ."

ELECTRIFYING   OHIO STATE GYMNASTICS

OHIO STATE MEN'S GYMNASTICS
FOR TICKETS CALL 1-800-GO-BUCKS OR VISIT OHIOSTATEBUCKEYES.COM

SPIRITED   BIG TEN GYMNASTICS

OHIO STATE WOMEN'S GYMNASTICS
FOR TICKETS CALL 1-800-GO-BUCKS OR VISIT OHIOSTATEBUCKEYES.COM

TWIST AND SHOUT   AT VALUE CITY ARENA

OHIO STATE WOMEN'S BASKETBALL
FOR TICKETS CALL 1-800-GO-BUCKS OR VISIT OHIOSTATEBUCKEYES.COM

CATCH THE ACTION   AT JESSE OWENS MEMORIAL STADIUM

OHIO STATE MEN'S SOCCER
FOR TICKETS CALL 1-800-GO-BUCKS OR VISIT OHIOSTATEBUCKEYES.COM

17.8. Ohio State has a huge athletic program, but men's football and basketball had so dominated that plenty of high-energy, well-played sports were neglected by the fans. Partly because of the program's size, there also was no perceived continuity among the teams. The goal of this campaign was to unify the brand (the athletic program), raise interest in smaller, less well-known sports, and increase ticket sales. By using an unusual—but appropriate—dissimilarity to complete each athlete's shape, these metaphorical "two-fers" surprise viewers, dramatize the energy of the sports, and pull the program together into a distinct brand.

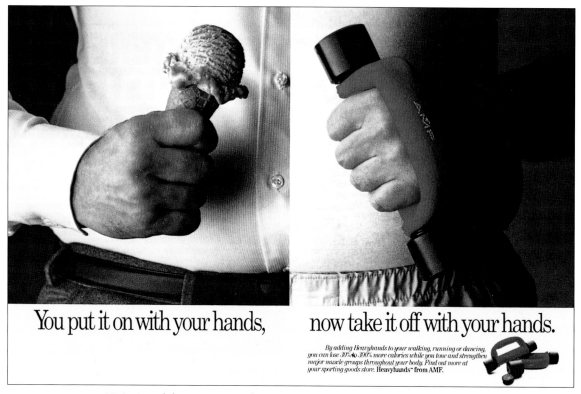

You put it on with your hands, **now take it off with your hands.**

By adding Heavyhands to your walking, running or dancing, you can lose 30% to 100% more calories while you tone and strengthen major muscle groups throughout your body. Find out more at your sporting goods store. Heavyhands™ from AMF.

17.9. An ad that seems to make more sense than it really does, thanks in part to tight visual and verbal parallelism. Eating with one's hands doesn't lead to any necessary wisdom in exercising with them, but it seems to, doesn't it? The "two-fer" format lends its rhetorical weight to the argument.

mom and dad

ATM

When you're broke, you look at things in a whole new way.
So for textbooks and stuff, hit ecampus.com. You'll save up to 50%. And shipping's always free.

eCAMPUS.com
Textbooks & Stuff Cheap

17.10. You can use "two-fers" to solve just about any problem. As this example shows, they're as creative as you are and work when you make them work.

18 ▪ Reversal

Discovery consists of looking at the same thing as
everyone else and thinking something different.
—Albert Szent-Gyorgyi,
Nobel Prize–winning biochemist

All great ads employ *reversal*: a technique by which something significant has been put in, left out, inverted, photographed oddly, colored wrong, talked about differently, or in some way had violence done to its ordinariness. Otherwise, if viewers' preconceptions have been fulfilled instead of violated, they'll be looking at clichés. They won't even blink because nothing has moved out of its same-as-usual spot.

If you want people to look, you've got to make them look, and that's where reversal comes in.[1] For example, a quintessential VW ad (fig. 18.1) took the American maxim "Think big" and reversed it to "Think small." It also ignored an advertising maxim —use the whole page to display the product—and instead filled the page with emptiness, sticking an itty bitty image of the VW Beetle up in the corner. The ad reversed viewers' expectations twice: once as users of clichés, and once as viewers of ads.

How to think in reverse

The best way to think backwards is to practice techniques that by definition *are* backwards.

WHEN EVERYONE IS GOING ONE WAY, GO ANOTHER

How well you can write has little to do with your success as a copywriter. Clients don't care what the words mean. No great campaign was ever bought because the client loved the sentences. Great campaigns happen when a creative sees the product differently than it has been perceived before.
—Mark Fenske,
advertising creative director

First you have to figure out the usual direction taken by ads in your product's category. How is the product usually sold? What expectations do people have when they encounter, say, a beer ad or a car ad? Violate those expectations. If you're selling a car, people expect to see it on a mountain road after a rain—so show it still on the boat from Korea; possible headline: "Every Hyundai comes with 6,000 miles on it." Or people expect to see it sitting on a page surrounded by lots of type—so show just part of the car, as VW has done, displaying only the engine underneath the headline "Introducing the 1981 Rabbit"; the point was that nothing else had changed.

How do most ads in your product's category talk? Talk some other way. For example, ads warning people not to drink alcohol excessively usually cite the dangers and are somber, serious, even scary. But the "Know when to draw the line" campaign created for Labatt by Axmith McIntyre Wicht, Toronto, headed in the opposite direction (see fig. 18.2). The glow-in-the-dark bull's-eye pillow says, "Hopefully you won't need this tonight." The poster's optically undulating visual is headlined "Feel familiar?" And a TV spot in the campaign is a funny take on a girl who wakes up married to an Elvis impersonator after a night of heavy drinking. Says writer Brian Howlett, "As far as we know, it's the first advertising that attempts to deliver this serious message in a light-hearted manner. The kids in research kept telling us they didn't want to see another 'drink responsibly' spot that had body bags or car crashes in it. Response has been fantastic."[2]

EXPLORE NEGATIVE SPACE

Often the most interesting angle in any problem is the negative. This area often seems more human; it has possibilities for entertainment and humor. You demonstrate how good you are by showing what you're

Think small.

Our little car isn't so much of a novelty any more.

A couple of dozen college kids don't try to squeeze inside it.

The guy at the gas station doesn't ask where the gas goes.

Nobody even stares at our shape.

In fact, some people who drive our little flivver don't even think 32 miles to the gallon is going any great guns.

Or using five pints of oil instead of five quarts.

Or never needing anti-freeze.

Or racking up 40,000 miles on a set of tires.

That's because once you get used to some of our economies, you don't even think about them any more.

Except when you squeeze into a small parking spot. Or renew your small insurance. Or pay a small repair bill. Or trade in your old VW for a new one.

Think it over.

18.1. This classic VW ad from 1960 may have created a longer ripple effect than any other single ad in the twentieth century. Its approach remains influential, both graphically and conceptually, even today.

not. The trick is to do it in such a way that the positive ultimately comes through.

—Sue Crolick,
Sue Crolick Advertising & Design

Artists talk about the *negative space* of an object: not the tree but the broken-up sky that interpenetrates it; not the model's fingers but the space that wraps itself around them. Artists learn to draw, not just the contour of the object, but also the contour of the space around it. They learn a different way of seeing.

Similarly, you can think about the negative space of a product, the "un-things" around it: the nonuses and wrong places and wrong times and wrong people for the product. Ask yourself:

- Who doesn't use the product?
- When isn't it used?
- What's an unusual use for it?
- Where don't you find it?
- When is the one time it *won't* come in handy?
- If it has lots of features, what *doesn't* it have?
- If it solves lots of problems, what problem *won't* it solve?

FEEL FAMILIAR?

KNOW WHEN TO DRAW THE LINE

Labatt

Hopefully you won't need this tonight. KNOW WHEN TO DRAW THE LINE *Labatt*

18.2. The light-hearted tone of this drink-responsibly campaign is 180 degrees from the voice of doom people expect in this genre.

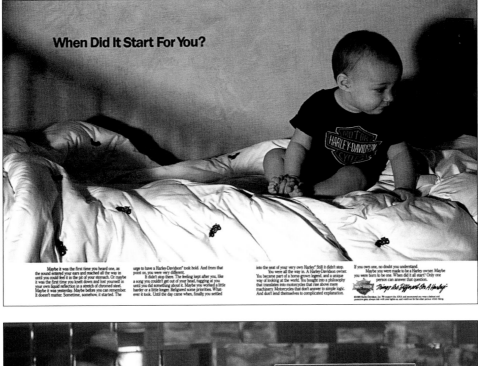

18.3. Exploring negative space. The Harley-Davidson ad uses the "wrong person," someone who doesn't (yet) use the product. What better way to indicate the long-standing loyalty that Harley-Davidson engenders than with a pre-rider? The Volvo airport sign points out something Volvo doesn't do in order to emphasize how well it does something else.

- How can it be placed out of context?
- What's an odd point of view from which to see it?
- What's the worst thing that can happen if you use it?

In other words, explore the empty, absurd areas around a product (see fig. 18.3).

SAY IT "WRONG"

Advertising should stun momentarily. It should *seem* to be outrageous. In that swift interval between the initial shock and the realization that what you are showing is not as outrageous as it seems, you capture the audience.

—George Lois, founder, Lois/USA

CANCER CURES SMOKING.

CANCER PATIENTS AID ASSOCIATION

18.4. Readers so hope to see a sentence that ends "... cures cancer" that the reversal stops them in their tracks, then makes its point.

Instead of taking a reasonable idea and reversing it into unreason, do something less extreme. Take that reasonable idea and simply reverse the way you say it. Invert the normal expression of a benefit. If your client's airline serves lots of cities, then there are some that it doesn't. One of Pan Am's benefits was that it flew more places than other airlines. But saying "more places than," "greater than," "the most number of," and the like is a cliché (as is drawing a bunch of arrows on a globe). So, in a moment of genius, the advertisers showed a photo of a cluster of penguins strolling past an ice floe in the Antarctic and said, "It's easier to remember where we don't go." Similarly, Volvo wrote the headline "It does 60 to 0 in 4 seconds flat," a nicely inverted way to express braking capability. An outdoor board for VW's New Beetle surprised viewers by saying, "0–60? Yes." A headline for Mercedes-Benz said,

BITCH AND COMPLAIN SOONER.

The Weather Network

18.5. Cast the benefit in terms of its opposite; find the downside of the upside. In this case, if people know the forecast sooner, they can be upset about it longer.

"Does your airbag come with a car?" (Figure 18.4 is an example of reversal that makes readers do a double take.)

Remember, when you gain one thing, you lose something else. If you get richer in some ways, you become poorer in others. If you gain freedom, you lose security. If you gain stature, you lose anonymity. The same reversals apply to products. Say the benefit backwards. Examine your list of straightforward benefits, asking how each could be said by emphasizing its opposite. The *Economist* magazine has expressed its contribution to subscribers' corporate success this way: "Lose the ability to slip out of meetings unnoticed." A loss that emphasizes the gain. Another *Economist* headline: "It's lonely at the top, but at least there's something to read." See figure 18.5 for an example of reversal that injects humor into the liability of gaining a benefit.

TURN DEFICITS INTO ASSETS

> Every artist knows that sunlight can only be pictured with shadows. And every good biographer shows us, as Boswell did, that only the faults of a great man make him real to us. But in advertising we are afraid of this principle, hence less convincing than we might be.
> —James Webb Young, *Diary of an Ad Man*

Every product has liabilities, but most advertising ignores the deficits and concentrates instead on making good seem better. Great campaigns, however, have been built on turning deficits into assets.

Make a list of all the reasons your client's target audience would *not* want to buy the product. What's wrong with it? Costs too much? Too little? Doesn't last long enough? Lasts too long? What? Then examine these perceived liabilities to see if you can flip one around—turn a deficit into an asset (see figs. 18.6 and 18.7). One problem with D'Amico Cucina, a restaurant in Minneapolis, is that it's open only in the evening. How to turn no lunch into a virtue? "We don't serve lunch. It takes us all day to prepare dinner."

An exemplary campaign was predicated on a liability of Bazooka chewing gum. If you've ever had Bazooka, you know that it's hard to chew at first— more like hard candy than gum. Most advertisers wouldn't even address that problem. Not Chiat/Day, whose campaign theme was "Bazooka chewing gum. If you're tough enough to chew the hard stuff."

18.6. Makes you want to
go, doesn't it?

18.7. Artists and designers often see
themselves as a hardy little band of
like-minded people in a world of "others." This campaign knows just what to
say: emphasize art school negatives
until they sound positively irresistible.
Other headlines: "Math. Our best
recruiter" and "Economics 101. We
don't have it. And based on junior
designer salaries, you don't need it."

WHAT WE LACK IN FRAT BOYS,
WE MAKE UP IN BITTER,
CHAIN-SMOKING INTROVERTS.

FOR TWO YEARS OF FOCUSED INSTRUCTION IN DESIGN, ILLUSTRATION AND ART DIRECTION, CALL 513-961-2484
CINCINNATI ACADEMY OF DESIGN

18.8. By mocking the cattle industry's own slogan ("Beef. It's what's for dinner"), this ad for a vegetarian deli goes right after the competition's soft underbelly.

18.9. You can't drink and drive. Or can you?

One TV spot had a close-up of a man starting to chew a piece to the soundtrack of a car trying to start and then stalling out. The voiceover: "It's harder to get started, but once it gets going, it never stops." Clever and memorable. And the campaign successfully differentiated the brand—no small feat in a category chock full of look-alike, taste-alike competitors about which it's hard to find much to say.

TURN THEIR ASSETS INTO DEFICITS

> The best and simplest way of selling a product is to say: "It is better than what you are about to buy."
>
> —Dave Trott, copywriter, BMP

Instead of taking a product's deficits and showing how they're really assets, take the competition's assets and show how they're really deficits. That is, push your product up by pushing the competition down, by arguing that competitors' apparent strengths are really weaknesses. Reposition the competition (see figs. 18.8 and 18.9).

Make a list of what's wrong with your product's competitors; better yet, find in that list weaknesses they think are strengths. Find a deficit in what is otherwise the strong position of the market leader. Point out Mr. Big's liabilities. For "offensive warfare" that repositions the leader, marketing experts Al Ries and Jack Trout give this advice: "Find a weakness [inherent] in the leader's strength and attack at that point."[3] For example, Coca-Cola for many years had virtually no significant competition, and its distinctive 6½-ounce bottle shape was its symbol. So in the late 1930s when Pepsi went after Coke, it attacked the bottle. Its key selling concept was a 12-ounce bottle for the same nickel, and the strategy worked.[4]

Royal's golf ball isn't exactly number one with Tiger Woods, Ernie Els, and other touring pros; they play Nike, Titleist, and other brands. So Royal simply took a close-up picture of a Royal golf ball resting on the grass and put on it the headline "Play the ball the pros ignore." Although Royal also wrote a lot of copy to explain why, the nervy headline alone challenges and intrigues, don't you think? (The slogan: "The perfect golf ball for the imperfect golfer.") This approach re-positioned the Big Boys; playing the ball the pros play now looked like a bad idea. And the ball-from-nowhere, the also-ran Royal, suddenly seemed more special, its humility entirely appropriate to all those imperfect golfers.

Final advice

> A safe ad is a bad ad. In fact, it's not an ad at all. If you're not prepared to get attention, you're not prepared to advertise.
>
> —Marsha Lindsay,
> president/CEO, Lindsay, Stone & Briggs

Working with reversals helps you take chances, but it's a difficult way to think. It runs counter to the copywriter's usual desire to make sense, plus it deliberately puts the client's product in jeopardy, creating a non sequitur from which you must then make sense follow. It's a tough technique—on both your client's product and your own brain. But remember the great ads and campaigns you've admired. Not one was a straightforward presentation of the traditional way of seeing a product, with the usual arguments for buying it. Each one jolted you by reversing some expectation. As a creative person, you are dedicating yourself to transcending clichés. Try the techniques I've suggested. After all, in the great work, upside down is indeed right side up.

19 ▪ Metaphor

> But the greatest thing by far is to be a master of metaphor. It is the one thing that cannot be learnt from others; and it is also a sign of genius, since a good metaphor implies an intuitive perception of the similarity in dissimilars.
>
> —Aristotle, *Poetics*

Consumers like to think they choose among products on the basis of what they can see, hear, feel, taste, and touch about those products. In other words, they make their judgments via *tangible* distinctions. Is this a good hamburger? Let's taste it. Is this a good car? Let's drive it. Does this shampoo get my hair soft? Let's wash with it and find out.

But what happens when consumers can't literally apprehend the product? Services are not concrete the way goods are, so often the product is itself *intangible*—people cannot see insurance or feel banking or test the plumpness of a college education with their finger—but they certainly demand a strong sense of a service's effectiveness before they buy it. Just as often an otherwise tangible good—that car, for example—offers *intangible* benefits that need expression, such as feelings of power or freedom or security. These don't literally adhere to the hardware, yet they're part of why consumers buy cars and ought to be part of how you sell them. Some goods, like computers, are too complicated to apprehend with the senses, while others—most packaged goods, for example—are shielded away from the immediate senses by tin, plastic, or cardboard. All these instances invite the advertising use of metaphor—talking about one thing in terms of something else—because the product's "one thing" is intangible, allowing the metaphor's "something else" to vivify it.

In short, when consumers can't apprehend the product's benefits with their senses—either before trial or ever—then they rely on substitutes, images that stand for those things. As Theodore Levitt notes, "Metaphors and similes become surrogates for the tangibility that cannot be provided or experienced in advance."[1] And while you'll primarily think of using metaphors in specific ads, consider the general point—it explains why IBM insists on a rigorous dress code for its employees; why Apple goes to such lengths with the package, product, and graphic design for its computers; why you carefully design your résumé and print it on expensive stock. Again, Levitt notes, "The less tangible the generic product, the more powerfully and persistently the judgment about it is shaped by the 'packaging'— how it's presented, who presents it, what's implied by metaphor, simile, symbol, and other surrogates for reality."[2]

How metaphors work

Think of all the insurance companies that use a metaphor or symbol to stand for the security they offer: Prudential's Rock of Gibraltar, the Travelers' umbrella, Hartford's elk, the "good hands" of Allstate, and so on. Since insurance is less a thing than a feeling or a state of mind, these metaphors help define the feeling, give consumers something to grasp in the absence of anything tangible. Metaphors don't always need to be visual images, either. They can be stated in the copy line or slogan—or, in the case of State Farm insurance, sung: "and like a good neighbor, State Farm is there."

A *metaphor*, of course, is a figure of speech in which one thing is talked about in terms of something else; a comparison is made between dissimilar things. If you compare Ohio State and Penn State or compare the Cleveland Browns and the Chicago Bears, you aren't making metaphors; you're making literal comparisons between similar things. But if you say, as Ralph Waldo Emerson

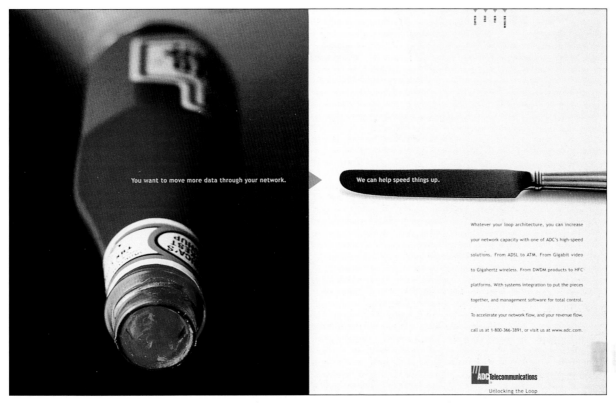

You want to move more data through your network.

We can help speed things up.

Whatever your loop architecture, you can increase your network capacity with one of ADC's high-speed solutions. From ADSL to ATM. From Gigabit video to Gigahertz wireless. From DWDM products to HFC platforms. With systems integration to put the pieces together, and management software for total control. To accelerate your network flow, and your revenue flow, call us at 1-800-366-3891, or visit us at www.adc.com.

ADC Telecommunications

Unlocking the Loop

19.1. How do you *show* slow communication systems and the solution to that problem? With a ketchup bottle, a knife, and a headline that links the tangible (the visual) with the intangible (the problem and its solution).

once did, that "an institution is the lengthened shadow of one man"[3] or that a football team is like a harnessed set of horses, then you are making metaphors. (Remember that a *simile*, which uses "like" or "as," is a kind of metaphor.)

Two ways to be metaphorical

When your're creating metaphors for ads, think of them as being of two kinds.

USE PURE METAPHOR

Sometimes you can just show something that isn't your client's product at all and say that it is. In this case, you're using a *pure metaphor*: something that stands in for the product (or its benefit or the feeling people get from it) and helps clarify and persuade. This is a good technique when the product is intangible but also when it's boring to look at or complicated or obscure or unknown. Or when someone else in that product category does one thing (show the car, for example), and you want to do something different.

I once saw a poster in a public library featuring

a big photo of a hiker with backpack pausing in a glorious solo trek through the Grand Canyon, the awesome spectacle looming over his shoulder. The poster could have been advertising Timberland gear or Arizona, but when I read the small headline, "Knowledge is free. Visit your library," I saw how well the visual worked. Going to the library *is* like an odyssey through immense, spectacular country; just think of what's there. The pure metaphor required me to leap to libraries and books from the Grand Canyon, but I could, and I felt invigorated by doing so. (See figures 19.1 and 19.2 for other examples of pure metaphor.)

> A metaphor forces everyone to look at your product in the simplest term. We get so caught up in the bells and whistles that we forget the basic function. The idea of any decent ad is to help us digest the information easily. Metaphor is a way of doing that.
>
> —Jennifer Solow, art director, Ammirati & Puris

19.2. An otherwise abstract situation is made concrete by a metaphor, which shows readers what the mortgage-lending process can be like.

CREATE A FUSED METAPHOR

Pure metaphors are rare. Why? Probably because it's easier to create fused metaphors, in which you take the product (or something associated with the product, the way a toothbrush is associated with toothpaste, a comb with hair care products, or the highway with cars) and fuse it with something else.

Objects that are "wrong," that have been assaulted or transformed in some way, are attractive to viewers, more so than unmodified ones. Unmodified images are really just clichés. For example, one of David Ogilvy's famous ideas was The Man in the Hathaway Shirt, who wore an eye patch and was thereby more interesting than a man who didn't. He wasn't just the cliché of hunk #119; he was a wounded, brave, singular fellow with a story to tell. Absolut Vodka has been metamorphosing its bottle in various amusing ways for years: turning it into a swimming pool for "Absolut L.A.," fogging it in for "Absolut San Francisco," blowing off its letters for "Absolut Chicago," and so on. Many other ads gain visual strength from a "what's wrong here?" approach.

Unlike pure metaphor, fused images help contextualize the selling argument; viewers don't have to leap quite as far when part of what they're looking at is what's for sale. You catch their attention and demonstrate your selling argument by metamorphosing the product into something new that expresses your selling idea.

How to fuse? Get in the habit of looking for latent pairs in whatever advertising problem you're working on; push two things together into one image. For example, if you're selling a home security system for Warner Amex, you could use a house and then metaphorically do something to it. Or you could begin with a lock or barbed wire or an armed guard and then "house-i-fy" that. A lot of arresting images are really a combination of the product and a metaphor, or of two aspects of the problem.

Photographer and art director Henry Wolf, famous for his conceptual work for *Esquire, Harper's Bazaar, Show,* and other magazines, worked frequently with metaphors and explained how he thought them through: "The working method that accomplishes these results [shock and surprise] is not easy to quantify. There are two major categories: addition—in which one or more elements are added to an image; and substitution—in which part of an image is replaced by another that does not normally belong with it."[4]

The power of graphic fusion comes from combining two clichés, symbols, or aspects of a situation into one new image. When you're working visually, think in terms of either *addition* (see figs. 19.3–19.5), adding something to an image, or *substitution,* replacing part of an image with something else (figs. 19.6–19.13).

Also when dealing with images, don't be too literal. Try to find metaphors that capture the psychological essence of a problem more than simply its external reality. Let's say that you're developing a poster to announce a seminar in business fundamentals for graphic designers, one called "The Business Primordial." You may start thinking of cavemen and clubs—clubs as felt-tip markers, business cards made out of stone, cavemen dressed in business suits, and so on. In other words, you try to

19.3. Just as makeup is garish and inappropriate on a baby's face, so too are additives in baby food, this company argues. Here readers see the power of fused metaphor: this claim may or may not be "true," but the transfer of belief from metaphor to claim lends it credence. A good instance of argument by analogy.

WHEN IT'S BUDGET CUTTING TIME, THEY ALWAYS START WITH THE EASIEST TARGETS.

Children can't stand up for themselves. Which makes them an easy mark for politicians when they're cutting back. Give children a voice. Yours. Kids can't vote, but you can. **THE CHILDREN'S DEFENSE FUND**

19.4. The bull's-eye is a simple, clear example of addition. The headline complements, rather than repeats, the visual, and the copy is well written, too. Read it; you'll be moved.

19.5. Another example of addition. How do you visually say "a very Italian Italian restaurant"? Why not add a distinctive tilt to the waiter?

fuse some image of business or graphic arts with some "primordial" image. But you don't have to. A visual of two dogs in a tug of war (a pure metaphor) can also express the psychological essence of basic business difficulties, but less obviously. It's a metaphor off to the side; the dogs symbolize not the thing, but the emotional center of the thing. They're unexpected but appropriate.

Headline advice for metaphors

Remember, if your visual is loud, then you can speak quietly, as the Grand Canyon/library poster did. It didn't scream, "Whole Worlds of Awesome Ideas!" It said simply, "Knowledge is free. Visit your library." So if you shout with the picture, whisper or make a little joke with the words, and vice versa. Don't shout twice.

And, of course, never resay in words what you show in pictures. *Marry* the headline and the visual. In the Warner Amex home security problem, if you show a house all wrapped up in barbed wire or a great big padlock on the roof, don't shout, "Lock Up Your World With Great Protection!" Readers can see and hear your image. Perhaps show that visual and then below it say, "Or call Warner Amex." See?

PAZZO
RISTORANTE

A VERY ITALIAN
ITALIAN RESTAURANT.

19.6. A terrific visual fusion for a motorcycle café and lounge, don't you think?

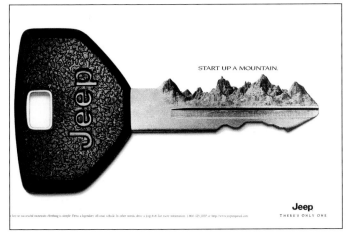

19.7. Metaphor as hyperbole.

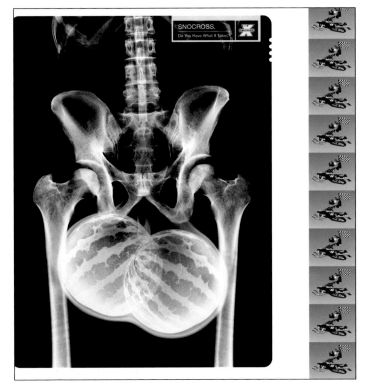

19.8. Creative copy substitutes for head and heart in posters for Athletes Helping Athletes.

19.9. The fusion of city sign and religious symbol. If too many churches are too remote from urban problems, this one sure isn't. Strong visual positioning.

19.10. Since language surrounds people in both consumer culture and public space, think about substituting new words for the expected ones.

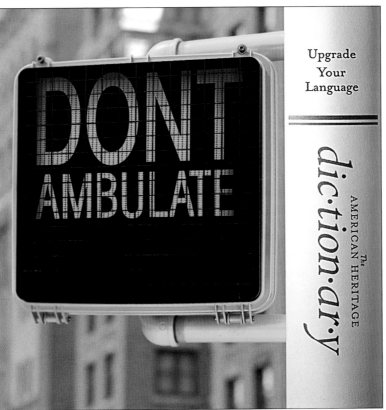

19.11. Logo/title of Margaret Edson's Pulitzer Prize-winning play about a witty English professor (a scholar of John Donne's witty poetry) dying of cancer. The professor takes punctuation seriously as an aspect of literary criticism, and since semicolons are end stops, the mark suggests both her passion and her predicament. Very clever, tight visual idea.

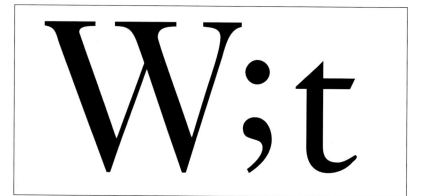

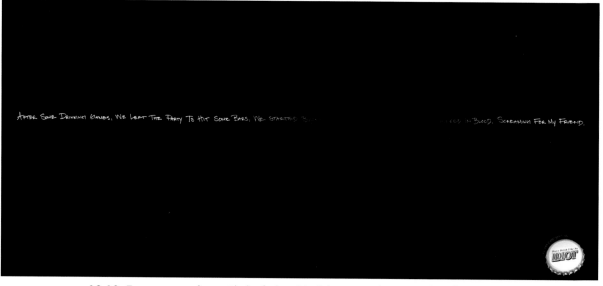

19.12. Type as metaphor, with the fade-to-black being analogous to the effects of excessive alcohol consumption. The way the language changes—going into the fade and coming out—is the shocker. The perils of too much drinking haven't been preached against; they've been demonstrated. Other headlines: "It was ladies' night. Everybody was there. We left the bar about 3 in the morning . . . how I got this unicorn tattoo on my butt" and "I met this really cute guy. He was so sweet. We danced and he bought me drinks and . . . with my panties around my ankles." In all the ads, the line on the beer cap says, "Don't drink like an idiot."

19.13. A stunner of an ad, seeing the problem in a new way—both visually and verbally. It's a disturbing image, and that's the point.

20 ▪ Verbal Metaphor

> Ideas do not need to be esoteric to be original and exciting. . . . What Cezanne did with apples, Picasso with guitars, Leger with machines, Schwitters with rubbish, and Duchamp with urinals makes it clear that revelation does not depend upon grandiose concepts. The problem of the artist is to defamiliarize the ordinary.
> —Paul Rand, *A Designer's Art*

Ads that people ignore are ones in which nothing seems amiss: expected imagery is accompanied by expected language; nothing is out of place. So consider another way to "defamiliarize the ordinary," to move things out of their clichéd resting places: verbal metaphor, the opposite side of the metaphor coin. Rather than changing the product visually, change it verbally, by putting it in another language system. Instead of making it "wrong" visually, call it by the "wrong" name—in other words, use *verbal metaphor*.

How the wrong name can be the right one

Not only does verbal metaphor gain attention by assigning something the wrong name, but it also helps sell products by elevating them. Often people don't want a product or service itself unless they can be persuaded that it isn't something regular, boring, and ordinary, but instead Something Else Real Important or Cool. As an advertiser, you want to reposition products in consumers' minds, make people reimagine those goods and services as something more than they seem.

For example, Club Med has called itself, cleverly, "the antidote to civilization." This is metaphor, a comparison between dissimilar things. Literally, Club Med is a vacation service; only metaphorically is it some kind of prescription for an illness. But the line makes a vacation seem like much more than just a regular getaway. Similarly, Royal Viking cruise lines has headlined ads, "The 7 day refresher course for those who have forgotten how to live." This is metaphor, too; after all, a cruise vacation is not literally a life-skills course. But both services have given themselves metaphorically appropriate names. They have talked about themselves using language associated with something else or language literally meaning something else. Thus they catch readers' attention, and with the logic of metaphor, they elevate their services in the process. This idea of inviting consumers to reimagine a product is so fundamental to advertising that once you begin to look for verbal metaphor, you will see it everywhere (see fig. 20.1).

Metaphor and simile

Even though your high school English teacher may have made these seem like two different things, they're just one: metaphor. Metaphor—talking about one thing in terms of something else—is the main idea; similes are simply a subset, the kinds of metaphor that use "like" or "as." Don't sweat the distinction. Compare your client's product to something dissimilar, and you're making metaphor (see fig. 20.2).

Consider using the following structures to help create verbal metaphor. Then either keep these structures in your headlines, or drop them off, if your meaning is clear without them:

Think of it as _____.
It's like a ____.
It's like a ____ for your ____.
If it were a ____, it would be a _____.

USE PERSONIFICATION

Personification, the giving of animate qualities to

**Hot, live gardening action
24 hours a day.**

garden.com

20.1. Verbal metaphor is widely used because of its obvious virtues: it's startling and often funny, and it quickly and memorably communicates a product benefit. It works well in outdoor advertising because you can say a lot without using many words.

**SOME SCENES MAY BE
DISTURBING TO VIEWERS.**

The
Weather
Network

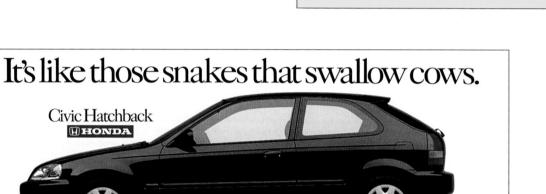

It's like those snakes that swallow cows.

Civic Hatchback
HONDA

20.2. Examples of the essence of verbal metaphor: say what the product is *like*. Rename it.

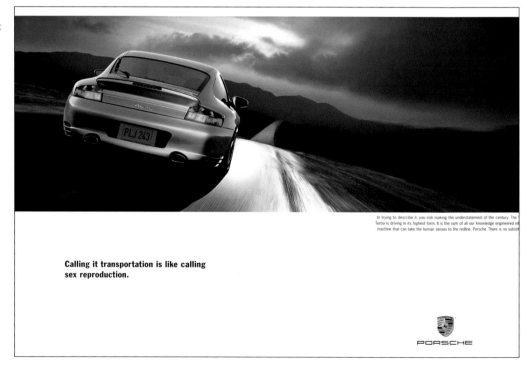

In trying to describe it, you risk making the understatement of the century. The
Turbo is driving in its highest form. It is the sum of all our knowledge engineered int
machine that can take the human senses to the redline. Porsche. There is no substi

**Calling it transportation is like calling
sex reproduction.**

PORSCHE

inanimate things, is a kind of metaphor: you're talking about one thing in terms of something else. Since people have relationships with products (they actually *love* many of their things), those products are alive, and people might as well admit it. So animate your client's product. Talk about it, or something associated with it, as though it were alive; or let it talk itself or behave as though it were alive:

> Safety marries performance. They elope. (Saab)

The following headlines in Crate & Barrel furniture ads, each showing an elegant piece of furniture, personify elements associated with each item:

> Loose change never had it so good. (comfy couch)

> Your remote just may decide to stay lost forever. (leather armchair)

> Just think of the positive effect it could have on a crumb's self-image. (dining table)

> Arouses feelings of intense jealousy among dust bunnies. (French sofa)

How to think about verbal metaphor

Shop around in your mind. If you had to call the product something else, what would it be? If you had to compare it to something else, what would it be? (An ad for Washington apples had this headline: "A snack so good, people even eat the wrapper" and this slogan: "The original health food.") How does it work? What does it do? (Headline on an ad showing a speeding Porsche: "Kills bugs fast." Headline above another Porsche: "Unclogs major arteries.") How does it differ from the competition (see fig. 20.3)? What's its highest possible benefit? What does it give people more of—time, power, love, money?

Always ask yourself, "What *is* this product?" For example, what *is* a car? Is it an investment? Durability on wheels? A reward for hard work? A mobile home? A comment on its owner? An exercise in rationality and sensible spending? (Hyundai outdoor board: "Use your mind more than your money.") Similarly, what's an iPod? A portable concert? A hearing aid? A privacy rite? The rhythm of life? "1,000 songs in your pocket"? Ask yourself,

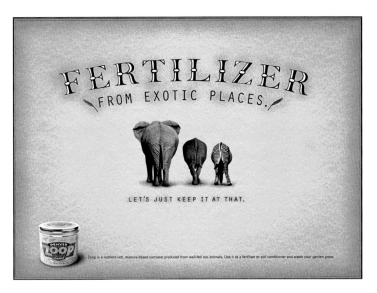

20.3. Funny headlines differentiate Zoop from all those other fertilizers out there.

"What is this product doing here? What is its real purpose? What do people go to it for?"

EXPLOIT LANGUAGE SYSTEMS AND CLICHÉS

Also consider whether there are any clichés associated with the brand, category, target market, or benefit that you might be able to exploit. What language does the target audience use? For example, Honda has placed "Multiple Choice," "Student Aid," and "Roads Scholar" headlines above its cars in ads aimed at students because a college audience speaks that language. Can you apply a language familiar to the target audience to your client's product (see fig. 20.4)? One quick way to investigate other language

20.4. The language of home construction aptly fits the product: customers decide what they want in it, then they get the custom-made product.

20.5. An important part of President Kennedy's administration was the space program and its culmination in a moon landing. A terrific way of re-seeing an image associated with JFK.

20.6. How to make mundane objects like shock absorbers and weed trimmers interesting? Don't get stuck looking only at the product. Move around. What else is involved? Who are other players in the drama? What's their point of view?

systems is to go to Web sites about whatever system you're considering. If you want to use psychological language, go to mental health or psychology sites, or go to amazon.com and peer inside psychology books. If you want judicial language, go to sites about the law. The Web is the new Roget's.

MOVE AROUND

In searching for verbal metaphor, try starting with visuals. Imagine the product in various settings and from various angles—from behind, in use, empty, just sitting there, in the driveway, in the showroom, and so on. With different visuals come different headlines. Many verbal metaphor ads do simply show the product sitting there in air, with a witty headline; but many others derive their relationship between headline and visual from some specific placement or view of the product—or of something associated with it. So think things out visually as well as verbally (see figs. 20.5 and 20.6).

DON'T JUST FILE YOUR LIFE INSURANCE AWAY, DRIVE IT.

There is a fountain of youth. You just have to swim laps in it.

Y.

20.7. Many great headlines do more than rename. Although it's smart to call a Volvo "life insurance," the idea gets even better if you say more. So, too, do the renamings of the swimming pool and the fishing reel.

A metal utensil used to eat a fish's lunch.

The Sigma 2200 reel: anodized aluminum, machine-tooled brass and stainless steel. Now that's bringing something to the table. *Shakespeare* SINCE 1897

CONSIDER SAYING MORE RATHER THAN LESS

A phrase can sometimes just sit there, inert, little more than a label. So once you rename the product, think about extending the phrase. For example, if you put "dental policy" beside a tube of toothpaste, readers might say, "Yes? So? What about it?" Remember that you're writing headlines, after all, so they can be sentences, commands, questions. Maybe, then, you'll want to give the new name more context and meaning by making it part of some-

thing longer. Consider the implications and circumstances that surround the phrase. See if you can add to it. The ads in figure 20.7 all extend the verbal metaphors with which they begin. A car really is a kind of "life insurance," but even more, it delivers a benefit missing from the kind on paper. Similarly, while it's smart to see a YMCA pool as a "fountain of youth," the observation gets smarter if you admit that some work is required. And if a fishing reel is "a metal utensil," yes, so? Keep going.

REMEMBER THAT THE LONGER THE LEAP, THE STRONGER THE METAPHOR

The farther away the language is from what people expect, the more surprising it is. So if you can pull words in from a long way off, you'll hook your audience harder. The title of Don Henley's greatest hits CD, "Actual Miles," for example, has been brought in from pretty far away. It's another way of talking about logging lots of tunes and stopping at some point to take stock of them. "Taking Stock" would convey the same idea but wouldn't be as fresh because it's not as much of a metaphorical leap.

"Inventory Clearance" would be negative. There's something, in this culture, almost heroic about lots of highway miles, yet who already thinks of miles as songs? Nice surprise, great title.

The ads in figures 20.8–20.11 gain power and surprise because the copywriters make unusual connections—seeing similarity in very dissimilar things. The surprise of each ad comes from the unexpectedness of the comparison, the audacity of the leap, if you will. Yet once readers think about the connection, they see its appropriateness and feel the selling power of the metaphor.

20.8. A controversial poster whose surprise and shock may just come from its honesty. Where did people think vintage clothing came from?

The lion is the king of beasts, because there are usually more lions than any of the others. He is a light tan color and always faces left. He is sweet and crispy and his rounded shape doesn't hurt your mouth when you eat him. The sheep tastes just like the lion, but he is somewhat taller. Unfortunately, it is hard to find a whole sheep because his thin front legs often break off in transport. Bears are best dipped in milk. You can't soak them in the milk too long, however, as they will get soggy and fall apart. Hippos are usually at the bottom of the box with the sheep's front legs and other assorted crumbs. Hippos just look like blobs from the back; you must see them from the front to even know they're hippos. Zebras too, are light tan like all the others. Their heads are kind of sharp though, which maybe makes them good ones to share with your friends.

It's hard to know what all God's creatures are really like if you can't see them first hand. Wouldn't a zoo in Broward County be great for you and your family? Contribute something, anything, to your educational future. Send your tax deductible contributions to Markham Park Zoo, Box 8844, Oakland Park, Florida 33310. For more information call 472-1976.

Markham Park Zoo
Broward County Zoological Society

20.9. To encourage the creation of a zoo, copy and headline explain animals in the endearing, odd, insufficient ways a child would whose only knowledge of them came from animal crackers. As sweet an idea as I've ever seen.

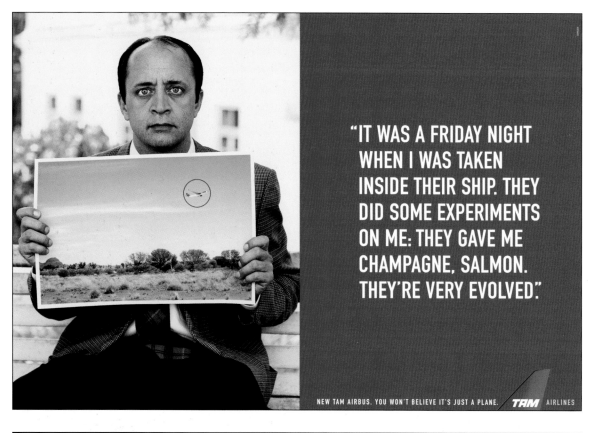

"IT WAS A FRIDAY NIGHT WHEN I WAS TAKEN INSIDE THEIR SHIP. THEY DID SOME EXPERIMENTS ON ME: THEY GAVE ME CHAMPAGNE, SALMON. THEY'RE VERY EVOLVED."

NEW TAM AIRBUS. YOU WON'T BELIEVE IT'S JUST A PLANE. *TAM* AIRLINES

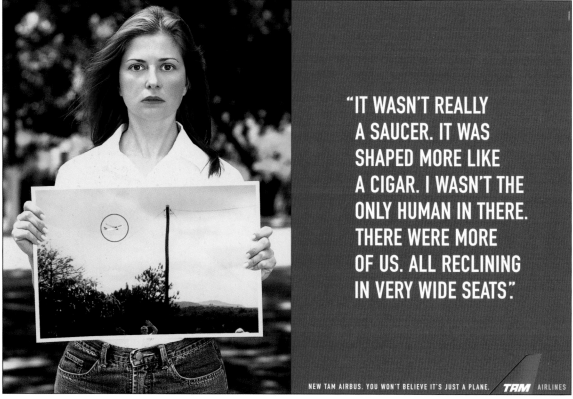

"IT WASN'T REALLY A SAUCER. IT WAS SHAPED MORE LIKE A CIGAR. I WASN'T THE ONLY HUMAN IN THERE. THERE WERE MORE OF US. ALL RECLINING IN VERY WIDE SEATS."

NEW TAM AIRBUS. YOU WON'T BELIEVE IT'S JUST A PLANE. *TAM* AIRLINES

20.10. Once you see something from a new point of view, everything changes. These ads use the tabloid conventions of UFO abduction stories to express the benefits of the New Tam Airbus: "You won't believe it's just a plane." Hilarious and wonderful work.

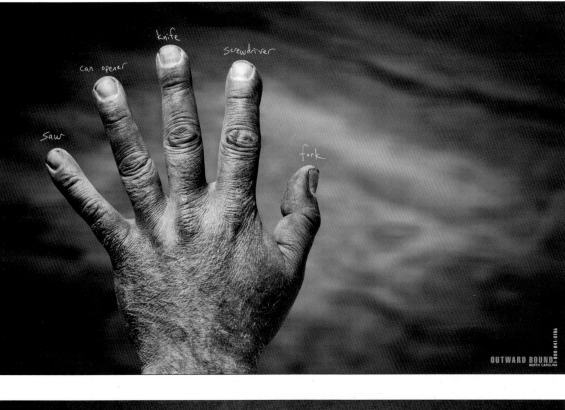

20.11. Outward Bound programs use wilderness survival to teach life lessons. The posters suggest other uses, other meanings, for familiar things. What better way to show ingenuity and self-reliance, the conquering of a new terrain, than by taking that wilderness experience and renaming it?

21 ▪ Postmodern Advertising

Any understanding of advertising in American culture must come to grips with the ironic game it plays with us and we play with it. If there are signs that Americans bow to the gods of advertising, there are equally indications that people find the gods ridiculous.

—Michael Schudson,
Advertising, the Uneasy Persuasion

What is postmodern advertising?

A lot of the ads in this book might be considered postmodern, and what they're doing—pushing against modernism—you'll often want to do, too. Modernism is, among other things, a belief in rationalism, a demand that form and function coincide. Implicit in modernism is a belief in progress, in creating new and better things.

Postmodernism is what comes after that, and simply within advertising it's a lot of things: an irreverent, I-know-this-is-an-ad attitude; an awareness that people are becoming increasingly cynical about advertising; an appreciation of advertising's past excesses; a critique of consumerism; a return to earlier advertising forms but now with an ironic attitude. Postmodernism is to advertising what David Letterman has been to the late night talk show: a subversion of the genre. Letterman made fun of being the only thing on NBC (later CBS); stuck his fingers on the camera lens; threw stuff off roofs; baited guests; talked, not to his audience, but to the stage hands; wandered off the set and into the city; in short, did any number of things that called attention to the artifice and highly mannered thing that was a talk show (much of it a rebellion against the genre's strictures). He not only demanded that viewers pay attention to the man behind the curtain, but he pulled the curtain away himself to reveal that, often enough, no one was there at all. He got past "talk showness." And all such shows since then have lived on that postmodern circuit. They've had to.

In many ways, copywriters have gotten to the same point with ads. Indeed, ads are highly man-

nered, artificial creations with unspoken assumptions, rules, and various built-in fakenesses. It's become okay—if not expected—that copywriters subvert those rules and get past them. Great ads can, of course, still play it straight, be good modernist stuff. But a lot of great ads bend something, do violence to the expectations inherent in the genre. They start with the assumption that advertising's language and forms have been used up, then go from there.

How to bend an ad

1. Ridicule the product. Traditional advertising thinks its job is to endorse the product. But consumers' immunity is such that it may be more effective to call the product's value into question, as do the "slider bar" ads shown in figure 21.1. Alan Russell, chief creative officer, DDB Canada, explains the idea: "TV12 has programming that pretty much appeals to the average couch potato. All the shows are light, fun and entertaining, and we felt that the brand personality should reflect that sentiment. We decided 'Truth in Advertising' was the way to go by poking fun at our own product. After all, when was the last time anyone watched Pamela Anderson for the riveting dialogue and profound subtext?"[1]

2. Make fun of the audience. Usually ads tell consumers they're smart for choosing a certain brand, but maybe consumers have heard that too much (see fig. 21.2).

3. Subvert the advertising category or format. If advertising's forms are used up—before

Donny & Marie
Weekdays 2 pm

TV12

Baywatch
Saturdays 4 pm

TV12

Seinfeld
Weeknights 6 pm and 10 pm
Sundays 7 and 7:30 pm

TV12

21.1. Ads can ridicule TV reruns even as they invite viewers to watch them.

21.2. Ads for an amusement park belittle the consumer (crying and vomiting in search of a good time) while also ironically mimicking the "Having a wonderful time. Wish you were here" postcard tradition that consumers associate with exotic vacation destinations.

21.3. A testimonial that violates expectations. This isn't happy talk from a happy person, testifying to the wonderful things his company can do for the consumer.

21.4. A liquor ad that—at first glance—looks like an item in an industrial products catalog. The copy, from the "scientists" at the "Rohol Institute," is designed and written to satirize the kinds of injunctions, pronouncements, product specs, and ancillary information that such advertising indulges in. *Rohol* means "crude oil" in German and is a liqueur, meant to be drunk as a shot, so the industrial strength metaphor and mind-numbed headline make more sense than they appear to at first.

21.5. Satirizing advertising's "money-back guarantee" works well for a parachute center. Flippancy bonds the center with daredevils, exactly the people most likely to exit a plane at altitude. Great first line of copy, too.

and after, comparison and contrast, testimonial, product feature, and so on—then use them ironically (see fig. 21.3). Or appropriate the forms of one kind of advertising and apply them to yours. What's an ad for your client's product supposed to look like? Can you use the look of another sort of product instead (see fig. 21.4)?

4. Speak with tongue in cheek. After all, the language of advertising is so worn out it's exhausted (see figs. 21.5–21.7).

5. Make old ads new. Find an old form and breathe a new sensibility into it. Remember the ads from your childhood for this thing you're selling? What were their conventions, what was their look? Can you use any of that ironically, spin it, update it? Look at other old ads—ones from as far back as the 1940s and 1950s or as recent as, say, the 1980s, however far back you have to go to be inside another aesthetic or series of assumptions (see fig. 21.8). Can you do anything with what you're seeing?

6. Import material from outside the genre; bring in stuff that's not supposed to be in an ad. Nike did this years ago with Beatle and John

21.6. One ad's headline satirizes the ubiquitous advertising claim "New!" while telling the literal truth. The other offers up a common advertising disclaimer, this time with tongue in cheek.

21.7. Adland clichés of overpromise are parodied, but in a voice just dumb enough to be a true beer drinker's. This ad gets readers coming and going.

Lennon songs, and a seminal Honda scooter TV spot used Lou Reed's "Walk on the Wild Side," both brands creating a new feel and a lot of media buzz. Bass ale has used Franz Kafka and Friedrich Nietzsche as spokespeople. Ads have parodied and manipulated great artwork (Rodin's *The Thinker,* Grant Wood's *American Gothic,* da Vinci's *Mona Lisa,* Michelangelo's Sistine Chapel ceiling), most of these so many times you'd think they'd be worn out, and

maybe they are. But lots of things aren't. Get busy. Inspiration can come from anywhere (see fig. 21.9).

7. Call attention to the ad's artifice. Make people notice that it's an ad. Share an understanding with your audience that, yep, they're looking at an ad. Maybe get them to smile about it (see figs. 21.10 and 21.11).

8. Do the opposite: don't look anything like an ad. Despite their best intentions, traditional

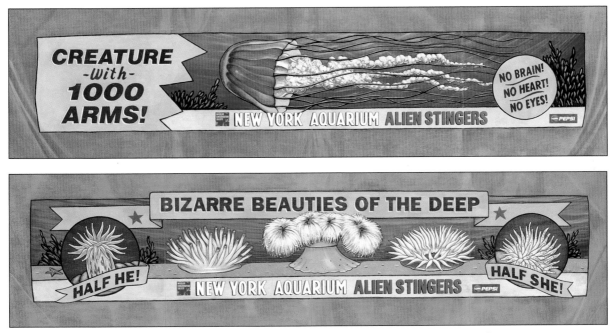

21.8. These ads invoke the language and style of the old-fashioned banners at fairs. They make readers smile while piquing their interest in the genuine oddity of these creatures from beneath the sea.

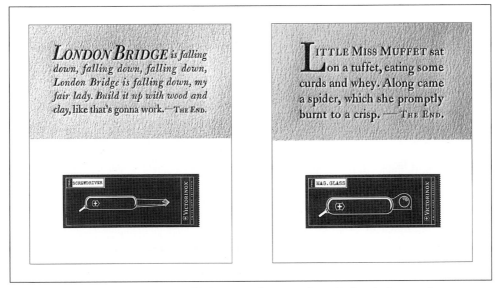

21.9. Nursery rhymes are an unlikely source for Swiss Army Knife ads, but not if you rewrite them. Here the old-time letterpress/literary look is undercut by the rewrite. The ads look one way, talk another. The format says old, sweet, harmless, cute; but the voice is tougher, hipper, more of a wise guy. Nice contrast.

ads fairly scream, "I'm an ad!" All right, make something else instead. Since people often hate ads and distrust them, they'll be grateful (see fig. 21.12).

9. Avoid direct, straight-ahead selling, no matter how winsome. Make no sales pitch whatsoever. Since ads are constantly hyping, be mute. Or make an anti-argument for the product (see those Playland ads in figure 21.2). Or look instead for the odd, perhaps dark, places in people's psyche. Get underneath the pitch to some shared collective space. Help your audience realize that everyone spends time there. Advertising writer Warren Berger and others

21.10. The small-space ad sections in the back of magazines provide the perfect place for a small-car ad, especially if it's hip enough to have fun with where it finds itself.

in his favor. (Hence "New Democrat," "New Paradigm," and all the other neologisms of the day.) For those lamenting the craven reluctance of the center left to challenge post-Gulf Bush, it was the sheer fact that Clinton was willing to run at all. He had a coterie of former Rhodes scholars who would support him unconditionally. And then there were those who liked him because he was willing to do anything at all to win.

I personally became powerfully nauseated by seeing Clinton up close in New Hampshire that year. His big, red-faced frame didn't seem so much "imposing" as simultaneously needy and greedy. He lied aggressively about Gennifer Flowers and, sitting next to his wife, let her do his marital propaganda for him. He fundraised as if there were no guidelines. When the polls seemed to sag, and he sought to burnish his tough-on-crime credentials, he flew back to Arkansas to oversee the execution of a brain-damaged black convict named Rickey Ray Rector. This episode isn't mentioned at all in Blumenthal's narrative, but it revolted a few people at the time, as it should have. By this stage Blumenthal was fully on board the candidate's train; and I'll never forget a Georgetown dinner, at which he was probably the most conservative person in attendance, where various liberals wondered aloud what the limits of "lesser evil" politics might be. One misgiving after another was mentioned, until Blumenthal impatiently quelled the bleats. "You don't understand," he said. *"It's our turn."*

There's no real trick to thinking like an apparatchik. You just keep two sets of ethical books. Thus, or in this case, only bad people get paid for their disclosures. Only Republicans ever use race in politics. And only reactionary thugs ever campaign as law-and-order exploiters of the death penalty. So Gennifer Flowers can be impugned, not for having a story to tell but for having a story to sell. Rickey Ray Rector can be given a lethal injection during a cliff-hanger primary because Clinton needs to show that he can't be "Willie Hortoned," as the saying then went. If Blumenthal can't mention, as he often does, that some of Clinton's critics made money on

have called such ads-beyond-ads "oddvertising."

10. Be deliberately primitive. Since ads have become too "slick," be so dumb it's scary. Dave Letterman, ambling through what he took to be the shambles of his show, would say, almost amazed, "You know, we're the only thing on NBC right now." He'd perfected the throw-it-all-away attitude that permeated so much of what he did. Okay, throw it all away.

Perhaps the best embodiment of throwing it all away I've ever seen was an E*Trade ad created by Goodby, Silverstein & Partners for the 2000 Super Bowl. Into the middle of all those expensively produced, extravagant TV ads came a spot showing two guys in a garage clapping for a chimp dancing to boom box music. That

was it. Thirty seconds of a chimp dancing and guys clapping. It closed with, "Well, we just wasted two million dollars. What are you doing with your money?" It was a wonderfully, awesomely crude ad, especially given its Super Bowl context. And one that couldn't have made more sense: yes, they *did* just waste two million dollars, and, come to think of it, what *was* I doing with my money?

Does postmodern advertising work?

A lot of people argue that the techniques described in this chapter are quickly seen by consumers as just another pitch—this time, the clever anti-pitch pitch. So rather than forming new relationships among consumers, their choices, and the ways they

A

B

C

D

E

F

G

21.11. Quirky spot for the Weather Network in which "clouds" waiting in the green room to go on TV end up in a shoving match—the dark, stormy clouds picking a fight with those gentle cumulus people. The casting director at first says, "Call for the Cumulus Clouds. White Cumulus Clouds." But as they get up, she quickly reverses herself: "Sorry. Make that Dark Rain Clouds. Call for Dark Rain Clouds." While the two sets of clouds jostle, a super reads, "Local forecasts every 10 minutes." This campaign sees its product as a TV station whose performing personalities are the weather itself. As in much postmodern advertising, viewers are being taken backstage; they share in watching the spots create themselves. Characters in other spots include Heavy Snow, three fat guys in white suits who like to fall on top of one another in a big pile, and Freezing Rain, a fellow in a slicker who slips and slides so much he can't stay on camera.

21.12. A magazine-insert ad is a flattened "milk carton," and consumers are invited to pop it open, shake it for their spouse to show that it's empty, and hop in the Mini for a trip to the grocery—a good excuse for some motoring. It's fun to contemplate this idea, and I don't feel pitched to. I smile when I think of the Mini now. Not bad advertising, after all.

understand those choices, these ads just work the old routes, albeit more cleverly. Many people also wonder how far off a sales pitch an advertiser can drift and still be selling anything. People may be amused and diverted, but if they're not also buying, then these techniques aren't working. As ad critic James B. Twitchell says, "What happens to advertising when it loses its grip on the product and becomes just another form of entertainment event is that it ceases to sell."[2]

> One peculiar characteristic of advertising is that it creates its own antibodies. One quickly learns, in reading the advertisements of one's own time, to build up automatically an immunity against their persuasions.
>
> —Frank Rowsome Jr., social historian

But from another point of view, ads use these techniques because they have to. Postmodern attitudes and assumptions have become part of consumers' cultural mindset. They form the world consumers live in now. Wieden + Kennedy's Dan Wieden explains:

Consumers today not only know they're being marketed to—they're actually judging how well it's being done. It's like when Toto pulls the curtain back: everybody knows the wizard is just that little guy back there with the machine. So it requires a freshness for the work to be effective now. It's not as simple as focus groups and philosophical formulas anymore. At the end of the day there has to be some fresh look . . . or something that jars your perspective and lets you see things from a different angle.[3]

22 · Human Truth

> Advertising is not about being clever; it's about
> finding a truth that connects the product to the user.
> —Wayne Best, creative director,
> Kirshenbaum Bond + Partners

Any great ad has a simplicity about it, a sense of inevitability, of an idea found very nearby ("Why didn't I think of this?") that makes it great. If you pick the ad up and shake it, it doesn't rattle. There's nothing complicated, extraneous, or superfluous about it. No extra moving parts. It's simple, often funny, true—and it works. It feels *found* as much as invented. Get in the habit, especially when your thinking has led you (as it so often leads all copywriters) into increasingly obscure and complicated solutions, solutions that still feel wrong and make no sense when you show them to other people—get in the habit of backing out and starting over. Be simple. Find the basic human truth.

"Raise the obvious to the conscious."

This is Wieden + Kennedy art director Todd Waterbury's advice.[1] Locate the obvious things consumers think and say and know about the product, product category, brand, even their habits with it, and write them down. Chances are that one of these things is, or with slight modification could become, your solution. That's what Waterbury means by "raise the obvious to the conscious," and it's excellent advice.

"Got milk?" is probably as pure an example of his advice as you can find. It's something people ask without even thinking, but it says everything: people don't miss milk until they don't have any, and they need it for lots of things—cookies, cereal, sandwiches, the kids, the cat, and so on. Jeff Goodby explains how his agency arrived at this idea:

> If we had started with the idea of milk as a glass of milk you drink alone, we would have ended up addresing the health benefits or the nostalgia of milk. Exactly as had been done in previous campaigns. Exactly wrong. We looked for the truth about milk. We asked people to go without milk for 2 weeks. "Sure, no problem," they said. They came back and told us how hard it was. What else goes with cereal? What are you going to do with a fresh-baked chocolate chip cookie? We arrived at the truth: Milk is never just milk. It is always ___ and milk. Milk as accompaniment. After that, everything fell into place.[2]

QUESTIONS TO HELP YOU FIND HUMAN TRUTHS

1. What do people say to themselves and each other about your client's product category or brand? What do people all notice but never remark on? What has your own inner speech been saying to you? (See fig. 22.1.)

2. Are there any myths or urban legends or other pop culture baggage surrounding your client's product? Any unspoken negatives? (See figs. 22.2 and 22.3.)

3. What's always part of the situation? What are the at-hand visuals and language that stick like Post-it notes to the product category, the product's competitors, or the brand? (See figs. 22.3–22.5.)

> At some point, a copywriter and art director cross over from wanting to tell you everything or show you everything to wanting to make you feel something. When you cross over, you are no longer an art director or a writer. You're an advertising person.
>
> —Susan Gillette, president, DDB Needham, Chicago

22.1. Comedian Steven Wright has built his career on noticing absurdist truths like this.

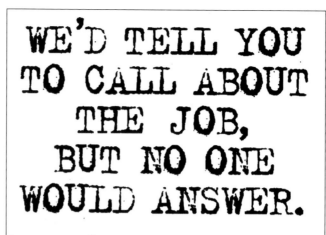

WE'D TELL YOU TO CALL ABOUT THE JOB, BUT NO ONE WOULD ANSWER.

Downtown ad agency needs a receptionist. Bad. Call Shay at 436-9400 to apply.

SEE DISTANT RELATIVES.
SAVE ENOUGH TO STAY IN A HOTEL.

Sun Country Airlines®

22.2. A clever way to tie a low-fare airline to a truth everyone has either experienced or wished for.

If other banks
are all about trust,

why are their pens
attached to chains?

For banking built on relationships.
952-431-4700.

MIDWAY BANK

22.3. Ever think of this? Why not? It's been right in front of you for years.

COMFORTABLE SEATS, FRIENDLY ATTENDANTS, CHOCOLATE CHIP COOKIES. WHAT IS THIS,
AN AIRLINE AD?

THE **BLOOD CENTER**

PULL ← PULL ← PUL

22.4. This ad finds a joke right there for the taking.

Day three: omelets and chocolate sauce.

Oregon. Things look different here.
Rafters grub at Cafe Campstove. Rogue River, Southern Oregon.
1.800.547.7842 www.traveloregon.com/south

22.5. When people go camping, sooner or later they're eating what's left—and enjoying it. Raising the obvious to the conscious, sharing human truths, is a powerful way to connect your client's brand with its audience.

They'll match everything in your ROOMMATE'S closet.

Wrangler

22.6. I don't know about your college roommates, but one of mine had great ties. I might still have a couple.

4. How do people *really* use the product? What habits are associated with using the product? (See figs. 22.6 and 22.7.)

What to do next? Write down all the truths about your client's product or brand that you can—not the Adland goody-goody stuff, but the real things that surround what you're selling. Develop a long, juicy list of stuff about the product, the brand, the situation. Now, which list items suggest directions for an ad campaign? Are there headlines lurking? Find the strongest, most resonant human truths and make them visible. Watch people smile with recognition.

Aim for the heart

Lots of ads are clever, witty, funny, spun out of a

Finals start next week.

Time to buy your books.

2338 Guadalupe
2410-B E.Riverside Dr.

22.7. How do students really approach college courses? This ad knows.

brainy place. And they work, they're good. But think of all the people in your target audience—they don't just appreciate brainy; they've all got hearts, too. If you can hang your product on the line between all those people and their feelings, between the members of that target audience and those they love, if you can find the center of a relationship and suspend your product from the invisible wires between, say, a grandfather and a grandson, between best friends, between people and their pets, between people and whatever feelings are associated with your product, then you have found your audience's heart. You've placed your product right on what matters in their lives, and by extension you've made the product matter because you've gotten it all tangled up in how they feel. It's part of what brings them their emotional daily bread.

The following copy, from the DeBeers "A diamond is forever" campaign, illustrates my point:

> Because she believes
> dogs have souls
> and angels have wings.
> Because she gave
> nine months of her life
> to watching someone grow.
> Because she named him
> after me.
>
> Diamonds.
> Just because you love her.

You're working on a little lump in your throat, and you know it. That's good. See figure 22.8 for another ad that tugs on those heartstrings.

Need another example? Let's consider Father's Day and the ever-popular but oh-so-boring gift: the watch. Father's Day obviously has emotional content, but watches don't. However, when you read the following copy, you'll see that an ad for a watch can really be all about how much you love that guy who is Dad. Somehow a watch becomes part of your love:

> *Headline:*
> Didn't ground you for shaving the dog's butt.
> *Visual:*
> Dad carrying son on his shoulders.

22.8. As strong as a logical appeal might be ("quit because smoking will kill you"), it would feel weak beside this one.

Copy:

Made you nutritious fish sticks and ice cream dinners. Let you sit on his lap and drive. Gave you CliffsNotes version of "Birds & Bees" speech. Snuck you first sip of brewski. Participated in the Great Cherry Bomb Mailbox Cover Up. Rode in death seat after you got your learner's permit, on third go round.

Dad. After all he's done for you. Getting him something great for Father's Day is the least you could do. At Watch Station you'll find over a thousand of the latest styles from names like Skagen. Call 1-888-22WATCH for a location near you. And while you're at it, it wouldn't kill you to pick up the telephone and call home once in a while.

Every detail about Dad as co-conspirator is specific and singular; none sounds off-the-rack. Although my father didn't have to cover up a cherry bomb prank, he covered up enough other stupid stuff I did. So, I'm betting, did yours. The copy's particulars speak to universals and show the power of drawing truths from one's own life. The copywriter was thinking of times that Dad's love really came through, and no doubt some of these details are taken from his own life.

Use *your* real life. It works. As Mark Fenske puts it, "Your fear of exposing what seems embarrassingly ordinary about your life denies your audience the only real story it wants. If two files were laid on your desk, one marked 'confidential' and the other one 'unconfidential,' which would you read?"[3]

23 ▪ Grace Notes

Wit is a delight. Be delightful when you can.
—Peggy Noonan, *On Speaking Well*

One beauty of being a copywriter is that you have all kinds of chances to improve the life around you. You've got big projects whose truths you can make interesting. But you've got countless small moments that you can bring wit and distinction to, and I hope you will. There are many places in people's lives where they expect to see the same old thing and too often find it. As a writer, you can do something about that.

Here is one such tiny moment. It's the top category of giving on a donation card for a nonprofit organization, in this case Thurber House. There are such traditional, expected terms for these categories ("Benefactor," "Sustainer") that it may never occur to a copywriter to surprise and please potential donors here, but Thurber House did by calling its highest level of giver "Godsend." Sweet, funny, and true. It's just one little word on a card, but it helps people feel the spirit behind the organization and invites them to share in it.

Here's another small moment that could have been perfunctory and boring—a "website under construction" page (fig. 23.1). The agency could have said exactly that and shown a crane, yellow

23.1. A Web page that's better than most pages *not* under construction. It also tells a lot about who works there, how they think, and, by implication, what they might be able to do for me if I were a client.

240

23.2. The meaning of "open" changes, and readers are surprised into a smile. A good pun that meets the definition of good advertising: effective surprise.

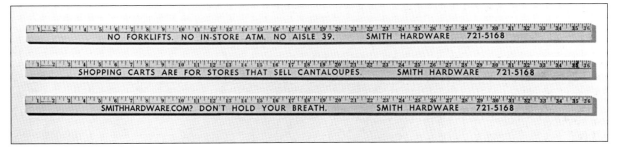

23.3. Yardsticks that bring a smile while positioning Smith Hardware as the antidote to big box madness. They're hip and nostalgic at the same time.

tape, or orange barrels. Everyone has seen such pages. To everyone's delight, this agency does better.

An open/closed sign on an art museum's front door doesn't have to be boring, either (see fig. 23.2).

Sometimes hardware stores give out yardsticks with their name and phone number. In figure 23.3, a hardware store invokes that tradition but takes the opportunity to do something more interesting, and more brand differentiating.

Business cards are often handsomely designed but rarely say more than the name and title of the person, contact information, and maybe the company's slogan. Why can't the words on these cards be more arresting? The advertising agency Crispin Porter + Bogusky took that question to heart, not only on its business cards but also on its letterhead and envelopes (see fig. 23.4).

It's possible to make anything good, even everyday exchanges between company and consumer. J. Peterman, the purveyor of exotic goods from distant lands, had a blow-in card in one of its catalogs inviting readers to send the catalog to their friends. Peterman was trolling for new business, new names for the mailing-list database. If you were writing this card, you could have said, "Would your friends like our catalog?" But Peterman showed a picture—exotic, tinted—of two turbaned people, sitting side by side, from who knows when or where, and said, "There's nobody else like you in

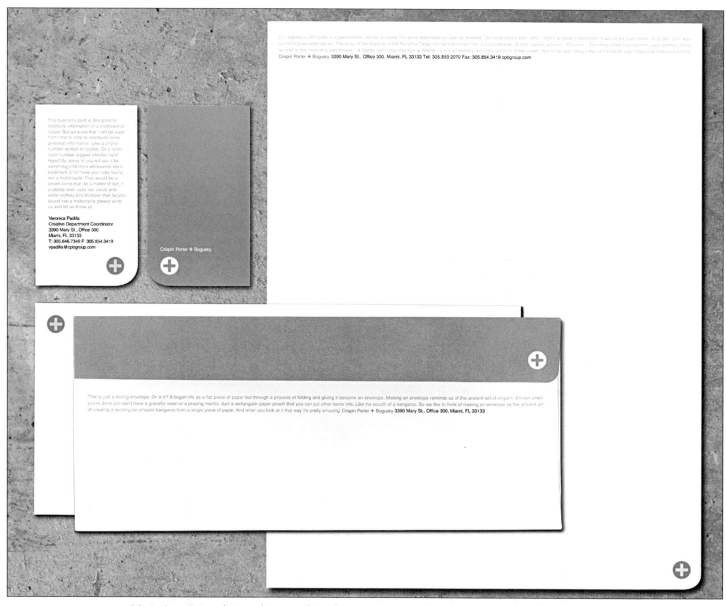

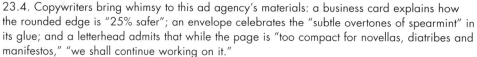

23.4. Copywriters bring whimsy to this ad agency's materials: a business card explains how the rounded edge is "25% safer"; an envelope celebrates the "subtle overtones of spearmint" in its glue; and a letterhead admits that while the page is "too compact for novellas, diatribes and manifestos," "we shall continue working on it."

the world. Or is there?" (see fig. 23.5). Very winning little moment that played off the brand image (exotica from elsewhere), flattered readers, and invited them in that very moment to name their best friends. I'm more inclined to pause over that than over a straightforward card. You too?

A press release isn't a little thing, but because a press release has an accepted format, you might think there's nothing to do except follow it—to say who, what, where, when, and maybe why and let it go at that. But good writers improve the form. Doug Dolan of the Toronto design firm Viva Dolan

wrote a press release announcing a new destination among a client's travel packages, a trip to Cuba (see fig. 23.6). He ultimately covered the who, what, where, and whens, but watch how he started out. He wanted to make sure his readers stuck around for the details.

Getting beyond ads

While it's easy to think of your work in traditional media as advertising, everything is advertising, really. Whenever you create anything for your client that consumers see, you are advertising to them. And these "touch points" are everywhere. So your opportunities to do good work for your clients while providing consumers with grace, wit, even beauty, are everywhere, too.

For a succinct expression of this larger idea of advertising, consider the following copy. I found it on the Web site for Crispin Porter + Bogusky's. It's part of the agency's employee handbook. CP+B is talking to its own people, but all copywriters should take what it says to heart:

WHY THE WORD ADVERTISING DOES NOT APPEAR ON YOUR BUSINESS CARD

Every person here and every client we have needs to be aware that while the ad that runs Monday is important and will get done, what's arguably more important is the stuff that orbits around the advertising. Like the message on the company voice mail. The line we spray paint on the sidewalk outside the industry convention. The T-shirt we mail to every employee. The wacked idea for a great new product. The bumper sticker every customer gets handed to them on a certain day. The cool new website home page. The letter to every member of Congress petitioning for a new national holiday. This is how brands are built now.[1]

As your work stretches beyond ad copy, as almost everything really does become an ad, it will bring with it an even greater responsibility to both client and consumer. For the client, you're entrusted with interpreting its brand in new ways. You're there to help deliver meaning across an array of media, developing and deepening relationships with consumers. And those relationships are a lot like marriage: both partners better be happy, or someone will be moving on.

To an audience already weighted down with sponsored messages—every American is exposed to 3,500 ads per day, according to one recent estimate[2]—you're about to make the load 3,501 and counting. You're taking up time, or asking for it,

23.5 You can always do more than what's expected, and you should.

There's nobody else like you in the world.

Or is there?

Attention:

Please send my friend

_____

a copy of your new Peterman catalogue right away.

_____

their address

_____

their city and state

_____

their zip code

Butterfield & Robinson

CONTACT
Press Relations
1-800-678-1147 or (416) 864-1354
www.butterfield.com

GETTING INTO CUBA

B&R's new biking trip winds from Old Havana, through sugar plantations and colonial towns, to beaches on the Caribbean

Toronto, Canada – How do you find out what Cuba is really like? You could buy tapes of Fidel's five-hour speeches and play them in the car. Or mix a pitcher of daiquiris and watch Robert Redford in *Havana*. Or put on a Buena Vista Social Club CD and light up a Cohiba (that's sounding better).

Or you could do something truly radical and join the hundreds of thousands of North Americans who visit Cuba each year. But to immerse yourself fully in this warm, vibrant, hospitable, sometimes controversial island, you can't stay in one of the resort compounds along the coast. You have to explore cobbled streets, colonial plantations and untouched beaches on your own terms – on the new Cuba Biking Expedition from Butterfield & Robinson, the leader in luxury active travel around the globe.

70 Bond Street
Toronto, Ontario
Canada M5B 1X3
1-800-678-1147
www.butterfield.com

23.6. The world is littered with press releases. To get people to read yours, you've got to hook them, then reel them in. The first two paragraphs of this press release show how wit, detail, and an unexpected opening can do just that.

from people already bearing up under too much visual and verbal noise, too many choices, too much muchness. What's more, you'll be invading their lives in ways traditional ads haven't.

Respecting your audience has always been an advertising principle. As David Ogilvy said so long ago, "The consumer isn't a moron; she is your wife."[3] As Rich Silverstein of Goodby, Silverstein & Partners said not so long ago, "We once had a debate—should we put 'advertising' on our business cards? No, because we don't want to be doing advertising. I'd never hire a person who 'does adver-tising.' We do *communications*. It's a way to move people. Make them think, laugh, cry. We like to treat the public with respect. We try to make advertising smart, intellectual."[4]

Now, in moving beyond advertising, you need not only to understand your client better than before but also to value your audience more—appreciate people's hectic lives, their constraints of time and interest, their desire for authentic, useful relationships. To add more crap to a system already waist deep in it becomes unconscionable.

Grace is in order.

ENDNOTES

CHAPTER 2: Researching Your Client's Product

1. William Bernbach, quoted in Marya Dalrymple, ed., *Is the Bug Dead? The Great Beetle Ad Campaign* (New York: Stewart, Tabori & Chang, 1983), 8–9.

2. Thomas Hine, *The Total Package* (Boston: Little, Brown, 1995), 269.

3. William Wells, John Burnett, and Sandra Moriarty, *Advertising: Principles and Practice* (Englewood Cliffs, NJ: Prentice Hall, 1989), 174.

4. Theodore Levitt, *The Marketing Imagination*, expanded ed. (New York: Free Press, 1986), 159.

5. Claude Hopkins, *My Life in Advertising & Scientific Advertising* (Lincolnwood, IL: NTC, 1991), 79.

6. Ernie Schenck, "The Story According to Schenck," *One*, Spring 1998, 8.

CHAPTER 3: Understanding Consumer Behavior

1. Theodore Levitt, *The Marketing Imagination*, expanded ed. (New York: Free Press, 1986), 76.

2. Based on Hierarchy of Needs from "A Theory of Human Motivation" in Abraham H. Maslow, *Motivation and Personality*, 3rd ed., revised by Robert Frager, James Fadiman, Cynthia McReynolds, and Ruth Cox. © 1954, 1987 by Harper & Row, Publishers, Inc. © 1970 by Abraham H. Maslow. Reprinted by permission of HarperCollins, Publishers, Inc.

3. Robert B. Settle and Pamela L. Alreck, *Why They Buy: American Consumers Inside and Out* (New York: Wiley, 1986), 24–27.

4. Casey Priest, quoted in Peg Tyre, "Clean Freaks," *Newsweek*, June 7, 2004, 43.

CHAPTER 4: Analyzing the Marketplace

1. The following discussion of segmentation categories is drawn from Art Weinstein, *Market Segmentation* (Chicago: Probus, 1987), 44–7, 108–27.

2. See Joel R. Evans and Barry Berman, *Principles of Marketing*, 2nd ed. (New York: Macmillan, 1988), 72–79.

3. Robert B. Settle and Pamela L. Alreck, *Why They Buy: American Consumers Inside and Out* (New York: Wiley, 1986), 292.

4. Fred Pfaff, "Levi's Dockers Weigh into Casuals," *Adweek's Marketing Week*, Sept. 24, 1990, 26–27.

5. The following discussion is drawn from Gary Armstrong and Philip Kotler, *Marketing: An Introduction*, 5th ed. (Upper Saddle River, NJ: Prentice Hall, 2000), 191–9.

6. "The Hearts of New-Car Buyers," *American Demographics*, Aug. 1991, 14–15.

7. Theodore Levitt, *The Marketing Imagination*, expanded ed. (New York: Free Press. 1986), 129.

CHAPTER 5: Defining Strategic Approaches

1. Jack Trout and Al Ries, *Marketing Warfare* (New York: NAL, 1986), 66.

2. Gary Knutson, quoted in Jim Johnston, "Howard, Merrell & Partners," *Communication Arts*, May/June 1993, 69.

3. John Hegarty, quoted in Warren Berger, *Advertising Today* (New York: Phaidon, 2001), 197.

4. Jack Trout and Al Ries published a three-part series on positioning in *Advertising Age* (April 24, May 6, and May 8, 1972), and put it all in a book, *Positioning: The Battle for Your Mind* (New York: McGraw-Hill, 1981).

5. Henry Louis Gates Jr., "Annals of Marketing: Net Worth," *New Yorker*, June 1, 1998, 48.

6. Trout and Ries, *Marketing Warfare*, 68–69.

7. David Ogilvy, *Ogilvy on Advertising* (New York: Random House, 1985), 14.

8. Lee Clow, quoted in Eleftheria Parpis, "Creative," *Adweek*, March 10, 1997, 28.

9. Dan Wieden, quoted in Joan Voight and Eleftheria Parpis, "Where Did the Magic Go?," *Adweek*, June 22, 1998, 30.

10. George W. S. Trow, *Within the Context of No Context* (Boston: Little, Brown, 1981), 8.

11. Jeff DeJoseph, quoted in Barbara Lippert, "Attitude Unbecoming," *Brandweek*, October 7, 1996, 38.

12. Rosser Reeves, *Reality in Advertising* (New York: Knopf, 1961), 82–83.

CHAPTER 6: Developing the Creative Brief

1. Norman Berry, "Norman Conquest" (interview) in *Creative Leaders Advertising Program*, (New York: *Wall Street Journal*, 1991), 7.

2. Bill Westbrook, quoted in Mill Roseman, "Bill Westbrook," *Communication Arts*, Mar./Apr. 1991, 51.

3. See Lisa Hickey, *Design Secrets: Advertising: 50 Real-Life Projects Uncovered* (Gloucester, MA: Rockport, 2002), 30–33.

4. See Warren Berger, "Creative Campaigns of the Year," *Graphis Advertising 98* (New York: Graphis, 1997), 12–13.

5. Roseman, "Bill Westbrook," 51.

6. Black Rocket and Goodby creative brief outlines courtesy of Steve Stone, founding partner, Black Rocket. For more about Goodby's approach, see Jon Steel, *Truth, Lies & Advertising* (New York: Wiley, 1998), 152–88.

7. Creative brief for Diamonds Direct courtesy of Christopher Cole. Written by Christopher Cole and Kim Portrate. The campaign was created at Chuck Ruhr Advertising by Christopher Cole, art director, and Mark Wegwerth, copywriter.

8. Christopher Cole, e-mail message to author, Oct. 18, 2004.

CHAPTER 7: Headlines and Visuals

1. See A. Jerome Jewler, *Creative Strategy in Advertising*, 3rd ed. (Belmont, CA: Wadsworth, 1989), 95–96; Philip B. Meggs, *Type & Image* (New York: Van Nostrand Reinhold, 1989), 64–65, 67.

2. Donald Hall (interview by George Myers Jr.), "For Man of Letters, Contradiction Is an Eternal Delight," *Columbus Dispatch*, September 23, 1990, G8.

3. Dick Wasserman, That's *Our New Ad Campaign . . . ?* (Lexington, MA: Heath, 1988), 28.

4. "Pong! Why Ping Pong Is Our Official Sport," Rethink Advertising, http://www.rethinkadvertising.com (accessed August 20, 2004).

5. Steve Hayden, quoted in Lawrence Minsky and Emily Thornton Calvo, *How to Succeed in Advertising When All You Have Is Talent* (Lincolnwood, IL: NTC, 1994), 112.

6. David Ogilvy, *Confessions of an Advertising Man* (1963; New York: Ballantine, 1971), 92.

CHAPTER 8: Body Copy I

1. M. H. Abrams, *A Glossary of Literary Terms*, 3rd ed. (New York: Holt, Rinehart and Winston, 1971), 123.

2. In this light all the Leo Burnett "critters"—the Jolly Green Giant, the Keebler elves, Tony the Tiger, and others—reveal their value. By taking these fellows home, consumers add to otherwise mundane products an imagined but nevertheless sustaining emotional and psychological content. When I buy Green Giant peas, I feel that I've put more in my cart than simply frozen peas; I've added the mythic presence of that character.

3. Alan Pafenbach, quoted in Bob Garfield, "VW: Best of All Media," *Advertising Age*, May 31, 1999, S22.

4. David Martin, *Romancing the Brand* (New York: AMACOM, 1989) 89, 96.

5. Elmore Leonard, "Easy on the Hooptedoodle," *New York Times*, July 16, 2001, E1.

6. Steve Hayden, quoted in Lawrence Minsky and Emily Thornton Calvo, *How to Succeed in Advertising When All You Have Is Talent* (Lincolnwood, IL: NTC, 1994), 115.

7. *Walden and Other Writings of Henry David Thoreau*, ed. Brooks Atkinson,

Modern Library ed. (New York: Random House, 1992), 3.

8. Jack Supple, "Pro File" (interview), *CMYK*, Fall 1996, 49.

9. Tracy Kidder, "Making the Truth Believable," in *Professional and Public Writing*, eds. Linda S. Coleman and Robert Funk (Upper Saddle River, NJ: Pearson/Prentice Hall, 2005), 18.

10. Bob Greene, "Nature Boy Goes the Final Round," *Chicago Tribune*, July 6, 1992, C1.

11. E.M. Forster, quoted in Lynn Z. Bloom, *Fact and Artifact: Writing Nonfiction*, 2nd ed. (Englewood Cliffs, NJ: Prentice Hall, 1994), 65. This line is so good that it has been attributed to a number of writers, among them W. H. Auden, Jerome Bruner, and Isak Dinesen, although it is most often associated with Forster.

CHAPTER 9: Body Copy II

1. Claude Hopkins, *My Life in Advertising & Scientific Advertising* (Lincolnwood, IL: NTC, 1991), 250.

2. William Strunk Jr. and E. B. White, *The Elements of Style*, 3rd ed. (New York: Macmillan, 1979), 23.

3. E. B. White, "Home-Coming," in *Essays of E. B. White* (New York: Harper & Row, 1977), 7.

4. Annie Dillard, "Living Like Weasels," in *Teaching a Stone to Talk* (New York: Harper & Row, 1982), 11.

5. James Webb Young, *Diary of an Ad Man* (Chicago: Advertising Publications, 1944), 214.

6. Joseph M. Williams, *Style*, 2nd ed. (Glenview, IL: Scott Foresman, 1985), 8.

7. E. B. White, "Will Strunk," in *Essays of E. B. White*, 258.

8. Chip Brown, "Ken Kesey Kisses No Ass," *Esquire*, September 1992, 160.

9. Alastair Crompton, *The Craft of Copywriting* (Englewood Cliffs, NJ: Prentice Hall, 1979), 152.

10. Elizabeth Hardwick, quoted in George Plimpton, ed., *The Writer's Chapbook* (New York: Viking, 1989), 111.

11. Barney Kilgore, quoted in Robert J. Samuelson, "How the WSJ Is Like Jell-O," *Newsweek*, April 22, 2002, 45.

CHAPTER 10: Television

1. See Maxine Paetro, *How to Put Your Book Together and Get a Job in Advertising*, 21st Century ed. (Chicago: Copy Workshop, 2002), 42–44. See also "The Ad School Review," *Creativity*, September 2004, 54–58, one of whose interviewees, Jan Jensen, creative manager, Deutsch/NY, says: "At least 95% of all the books I see for entry-level positions consist of print ads alone, and that's fine by me. When reviewing junior portfolios, I look for concepts and ideas over polished executions. TV is something

they can learn once they get into an agency with creative directors to guide them" (57).

2. Quoted in Mark Crispin Miller, "Hollywood: The Ad," *Atlantic*, April 1990, 50.

3. V. C. Strasburger, *Pediatrician*, Spring/Summer 1986, cited in "Vital Statistics," *In Health*, July/August 1990, 12.

4. Neil Postman, "She Wants Her TV! He Wants His Book!," *Harper's*, March 1991, 48.

5. Kinka Usher, quoted in "Understanding Usher," *One*, Spring 1998, 12.

6. Bruce Bildsten, quoted in *Adweek*, February 4, 1991, C.R. 14.

CHAPTER 11: Radio

1. Both facts from *Stereophile* staff, "News Desk: Get Ready for Audio Bits in Space," *Stereophile*, October 11, 1998 (accessed September 30, 2004). http://www.stereophile.com/news/10284/

2. Bob Schulberg, *Radio Advertising: The Authoritative Handbook* (Lincolnwood, IL: NTC, 1989), 145.

3. J. Thomas Russell and W. Ronald Lane, *Kleppner's Advertising Procedure*, 11th ed. (Englewood Cliffs, NJ: Prentice Hall, 1990), 209.

4. Bill West, "We're Not As Big As P&G: Case Study: John Moore Plumbing" (address, *Advertising Age* Creative Workshop, Chicago, August 10, 1990).

5. Bill West and Jim Conlan, "Funny, You Should Say That: Five Rules for Writing Radio Dialogue," *Advertising Age's Creativity*, September 1999, 33.

6. Robert Frost, quoted by Amy Clampitt in Robert E. Hosman Jr., "Amy Clampitt, The Art of Poetry XLV" (interview), *The Paris Review* 126 (Spring 1993), 92.

7. Jeff Goodby, quoted in Dyann Espinosa, "Radio Pays," *Advertising Age's Creativity*, September 1999, 26.

CHAPTER 12: Other Media and Genres

1. Keith Reinhard, "Keith's Beliefs" (interview) in *Creative Leaders Advertising Program* (New York: *Wall Street Journal*, 1991), 40.

2. A. Jerome Jewler and Bonnie L. Drewniany, *Creative Strategy in Advertising*, 7th ed. (Belmont, CA: Wadsworth/Thompson, 2001), 194.

3. Bob Stone, *Successful Direct Marketing Methods*, 4th ed. (Lincolnwood, IL: NTC, 1988), 334–35.

4. Barry Tarshis, *How to Write Like a Pro* (New York: New American Library, 1982), 63.

5. Michael D. Liss, quoted in "The Road Less Traveled," *@issue*, vol. 8, no. 2, (Fall 2002), 9.

6. Frank Viva, quoted in "The Road Less Traveled."

7. Doug Dolan, quoted in "The Road Less Traveled."

8. Rob Morris, quoted in Rogier Van

Bakel, "Outdoor Advertising: Primer Alfresco," *Advertising Age's Creativity*, March 1998, 34, 36.

9. Dan Sutton, quoted in *Creativity*, May 1999, 10.

10. Charles Austin Bates, *Short Talks on Advertising* (New York: Charles Austin Bates, 1898), 1.

11. See Catherine P. Taylor, "Playing Chicken," *Adweek*, April 19, 2004, 19.

12. Jonathan Bond, quoted in Bernice Kanner, "On Madison Avenue: Brats No More," *New York*, July 20, 1992, 12.

13. Warren Berger, *One*, Winter 2003, 3.

14. See Karen Gaudette, AP article reprinted as "Bumpers Are Pair's Billboards," *Columbus Dispatch*, January 6, 2001, 1F.

15. See Emma Hall and Normandy Madden, "Ikea Courts Buyers With Offbeat Ideas," *Advertising Age*, April 12, 2004, 10.

16. Lisa Hickey, *Design Secrets: Advertising: 50 Real-Life Projects Uncovered* (Gloucester, MA: Rockport, 2002), 169.

17. See "Singapore sensibility" (interview), Chris Lee, *One*, Summer 2002, 15. Lee is managing partner, Fallon/Duffy Asian offices.

18. Ian Batey, quoted in "Singapore Sensibility," *One*, Summer 2002, 15.

19. See Anita Santiago, "When Leche Is Love" (interview), *One*, Fall 2003, 12–13. Santiago is president of Anita Santiago Advertising, whose agency worked with Goodby to develop milk advertising for the Spanish-speaking Hispanic market.

20. José Mollá, "Adding Loco Humor to Hispanic Advertising" (interview), *One*, Fall 2003, 4–5.

21. See Laurel Wentz, "Banks Tailor Efforts to Homesick Hispanics," *Advertising Age*, April 5, 2004, 30.

22. J. Walker Smith, quoted in Karen Benezra, "The Fragging of the American Mind," *Brandweek*, June 15, 1998, S19.

23. Keith Byrne, "Web Design: Click Here!," *Advertising Age's Creativity*, June 1998, 45.

24. Adapted from Raymond Pirouz, *Click Here* (Indianapolis: New Riders, 1997), 18.

25. Paul Roberts, "Virtual Grub Street," *Harper's*, June 1996, 72.

CHAPTER 13: How to Be Creative

1. John Vitro, "Vitro Talks," *One*, Winter 1998, 8.

2. Eva Zeisel, quoted in Richard Rhodes, *How to Write* (New York: Morrow, 1995), 56.

3. Peter Elbow, *Writing without Teachers* (New York: Oxford University Press, 1973).

4. Edward de Bono, *Lateral Thinking* (New York: Harper & Row, 1973), 107, 108.

5. Bill Westbrook, quoted in *Communication Arts*, March/April 1991, 46.

6. Mike Roe, e-mail message to author, November 8, 2004.

7. Paula Scher, quoted in Anna Muoio, "They Have a Better Idea . . . Do You?," *Fast Company*, August, September 1997, 73, http://www.fastcompany.com/magazine/10/one.html (accessed November 11, 1997).

8. Ibid.

9. Jay Chiat, quoted in Marilynn Milmoe, "Aspen," *Communication Arts*, September/October 1987, 91.

CHAPTER 14: How to Write a Headline

1. Lee Clow, quoted in Lynda Twardowski, "On the Inside: TBWA Chiat/Day: Behold the Second Coming," *CMYK*, Winter 1998, 55.

2. Ken Macrorie, *Telling Writing*, 3rd ed. (Rochelle Park, NJ: Hayden, 1980), 136–37.

3. Woody Allen, "Death (A Play)," in *Without Feathers* (New York: Random House, 1975), 99.

4. The source of this quote is uncertain. Thompson wrote a similar line in *Generation of Swine: Tales of Shame and Degradation* (New York: Summit, 1988, p. 43), but the thought itself has become an urban legend, spreading widely in various forms, none of them quite the Thompson original. Its omnipresence is testimony not only to Thompson's hot-rocks style but, with its laugh-out-loud last sentence, to the power of misdirection.

5. David Denby, "Traffic Jams," *New Yorker*, June 16 & 23, 2003, 201.

6. Voltaire, quoted in John Bartlett, *Familiar Quotations*, 16th ed. (Boston: Little, Brown, 1992), 305.

7. Ezra Pound, *ABC of Reading* (Norfolk, CT: New Directions, [nd]), 28.

8. William S. Burroughs, from RE/SEARCH #4/5, 1982. http://www.lazaruscorporation.co.uk/explanations/explanations2.htm (accessed July 11, 2003).

9. Goodby, Silverstein & Partners, quoted in Andrea Birnbaum, ed., *Top Ten in Advertising* (New York: Graphis, 2001), 74.

10. Dan Wieden, quoted in Steve Woodward, "MIND-SET/slogans," *Oregonian*, December 14, 2003, adslogans.com/mediadesk/pdf/AdSlogans_Oregonian.pdf (accessed July 5, 2004).

11. Danny Altman, quoted in Josh Rottenberg, "How to Invent a Brand Name," *New York Times Magazine*, April 8, 2001, http://www.ahundredmonkeys.com/nytimes_article2.html (accessed June 5, 2001).

12. Danny Altman, quoted in Cheryl Dahle, "How to Make a Name for Yourself," *Fast Company*, September 2000, http://www.fastcompany.com/online/38/100monkeys.html (accessed June 5, 2001). For a good discussion of naming techniques, also see Beth Brosseau, "How to Win the Naming Game," *Critique*, Spring 1997, 57–63.

CHAPTER 16: Testimonials

1. Dave Schiff, quoted in "PrintCritic E-mail," *Creativity's AdCritic.com*, http://adcritic.com/printercritic/email (accessed July 28, 2004).

2. Ibid.

CHAPTER 18: Reversal

1. I owe the title of this chapter and some of my thinking to Edward de Bono's *Lateral Thinking* (New York: Harper & Row, 1990).

2. Brian Howlett, quoted in "Exhibit," *Communication Arts*, January/February, 1997, 125.

3. Al Ries and Jack Trout, *Marketing Warfare* (New York: McGraw-Hill, 1986), 70. As its title indicates, this engaging book likens marketing to the battlefield and explains fundamental strategies in its terms.

4. Ibid., 117–36.

CHAPTER 19: Metaphor

1. Theodore Levitt, "Marketing Intangible Products and Product Intangibles," *The Marketing Imagination*, expanded ed. (New York: Free Press, 1986), 97.

2. Ibid., 98.

3. Ralph Waldo Emerson, "Self-Reliance," *Selected Essays*, ed. Larzar Ziff (New York: Penguin Books, 1982), 185.

4. Henry Wolf, *Visual Thinking: Methods for Making Images Memorable* (New York: American Showcase, 1988), 14.

CHAPTER 21: Postmodern Advertising

1. Alan Russell, e-mail message to author, July 21, 2004, quoting his comments in "Gold on Gold," *The One Show*, vol. 21 (Hove, East Sussex, UK: Rotovision SA, 1999), 105.

2. James B. Twitchell, *Twenty Ads That Shook the World* (New York: Crown, 2000), 192.

3. Dan Wieden, "On Global Ambitions, Turning 17, and Memories of 'Revolution': Dan Wieden Reflects" (interview), *One*, Winter 1998, 6.

CHAPTER 22: Human Truth

1. Todd Waterbury, address, Columbus Society of Communicating Arts, Columbus, Ohio, October 16, 1997.

2. Jeff Goodby, quoted in *Advertising Age* "The Age of Ideas" advertising campaign, "This is not milk," print ad, in *Ad Age's Creativity*, December 2000–January 2001, 30–31.

3. Mark Fenske, "My Art Center Class in 800 Words or Less," *CMYK*, Fall–Winter 1998, 64.

CHAPTER 23: Grace Notes

1. Excerpt from New Employee Handbook, "Employment" section, Crispin Porter + Bogusky Web site, http://www.cpbmiami.com/ (accessed December 29, 2003).

2. Lisa Sanders, "Fight for the Streets," *Advertising Age*, May 31, 2004, 58.

3. David Ogilvy, *Confessions of an Advertising Man* (1963; New York: Ballantine Books, 1971), 84.

4. Rich Silverstein, quoted in Chris Barnett, "Cruising a Steady Course: Goodby, Berlin & Silverstein," *Graphis*, 46, no. 265 (January/February 1990), 50.

RECOMMENDED READING

CREATIVE THINKING

Adams, James L. *Conceptual Blockbusting: A Guide to Better Ideas*. 3rd ed. New York: Addison-Wesley, 1986. A book that takes its title seriously: breaking the blocks that inhibit our creativity.

De Bono, Edward. *Lateral Thinking*. New York: Harper & Row, 1973. This is his best-known book about creativity, but he has written a number of others.

Von Oech, Roger. *A Whack on the Side of the Head*. 3rd ed. New York: Warner, 1998. *A Kick in the Seat of the Pants*. New York: Harper & Row, 1986. Both books seem almost too simple: easy to read, easy on the eyes, funny. But both are head stretchers.

VISUAL THINKING

Heller, Steven, and Gail Anderson. *Graphic Wit: The Art of Humor in Design*. New York: Watson-Guptill, 1991. This really powers up your visual acuity. There's a revised version: Heller, Steven. *Design Humor: The Art of Graphic Wit*. New York: Allworth, 2002. Heller has written or edited a number of books on design, all of them interesting.

McAlhone, Beryl, and David Stuart. *A Smile in the Mind: Witty Thinking in Graphic Design*. rev. ed. Boston: Phaidon Press, 1998. A feast of graphic wit, categorized and analyzed. Add to your own visual thinking and study how the words work.

McKim, Robert H. *Experiences in Visual Thinking*. 2nd ed. Boston: PWS Engineering, 1980. A good corrective for those who equate thinking with thinking verbally.

WRITING

Anderson, Chris. *Free/Style*. Boston: Houghton Mifflin, 1991. This brief book is out of print but shouldn't be. You'll write better, more interesting sentences after reading it. Out-of-print books are easy to find via Web sites like alibris.com, amazon.com, bookfinder.com, and my favorite, abebooks.com. Find those great ones; they're still out there.

Hale, Constance. *Sin and Syntax: How to Craft Wickedly Effective Prose*. New York: Broadway, 2001. Hale organizes her advice by the parts of speech and draws from fresh, unusual sources.

Marius, Richard. *A Writer's Companion*. 4th ed. Boston: McGraw-Hill College, 1999. Marius is talking to college students about how to write essays, but we can easily slip into the room. Our copy will thank us.

Strunk, William, Jr., and E. B. White. *The Elements of Style*. 4th ed. Boston: Allyn and Bacon, 2000. This classic little book combines Strunk's gruffness with White's grace. If you haven't read it, you should.

Trimble, John R. *Writing with Style: Conversations on the Art of Writing*. 2e. Upper Saddle River, NJ: Prentice Hall, 2000. This is another classic, though less well known than *The Elements of Style*. Trimble, like Marius, is a professor talking to college students about how to write essays. Proof that the best profs are always worth listening to.

Williams, Joseph M. *Style: Ten Lessons in Clarity & Grace*. 7th ed. New York: Longman, 2003. If you really want to study the engine of style, this book opens the hood. He has also written a cut-to-the-chase version: *Style: The Basics of Clarity and Grace*. New York: Longman, 2003.

Zinsser, William. *On Writing Well*. 25th anniv. ed. New York: HarperResource, 2001. A much-admired book full of practical, sound advice. I think it's the single best book on how to write.

COPYWRITING

Aitchison, Jim. *Cutting Edge Advertising*. Singapore: Prentice Hall, 1999. I don't know another book in which the thoughts of advertising creatives have been as usefully organized. Rather than presenting his subjects one by one, he integrates their comments into chapters that track how you'd work on a problem, from beginning to end.

Bendinger, Bruce. *The Copy Workshop Workbook*. 3rd ed. Chicago: Copy Workshop, 2002. An energetic potpourri of advice and resources. You'll want to make ads after reading it.

Bly, Robert W. *The Copywriter's Handbook*. Updated ed. New York: Holt, 1990. Conservative, no-nonsense features-and-benefits approach to advertising. Read this book when you're starting out, then consider breaking its rules as your talent and experience tell you to.

The Copy Book: How 32 of the World's Best Advertising Writers Write Their Copy. Crans, Switzerland: Designers and Art Directors Association of the United Kingdom and Rotovision, 1995. Great copywriters show their work and talk about how they did it. Most are British; much of the work you may not have seen. (A paperback edition is entitled *The Copywriter's Bible*.)

Sullivan, Luke. *Hey, Whipple, Squeeze This: A Guide to Creating Great Ads*. 2nd ed. Hoboken, NJ: Wiley, 2003. It's hard to be either funny or wise. Sullivan is effortlessly both. A great book. If you read only one on how to make ads, this is it.

HISTORY OF ADVERTISING

Berger, Warren. *Advertising Today*. New York: Phaidon, 2001. A great big dreamboat of a book. (Takes two hands and a strong lap.) Lots of handsomely reproduced ads (from the 1960s on—many you've seen, many you haven't), interviews with major players, and, not least, a fine writer on the bridge. Ask for it for your birthday. Or give it to yourself.

Goodrum, Charles, and Helen Dalrymple. *Advertising in America: The First 200 Years*. New York: Abrams, 1990. Beautifully illustrated, well researched, clearly written. Organized chronologically within categories: cosmetics, automobiles, travel, causes, etc. Out of print, but that's not a problem. (See Web sites listed in Anderson entry under "writing," above.)

Twitchell, James B. *Twenty Ads That Shook the World*. New York: Crown, 2000. Smart, wide-ranging analyses of seminal ads. History in bite sizes.

ADVERTISING AND MARKETING

Minsky, Laurence, and Emily Thornton Calvo. *How to Succeed in Advertising When All You Have Is Talent*. Lincolnwood, IL: NTC, 1994. Substantial interviews with people like Steve Hayden, Lee Clow, Tom McElligott, and Ed McCabe—about their careers and experiences. Lots of advice about how to think, how to solve advertising problems, and how to grow in the profession.

Paetro, Maxine. *How to Put Your Book Together and Get a Job in Advertising*. 21st century ed. Chicago: Copy Workshop, 2002. This book's title fits it like a lid fits a jar. Q&As with Paetro, an ad agency headhunter, and lots of advice from industry professionals. If you're just leaving college with advertising as a career goal, buy this book immediately.

Ries, Al, and Jack Trout. All of their books are fast reads that simplify marketing principles just enough to make them useful: *Bottom-Up Marketing*. New York: McGraw-Hill, 1989; *Marketing Warfare*. New York: McGraw-Hill, 1986; *Positioning: The Battle for Your Mind*. 20th anniv. ed. New York: McGraw-Hill, 2001; *The 22 Immutable Laws of Marketing*. New York: HarperBusiness, 1993.

Steel, Jon. *Truth, Lies & Advertising: The Art of Account Planning*. New York: Wiley, 1998. How they think things through at Goodby, Silverstein & Partners from someone who should know. Steel starts from the consumer's point of view, which is where ads themselves should start but too often don't. He helps you see into the psychology that underlies great advertising.

ILLUSTRATION CREDITS

1.1. Courtesy of Reader's Foundation and Ruhr/Paragon.

1.2. Courtesy of Reader's Digest Foundation and The Martin Agency.

1.3. Scarred face ad courtesy of Chiat/Day/Mojo. Obituary notice ad courtesy of Bozell, Inc., and Reader's Digest Foundation.

2.1. Courtesy of Volkswagen of America, Inc.

2.2. "Daddy fought in the war" ad © 2004, Motorola, Inc. Reproduced with permission from Motorola, Inc. Humboldt penguin ad courtesy of World Wildlife Fund.

2.3. "Block out harmful rays" ad developed by Goodby, Berlin & Silverstein, advertising agency for the *San Francisco Examiner*. Reprinted by permission. Coupon-off-the-TV-screen ad courtesy of *The Oregonian*.

2.4. Courtesy of Piaggio USA.

2.5. Courtesy of BVK.

2.6. Courtesy of L.L.Bean and Martin|Williams. Creative director, Jim Henderson; art director, Tim Tone; copywriter, Jan Pettit.

2.7. Courtesy of True Fitness Public Relations, ORCA Partnership.

2.8. Courtesy of Fallon.

2.9. Courtesy of Howard, Merrell & Partners.

2.10. Courtesy of Chopin Vodka and Clarity Coverdale Fury. Creative director, Jac Coverdale; art director, Glenn Gray; copywriter, Kelly Trewartha.

3.1. Courtesy of Starkey Labs.

3.2. Courtesy of Kohnke Hanneken Advertising, Inc.

3.3. Courtesy of BBDO Canada.

3.4. Courtesy of Sawyer Riley Compton. Creative director/art director, Bart Cleveland; copywriter, Al Jackson; photographer, Jim Erickson.

3.5. Courtesy of the Animal Humane Society and Sally J. Wagner, Inc.

3.6. Courtesy of Rethink.

3.7. Courtesy of Holmes & Lee.

3.8. Courtesy of Sawyer Riley Compton. Creative director/art director, Bart Cleveland; copywriter, Al Jackson; photographer, Jim Erickson.

3.9. Courtesy of Martin|Williams.

3.10. Courtesy of Gibson Guitar Corp., Carmichael Lynch, and Shawn Michienzi, photographer.

4.1. Courtesy of Black Rocket.

4.2. Courtesy of Winnebago Industries, Inc.

4.3. Courtesy of Paul Carek. Terry Rietta, art director.

4.4 Courtesy of L.L.Bean and Martin|Williams.

4.5. Courtesy of Harley-Davidson, Carmichael Lynch, and Chris Wimpey, photographer.

4.6. Courtesy of Sawyer Riley Compton. Creative director, Bart Cleveland; art director, Kevin Thoem; copywriters, Kevin Thoem/Ari Weiss.

4.7. Courtesy of White Wave.

4.8. Volvo ad courtesy of Volvo. Used by permission. Porsche ad courtesy of client, Porsche Cars North American; agency, Carmichael Lynch; and photographer, Georg Fischer.

PORSCHE, BOXSTER, CARRERA, and the Porsche Crest are registered trademarks and the distinctive shape of PORSCHE automobiles are trade dress of Dr. Ing. h.c. F. Porsche AG. Used with permission of Porsche Cars North America, Inc. Copyrighted by Porsche Cars North America, Inc.

4.9. Courtesy of Viking & Indianhead Councils, BSA; and Carmichael Lynch.

4.10. Courtesy of Kohnke Hanneken.

4.11. Courtesy of Church Ad Project (www.churchad.com).

4.12. Courtesy of Tom Bedecarré, AKQA.

5.1. Honda ad courtesy of American Honda Motor Co., Inc. For Eyes ad courtesy of DeVito/Verdi, New York.

5.2. "The Day The Earth Stood Still" courtesy of Cellular One®—Washington/Baltimore. "200 minutes" courtesy of Jim Schmidt, McConnaughy Stein Schmidt and Brown.

5.3. Courtesy of Howard, Merrell & Partners.

5.4. Courtesy of BVK.

5.5. MINI and MINI Cooper are registered trademarks of BMW NA, LLC. All rights reserved. Ad used by permission.

5.6. Courtesy of DeVito/Verdi, New York.

5.7. Courtesy of BVK.

5.8. Courtesy of BVK.

5.9. Courtesy of Big Bang Idea Engineering, San Diego, CA. Creative director, Wade Koniakowsky.

5.10. Courtesy of Volkswagen of America, Inc., and Arnold Worldwide. Photography © Smari. Used by permission.

5.11. Courtesy of Butch Blum, Inc.

5.12. Courtesy of Ace Asphalt.

6.1. © Schwinn Bicycles. Reprinted with permission of Pacific Cycle.

6.2. Courtesy of L.L.Bean and Martin|Williams.

6.3. Courtesy of American Standard, Carmichael Lynch, and Shawn Michienzi, photographer.

6.4. Courtesy of Christopher Cole. Art director, Christopher Cole; copywriter, Mark Wegwerth.

7.1. VW ad courtesy of Volkswagen of America, Inc. "Don't Vote" courtesy of Borders Perrin Norrander.

7.2. © Amtrak. Reprinted with permission.

7.3. Excedrin ad courtesy of Bristol-Myers Squibb Company. "Elephants in a box" ad courtesy of World Wildlife Fund. Illustrations used with the permission of Bristol-Myers Squibb Company and World Wildlife Fund.

7.4. Stock footage ad courtesy of Crosspoint. Coffee ad courtesy of Cityscape Deli.

7.5. Courtesy of Crystal Springs Bottled Water.

7.6. Courtesy of Serve Marketing.

7.7. Courtesy of Whitewater Excitement and See of San Francisco.

7.8. Courtesy of McClain Finlon Advertising.

7.9. Courtesy of Pillsbury and Clarity Coverdale Fury. Creative director,

Jac Coverdale; art director, Jac Coverdale; copywriter, Troy Longie.

710. Courtesy of Mullen.

7.11. Courtesy of Serve Marketing.

7.12. Courtesy of Sawyer Riley Compton. Creative director, Bart Cleveland; art director, Kevin Thoem; copywriter, Ari Weiss.

7.13 Courtesy of BVK.

7.14. Reprinted with permission from Shimano American Corporation.

7.15. Courtesy of Concepts Marketing Group, Indianapolis, IN. Creative director, Larry Aull; art director, Tony Fannin; copywriter, Mark LeClerc; client, Columbus Hockey, Inc., Columbus, OH.

8.1. Courtesy of Volkswagen of America, Inc., and Arnold Worldwide. © Bill Cash Photography. Used by permission.

8.2. Courtesy of Nike, Inc.

8.3. Courtesy of Royal Viking Line.

8.4. "Accepted at more schools" courtesy of Visa. "Spend the difference" courtesy of Black Rocket. "Row, row, row" courtesy of North Carolina Division of Tourism and Film and Loeffler Ketchum Mountjoy.

8.5. Parrot ad courtesy of *The Des Moines Register*. Cigar ad courtesy of Loeffler Ketchum Mountjoy.

8.6. Courtesy of *The Village Voice*, New York, NY.

8.7. Courtesy of Reebok International Ltd.

8.8. Courtesy of Clarion Sales Corporation, Gardena, CA, and Stein Robaire Helm, Los Angeles.

8.9. Courtesy of Mullen.

8.10. Courtesy of Millennium Import LLC and Hunt Adkins.

8.11. Courtesy of KVOS TV and Palmer Jarvis DDB.

8.12. Courtesy of the Peace Corps and Backer Spielvogel Bates.

9.1. Courtesy of Mitsubishi and Chiat/Day.

9.2. Copy of advertisement used by permission of Porsche Cars North America, Inc. Porsche and the Porsche crest are registered trademarks of Dr. Ing. h.c. F. Porsche AG.

9.3. Courtesy of L.L.Bean and Martin|Williams.

9.4. Courtesy of The Nature Company.

9.5. Courtesy of American Honda Motor Co., Inc.

10.1. Courtesy of DeVito/Verdi, New York.

10.2. Courtesy of McGarrah/Jessee.

10.3. Courtesy of Rethink.

10.4. Courtesy of Volkswagen of America, Inc., and Arnold Worldwide. Photography © 2002 Malcolm Venville and Anonymous Content. Used by permission.

10.5. Courtesy of Black Rocket.

10.6. Reprinted by arrangement with Sears, Roebuck and Co.

10.7. Courtesy of Wolverine Worldwide, Inc.

10.8. Courtesy of McGarrah/Jessee.

11.1. Courtesy of DeVito/Verdi, New York.

11.2. Courtesy of Black Rocket.

11.3. Courtesy of Borders Perrin Norrander.

11.4. Courtesy of DeVito/Verdi, New York.

12.1. Courtesy of Quality Paperback Book Club.

12.2. © 1999–2000 Blue Nile, Inc. All rights reserved. BLUE NILE and the BLUE NILE logo are registered trademarks of Blue Nile, Inc., in the United States and other countries. Reproductions from the booklet used by permission.

12.3. © 2000 Viva Dolan Communications and Design Inc. Used by permission.

12.4. © 1999 Viva Dolan Communications and Design Inc. Used by permission.

12.5. Courtesy of Fallon McElligott; photography by Rick Dublin.

12.6. Courtesy of Rethink.

12.7. "Parking. How sad" ad used by permission of BMW NA, LLC. All rights reserved. MINI and MINI Cooper are registered trademarks of BMW NA, LLC. Weather Network quotes ad courtesy of Holmes & Lee. "If this bus hit you . . ." ad courtesy of DeVito/Verdi, New York. "Repels all of the above" ad courtesy of Borders Perrin Norrander.

12.8. Courtesy of Interfaith Airport Chapel.

12.9. Andy Warhol, Self Portrait, 1986 © AWF. Courtesy of The Andy Warhol Museum, Pittsburgh, PA (www.warhol.org).

12.10. MINI and MINI Cooper are registered trademarks of BMW NA, LLC. All rights reserved. Ad used by permission.

12.11. Courtesy of Kirshenbaum & Bond.

12.12. Courtesy of The Jupiter Drawing Room, Cape Town, South Africa.

12.13. Courtesy of M&C Saatchi.

12.14. Courtesy of la comunidad.

12.15. Courtesy of Corona, imported by Barton Beers Ltd., Chicago, IL.

12.16. Courtesy of Sawyer Riley Compton. Creative director/art director, Bart Cleveland; copywriter, Jackie Hathrimani.

13.1. Courtesy of Schmeltz + Warren.

13.2. Courtesy of Mike Roe and Jason Wood.

13.3. Courtesy of DeVito/Verdi, New York.

13.4. Courtesy of McClain Finlon Advertising.

13.5. Courtesy of USA WEEKEND and Cabell Harris.

14.1. Courtesy of Borders Perrin Norrander.

14.2. Courtesy of Borders Perrin Norrander.

14.3. Courtesy of United Hospital and Clarity Coverdale Fury. Creative director, Jac Coverdale; art director, Simon McQuoid; copywriter, Jerry Fury.

14.4. Courtesy of Borders Perrin Norrander.

14.5. "Happy?" ad courtesy of Checkered Past Records. Creative directors, Erik Johnson and Tom Cheevers; art director, Tom Cheevers; copywriter, Erik Johnson; pro-

EPIGRAPH AND PULL QUOTE CREDITS

Ansel Adams, quoted in *Wordsmith,* November 15, 1998, http://wordsmith.org/awad/archives/1198.

Ron Anderson, "Right On, Ron" (interview), in *Creative Leaders Advertising Program* (New York: Wall Street Journal, 1991), 4.

Aristotle, *Poetics,* in *The Complete Works of Aristotle,* rev. Oxford trans., ed. Jonathan Barnes (Princeton, NJ: Princeton University Press, 1984), 2:2334–35.

Matthew Arnold, quoted in Joseph M. Williams, *Style,* 3rd ed. (Glenview, IL: Scott, Foresman, 1989), 1.

David Baldwin, "Nobody Cares That You Only Had the Weekend," *Communication Arts,* January/February 2002, 34.

James Baldwin, quoted in George Plimpton, ed., *The Writer's Chapbook* (New York: Viking, 1989), 126.

Jamie Barrett, "On the Spot" (interview by Celeste Ward), *Adweek,* June 14, 2004, 31.

Charlotte Beers, quoted in James Atlas, "The Million-Dollar Diploma," *New Yorker,* July 19, 1999, 46.

William Bernbach [p. 63], quoted in Bob Levenson, *Bill Bernbach's Book* (New York: Villard, 1987), 116. **[p. 136]** Ibid., 210.

Wayne Best, quoted in Lauren Slaff, "Before You Send Out That Book, Read This," *CMYK,* no. 22, 80.

Victor Borge, quoted in Dick Wasserman, *That's Our New Ad Campaign . . . ?* (Lexington, MA: Heath, 1988), 66.

Leo Burnett, quoted in *100 Leo's: Wit & Wisdom from Leo Burnett* (Lincolnwood, IL: NTC, 1995), reprinted in "Wit and Wisdom from 'Chairman Leo,'" *Advertising Age,* July 31, 1995, LB-14.

Lewis Carroll, *Alice's Adventures in Wonderland,* in *Alice in Wonderland,* ed. Donald J. Gray (New York: Norton, 1971), 94.

Chaucer, quoted in Donald M. Murray, *Write to Learn,* 2nd ed. (New York: Holt, Rinehart and Winston, 1987), 264.

Chuck Close, "What I've Learned" (interview by Andy Ward), *Esquire,* January 2002, 95.

John Colasanti, "The Simpler the Better," *Adweek,* April 5, 2004, 16.

Sue Crolick, quoted in Sally Prince Davis, *The Graphic Artist's Guide to Marketing and Self-Promotion* (Cincinnati: North Light, 1991), 35.

Laurel Cutler, quoted in "Is Any Niche Too Small for U.S. Automakers," *Advertising Age,* April 9, 1990, 52.

Leonardo da Vinci, quoted in Jack Foster, *How to Get Ideas* (San Francisco: Berrett-Koehler, 1996), 108.

Miles Davis, quoted in Joel Saltzman, *If You Can Talk, You Can Write* (New York: Warner, 1993), 98.

Edward de Bono [p. 147], *Lateral Thinking* (New York: Harper & Row, 1973), 13. **[p. 160]** Ibid., 132.

Antoine de Saint-Exupéry, from *The Wisdom of the Sands,* quoted in *Wordsmith,* September 13, 2004, http://wordsmith.org/awad/archives/0299.

Peter de Vries, quoted in Donald M. Murray, *Write to Learn,* 2nd ed. (New York: Holt, Rinehart and Winston, 1987), 210.

Phil Dusenberry, "Getting Started," in Maxine Paetro, *How to Put Your Book Together and Get a Job in Advertising,* 21st Century ed. (Chicago: Copy Workshop, 2002), 151.

Peter Elbow, *Writing without Teachers* (New York: Oxford University Press, 1973), 6.

Barbara S. Feigin, quoted in Randall Rothenberg, *Where the Suckers Moon* (New York: Knopf, 1994), 121.

Mark Fenske [p. 147], "How to Know When You've Done a Good Ad" (print advertisement for ibidphoto.com), *One,* Summer 2002, 24. **[p. 201]** Mark Fenske, "My Art Center Class in 800 Words or Less," *CMYK,* Fall–Winter 1998, 64.

Craig Frazier, quoted in *Communication Arts,* Design Annual 1989: 143.

Cliff Freeman, "Cliff's Notes," in Maxine Paetro, *How to Put Your Book Together and Get a Job in Advertising,* 21st Century ed. (Chicago: Copy Workshop, 2002), 158.

John Kenneth Galbraith, quoted in Donald Murray, *Write to Learn,* 2nd ed. (New York: Holt, Rinehart and Winston, 1987), 53.

Walker Gibson [p. 86], *Persona* (New York: Random House, 1969), 68. **[p. 88]** Ibid., 51.

Susan Gillette, quoted in Lawrence Minsky and Emily Thornton Calvo, *How to Succeed in Advertising When All You Have Is Talent* (Lincolnwood, IL: NTC, 1994), 41.

Seth Godwin, *Permission Marketing* (New York: Simon & Schuster, 1999), 155.

Joy Golden, quoted in Mill Roseman, "Joy Radio," *Communication Arts,* January/February 1989, 69.

Jeff Goodby, "The Next Golden Age," *Advertising Age,* February 10, 2003, 23.

Howard Gossage [p. 64], *Is There Any Hope for Advertising?* (Urbana: University of Illinois Press, 1986), xv, xix.

Nancy Hale, quoted in Donald Murray, *Write to Learn,* 2nd ed. (New York: Holt, Rinehart and Winston, 1987), 53.

Steve Hayden, quoted in *The Copy Book* (Hove, England: Designers and Art Directors Association of the United Kingdom, 1995), 68.

Melvin Helitzer, *Comedy Writing Secrets* (Cincinnati: Writer's Digest, 1987), 37–38.

Mark Hillman, e-mail message to author, December 10, 1999.

Sally Hogshead, "'The Agency with the Best Softball Team Does the Worst Creative' (and Other Unshakable Truths of Advertising)," *One,* Winter 1998, 12.

Claude Hopkins, *My Life in Advertising & Scientific Advertising* (Lincolnwood, IL: NTC, 1991), 148.

Harry Jacobs, "Wild about Harry" (interview), in *Creative Leaders Advertising Program* (New York: Wall Street Journal, 1991), 19.

Ben Jonson, quoted in George Plimpton, ed., *The Writer's Chapbook* (New York: Viking, 1989), 101.

Don Kanter, quoted in Bob Stone, *Successful Direct Marketing Methods,* 4th ed. (Lincolnwood, IL: NTC, 1988), 324.

Crawford Kilian, "An Audience of One," *Content Spotlight,* June 18, 2001; *Content Exchange,* July 22, 2001; http://www.content-exchange.com/cx/html/newsletter/3-2/ck3-2.htm.

Rod Kilpatrick, quoted in Jack Haberstroh and Paul D. Wright, eds., *Copywriting Assignments from America's Best Advertising Copywriters* (Englewood Cliffs, NJ: Prentice Hall, 1989), 17.

Theodore Levitt [p. 13], *The Marketing Imagination,* expanded ed. (New York: Free Press, 1986), 135. **[p. 31]** Ibid., 128.

Marsha Lindsay, quoted in Jeanette Smith, *The Advertising Kit* (New York: Lexington, 1994), 255.

George Lois, "Oldest Living Creative Tells All," *Advertising Age's Creativity,* May 1998, 24.

John Lyons, *Guts* (New York: AMACOM, 1987), 124.

John Newton, quoted in John Bartlett, *Familiar Quotations,* 16th ed. (Boston: Little, Brown, 1992), 327.

Peggy Noonan, *On Speaking Well* (New York: Regan, 1999), 15.

David Ogilvy, *Ogilvy on Advertising* (New York: Random House, 1985), 14.

Charles Osgood, quoted in Bob Schulberg, *Radio Advertising: The Authoritative Handbook* (Lincolnwood, IL: NTC, 1989), ix.

John Pearson, quoted in Leslie Savan, "Morality Plays on 42nd Street," *The Village Voice Worldwide,* http://www.villagevoice.com/ (accessed July 13, 1997).

Steffan Postaer, quoted in Lisa Hickey, *Design Secrets: Advertising: 50 Real-Life Projects Uncovered* (Gloucester, MA: Rockport, 2002), 29.

Paul Rand, *A Designer's Art* (New Haven: Yale University Press, 1985), 45.

Keith Reinhard [p. 47], "Keith's Beliefs" (interview), in *Creative Leaders Advertising Program* (New York: Wall Street Journal, 1991), 40. **[p. 49]** Keith Reinhard, quoted in David Martin, *Romancing the Brand* (New York: AMACOM, 1989), 92.

Hal Riney, "How Now, Hal?" (interview), in *Creative Leaders Advertising Program* (New York: Wall Street Journal, 1991), 42.

Jean Robaire, quoted in Julie Pren-diville, "Stein Robaire Helm," *Communication Arts,* May/June 1992, 66.

Alice Roosevelt, quoted in Philip Hensher, "Books & Critics: The Country and the City," *Atlantic Monthly,* September 2001, 131.

Frank Rowsome Jr., *They Laughed When I Sat Down* (New York: Bonanza, 1959), 3.

Michael Schudson, *Advertising, the Uneasy Persuasion* (New York: Basic, 1984), 227.

Mike Shine, "Shine On," *One,* Winter 1998, 8.

Jennifer Solow, quoted in Stefani Zellmer, "Visual Metaphor: How Art Directors Articulate the Unspeakable," *Art Direction,* January 1995, 46.

William Stafford, "A Course in Creative Writing," in *A Glass Face in the Rain* (New York: Harper & Row, 1982), 65.

Albert Szent-Gyorgyi, quoted in Jon Steel, *Truth, Lies and Advertising* (New York: Wiley, 1998), 269.

James Thurber, quoted in Thomas Kunkel, *Genius in Disguise: Harold Ross of* The New Yorker (New York: Random House, 1995), 248.

Dave Trott, "They Would Be Better Off Hiring Your Mother," *One,* Fall 1998, 31.

Jack Trout and Al Ries, *Marketing Warfare* (New York: NAL, 1986), 7.

John Updike (address, Thurber House Evenings with Authors, Columbus, Ohio, October 14, 1989).

Jeff Weiss, "How Jeff Weiss Gets in the Groove" (interview), *One,* Fall 2000, 10.

E. B. White, letter to Katharine S. White, 4 February 1942, in *Letters of E. B. White* (New York: Harper & Row, 1976), 225.

Dan Wieden, quoted in Ron Lieber, "Creative Space," *Fast Company,* January 2001, 141.

Tracy Wong [p. 130], quoted in Anthony Vagnoni, "The 1995 Obie Awards," *Advertising Age,* May 8, 1995, O-6. **[p. 146]** Tracy Wong, "Tracy Wong's Approach," *One,* Fall 1998, 8.

Virginia Woolf, "The Patron and the Crocus," in *The Common Reader* (New York: Harcourt, Brace & World, 1925), 213-14.

Lester Wunderman, "Is Direct Marketing a 'Weary Revolution'?," *Advertising Age,* May 25, 1998, 23.

James Webb Young [p. 150–51], *A Technique for Producing Ideas* (1940; repr., Chicago: Crain, 1975), 35–36. **[p. 204]** James Webb Young, *Diary of an Ad Man* (Chicago: Advertising Publications, 1944), 68.

Warren Zevon, quoted in Dan DeLuca, "Cancer Claims 'Excitable Boy' 12 Days after Release of Farewell Album," *Columbus Dispatch,* September 9, 2003, D6.

William Zinsser, *On Writing Well,* 6th ed. (New York: HarperCollins, 1998), 178.

Page numbers in *italics* refer to illustrations.

659.1
F326

117089